Essentials
of
Risk Management
Volume II

Essentials
of
Risk Management
Volume II

GEORGE L. HEAD, Ph.D., CPCU, ARM, CSP, CLU
Vice President
Insurance Institute of America

STEPHEN HORN II, CPCU, ARM, AAI

HAEC
STUDIA
ADOLESCENTIAM
ALUNT

Second Edition • 1991

INSURANCE INSTITUTE OF AMERICA
720 Providence Road, Malvern, Pennsylvania 19355-0770

Table of Contents

CHAPTER 8

Examining Alternative Risk Management Techniques

Examining alternative risk management techniques—assessing the feasibility and the costs and benefits of various risk control and risk financing options—is the second step of the risk management decision process. In sequence, it lies between the first step of identifying and analyzing loss exposures (the subject of Chapters 3 through 7 of this text) and the third step of selecting the apparently best risk management techniques (which will be the focus of Chapters 9 through 12).

Systematically examining alternative risk management techniques is a crucial, yet often overlooked, step in the practice of sound risk management. It is crucial because an alternative cannot be chosen unless it is recognized. The overlooked alternative may turn out to have been the most cost-effective choice. Restricting risk management choices to, say, just the traditional insurance or safety measures that senior management has accepted for years prevents many organizations' risk management programs from contributing fully to profits or operating efficiency. All too often, the rush to deal with a particular loss exposure leaves too little time for carefully exploring all risk management options. (Once an exposure has been identified, there is often pressure to deal with it immediately even though the immediately apparent option may not be the best choice.)

A risk management professional can minimize these oversights by using the catalog of risk management techniques presented in this chapter to examine all the major categories of risk management techniques, determine which of them are sufficiently feasible to merit at least more detailed examination, and identify the broad types of costs and benefits that each technique is likely to entail. With practice, this catalog of techniques will become "automatic" for the risk management profes-

1

sional. Every time he or she considers how to treat an exposure, this outline of alternatives will come to mind so that none will be overlooked.

This analysis enables the risk management professional to do the following:

- Describe and distinguish among each of the various risk control and risk financing techniques.
- *Imagine* how, if at all, each technique could be applied to any specific property, net income, liability, or personnel loss exposure an organization faces.

Notice that "imagine" is italicized in the statement above. Imagination is important in considering alternatives because, at this stage in the risk management process, free thinking (even "brainstorming") should be encouraged. Here the objective is to identify as many feasible alternatives as possible. The inferior options can then be discarded in the third step of selecting which technique(s) to implement. In the second step, however, no reasonable alternative should be rejected—any option overlooked here may be lost forever. Further, failing to take the time for this second, creative step—going directly from exposure identification to the selection of risk management techniques—can rob a risk management program of much of its vitality and capacity for innovation.

This chapter outlines the thirteen alternative risk management techniques. For each technique, the chapter first defines the technique in question and, where appropriate, differentiates it from other techniques and, second, illustrates how that technique could be applied, or why it could not be applied, to particular property, net income, liability, and personnel losses facing Promontory Point Railroad and Sheltering Arms Hospital. This discussion lays the foundation for the third step in the risk management process, selecting the apparently best (most cost-effective, profitable, or efficient) risk management technique(s), a step detailed in Chapters 9 through 12.

EXPOSURES TO BE MANAGED

This chapter focuses on eight loss exposures—one property, one net income, one liability, and one personnel loss exposure each for Promontory Point Railroad and Sheltering Arms Hospital. The following are possible losses:

Property exposures to:
- Promontory Point Railroad from fire damage to its headquarters building, which it owns, partially occupies, and partially rents to other office tenants

- Sheltering Arms Hospital from highway accident damage to the six ambulances it owns for transporting its patients

Net income exposures to:
- Promontory Point Railroad from damage to its headquarters building
- Sheltering Arms Hospital from a nurses' strike, forcing shutdown of the hospital's nonessential activities

Liability exposures to:
- Promontory Point Railroad from loss of, or damage to, passengers' luggage
- Sheltering Arms Hospital from medical malpractice claims from open-heart surgery patients

Personnel exposures to:
- Promontory Point Railroad from disability of the chief of its computer operations, on which both the railroad's scheduling and accounting activities are dependent
- Sheltering Arms Hospital from the death of its widely respected chief of staff, who also served as chairman of its finance committee

While somewhat random, these exposures exemplify the wide range of exposures with which risk management professionals must often deal and illustrate appropriate uses of the range of risk control and risk financing techniques. Learning how to apply various risk management techniques to these exposures equips a risk management professional to be equally creative in applying these techniques to many other routine and unusual exposures.

This chapter's examples of how to apply particular risk management techniques to specific loss exposures is not exhaustive. With respect to loss prevention, there may be thirty or forty measures Promontory Point could take to reduce the frequency of fire losses to its headquarters building. This chapter discusses only the most apparent measures; risk management professionals will be able to think of many others (indeed, one of the objectives of this chapter is to stimulate such creative thinking).

This discussion also makes no attempt to take account of any legal restrictions that may limit an organization's choices among various risk management techniques. Thus, the following paragraphs ignore the possibility that a statute may require an organization to install a fire-fighting system even though such an installation may not be in an organization's best financial interest. Likewise, this discussion assumes that no requirements imposed by bond holders, other creditors, or those with whom the organization has entered into business contracts require it to purchase insurance rather than choosing, for example, to retain the financial burden of those accidental losses it may wish to absorb directly. Similarly, this discussion assumes that if an organization wishes to establish a funded reserve or rely on any other recognized risk financing technique, no statutes preclude it from doing so. While these assumptions are generally valid for profit-seeking organizations, some state statutes or local ordinances may restrict the options that some organizations—particularly public entities—might wish to exercise. In practice, every organization's risk management professional should check for such legal limitations on a particular organization's risk management choices. Where such restrictions apply, the affected organization should comply with them or work to have them changed.

Finally, a particular measure may involve elements of two or more risk management techniques. For example, with respect to damage to Sheltering Arms' ambulances in highway accidents, driving at reduced speeds can involve both loss prevention (reducing the frequency with which these accidents occur) and loss reduction (reducing the severity of accidents because of the reduced energy involved in any collisions). The fact that a given measure involves two or more risk management techniques does not make it any less valid as an example provided that both the loss prevention and loss reduction effects are separately distinguished.

RISK CONTROL TECHNIQUES

Risk management techniques include both risk control and risk financing techniques. Exhibit 8-1 presents thirteen alternative risk management techniques. For the second step in the risk management process, where the objective is to consider all alternatives in a systematic fashion, this sequence is very efficient. However, it bears no relationship to the relative practical significance of various risk control and risk financing techniques. For example, exposure avoidance — treated first among the risk control techniques because, conceptually, it is the most complete form of risk control—is quite rare. Exposure avoidance requires sacrificing all the potential benefits from the asset or activity associated with the avoided exposure. The risk control techniques of loss prevention and reduction, discussed second and third, are used much more frequently. Segregation of exposure units and contractual transfer apply less frequently, but can be very effective.

Exposure Avoidance

Exposure avoidance is acting so as not to create the particular loss exposure being avoided or to eliminate completely any existing exposure,

Exhibit 8-1

Thirteen Alternative Risk Management Techniques

Risk Control Techniques	Risk Financing Techniques
1. Exposure Avoidance	Retention through:
2. Loss Prevention	7. Current expensing of losses
3. Loss Reduction	8. Unfunded reserve
Segregation of Exposure Units	9. Funded reserve
4. Separation	10. Borrowed funds
5. Duplication	11. Affiliated ("captive") insurer
6. Contractual Transfer for	12. Contractual Transfer for
Risk Control	Risk Financing
	13. Commercial Insurance

thereby reducing the probability of any loss absolutely to zero for any one person, firm, or society as a whole. For example, a person who chooses to "not go near the water" under any circumstances avoids the exposure to drowning in water—the person does not allow that exposure to exist. The swimming pool owner who fills in his or her pool with concrete avoids the exposure of being found liable to the heirs of someone who might have drowned in the pool. Properly practiced, exposure avoidance is a completely self-sufficient risk management technique. An exposure that has been completely avoided cannot produce a loss. Therefore, there is no further need to try to prevent, reduce, or pay to restore the impossible loss. This reasoning assumes that the probability of loss from the avoided exposure is absolutely zero, and not merely some very small number (in which case, some other risk management technique(s) would be appropriate).

While exposure avoidance is the complete risk management technique, it has only very limited application. To avoid the exposure of drowning in water, for example, a person must literally *never* go near any water in which he or she can drown. This person cannot, for instance, wash in customary ways, drink or otherwise consume water in quantities that could cause drowning, or take airline flights over any bodies of water into which the airplane might crash. (In reality, there is no way a person can avoid the exposure to drowning in water.)

In short, simply existing unavoidably subjects individuals and organizations to some exposures to loss. The only way to avoid all types of property loss is to possess no property whatever. Furthermore, only by never earning (and never hoping to earn) any net income can an individual or organization avoid all exposures to net income loss. Therefore exposure avoidance is not a feasible alternative against the broad categories of loss exposure.

Certain narrower exposures can definitely be avoided. Suppose a manufacturing company, located on an island and concerned about the weakened condition of the one bridge over which trucks carry its output to market, wishes to avoid the exposure of losing a shipment in a bridge collapse. The company can avoid this exposure by transporting its output to the mainland on boats (which do not pass under the bridge lest they be damaged in a possible bridge collapse). Using boats avoids the exposure to trucks being lost in a bridge collapse, but this action exposes shipments to boating accidents. Avoiding one loss exposure often creates another.

If this company's real concern is not with exposure to bridge collapse as such, but rather with the broader exposure to damage of its output while in transit to the mainland, boats may be no better than trucks. The only ways to avoid the exposure to damage to its output in transit over water are not to transport to the mainland at all or to move its manufacturing plant to the mainland.

Exposure avoidance is often mistaken for either loss prevention or contractual transfer for risk control. The proper distinctions among them appear in the discussions of loss prevention and of contractual transfer for risk control.

Property Exposures. For fire damage to Promontory Point's headquarters building and physical damage to Sheltering Arms' ambulances, exposure avoidance may not be feasible. Exposure avoidance would require Promontory Point to function without a headquarters building or Sheltering Arms to function without ambulances. No organization can operate without some sort of headquarters, and few hospitals function without ambulances to bring patients to their facilities. (As will be discussed in connection with contractual transfer for risk control, both Promontory Point and Sheltering Arms might be able to operate with *leased* facilities, but leasing would merely shift the loss exposure to the lessor/owner of the building or ambulances, not avoid the exposure.)

Net Income Exposures. The two net income exposures for which this chapter explores the feasibility of alternative risk management techniques are, first, Promontory Point's reductions in revenues or increases in expenses because of fire damage to its headquarters and, second, loss of revenues or increased expenses Sheltering Arms may suffer if its nurses strike, partially shutting down the hospital.

Avoiding either of these exposures is not feasible. As long as Sheltering Arms has nurses who may strike (whether legally or illegally), disruption of the hospital's activities stemming from such a strike is inevitable. As long as Promontory Point has a headquarters, fire damage to that facility, making it untenantable, would raise the railroad's operating expenses. Promontory Point also has the exposure to loss of its rental income from the portion of the building it rents to others. The only way this exposure can be avoided would be to discontinue, or fail to renew, all leases. In this way, the railroad would no longer have tenants from whom it would receive rental income.

Liability Exposures. In general, any liability exposure can be avoided only by refraining from the activity that may give rise to that liability. For example, Promontory Point could avoid liability for damage to passengers' luggage by refusing to transport, handle, or otherwise be responsible for any passenger's luggage. The railroad's rules would have to stipulate that no passengers may carry any luggage, even hand luggage, on board its trains. Similarly, Sheltering Arms could avoid its exposure to liability for medical malpractice stemming from open-heart surgery by not performing any such surgery and forbidding any of its surgeons from performing such surgery.

Although avoiding these liability exposures is conceivable in these two examples, there are serious questions about whether or not avoidance is advisable, or even practical, in the real world. A railroad refusing passengers with luggage, even executives with briefcases, will soon have few passengers. Avoiding open-heart surgery is also impractical. A patient brought to Sheltering Arms' emergency room may require such surgery and the hospital's refusing to perform it (or sending the patient to some other hospital for the surgery) may itself constitute malpractice.

Furthermore, rules instructing employees or agents to refrain from certain activities may be broken. Some Promontory Point train conductor may allow a passenger to carry luggage. Perhaps in the midst of another surgical procedure, a surgeon at Sheltering Arms could decide that immediate open-heart surgery is essential for the patient's recovery. These breaches of regulations compromise any efforts to avoid the exposures to which the regulations are directed. Furthermore, these regulations would provide the railroad or the hospital no legal defense if, as a result of these breaches, someone were injured and brought suit against the railroad or the hospital. (If the railroad or hospital were held liable for an employee's conduct in breach of an established rule, the railroad or hospital may be able to recover its liability loss from the wrongdoing employee, but this recovery does not eliminate the railroad's or hospital's initial liability for the harm done by its employee.)

Despite the inherent difficulties of applying exposure avoidance, an organization should attempt to avoid a liability exposure whenever the expected value of the liability losses from engaging in a particular activity (and employing any other risk management technique except exposure avoidance) outweigh the expected benefits of engaging in that activity. Thus, it may be quite reasonable for Sheltering Arms to attempt to reduce (but probably not completely avoid) its exposure to medical malpractice liability from open-heart surgery by referring all such surgical patients to another hospital whenever reasonably possible.

On the other hand, Promontory Point Railroad probably should not even attempt to avoid its liability exposure from passengers' luggage. Because most passengers would not be willing to travel without luggage, the only reasonable way to avoid the exposure would be for Promontory Point to discontinue passenger service—an option probably not worth the loss of revenue it would require. The benefits of transporting luggage—and the passengers who travel with it—almost certainly outweigh the costs of the liability exposures involved. The practice of sound risk management would call for other ways of dealing with these liability exposures.

Personnel Exposures. The only way to avoid exposure to loss of a key person is to eliminate the organization's dependence upon his or her hard-to-replace services. However, if the services of such persons were not essential, they would not be "key" persons. This is certainly true for the two personnel loss exposures used as examples in this chapter. Promontory Point cannot do without the special skills of the chief operator of its computer used for scheduling its trains and maintaining its accounting system, nor can Sheltering Arms do without the special prestige and executive talents of the renowned surgeon who serves as both its chief of staff and chairman of its finance committee.

Loss Prevention

Loss prevention is any measure that reduces the probability, or *frequency*, of a particular loss but does not completely eliminate all possibility of that loss, as does exposure avoidance. Loss prevention reduces loss frequency without completely eliminating all chance of loss and without necessarily having an effect on the likely severity of loss. Conceptually, loss prevention differs from exposure avoidance because loss prevention does not eliminate all chance of loss.

Loss prevention is also distinct in principle from loss reduction because loss reduction focuses on reducing the *severity* of losses, not on their probability or frequency. In practice, a risk management action may combine elements of both loss prevention and loss reduction, as when the reduction in the legal highway speed limit in the late 1970s cut both the number of automobile accidents (because drivers had more time to react to dangerous situations) and the seriousness of those accidents that did occur (because less kinetic energy was released when slow-moving vehicles collided with any other object).

The differences among exposure avoidance, loss prevention, and loss reduction are highly important. Since exposure avoidance eliminates all possibility of loss, it is the self-sufficient risk management technique in those rare situations when it can be successfully and thoroughly applied. When exposure avoidance completely eliminates a risk exposure, no other risk control or risk financing technique is needed. If, however, a safety measure only reduces probability of loss, then sound risk management calls for at least some risk financing plan, and perhaps further risk control measures, for coping with the remaining exposure.

Similarly, the distinction between loss prevention and loss reduction is critical to effective risk management. A safety measure that reduces the likely frequency of loss (but does nothing to reduce the probable severity of the losses that do occur—for example, "No Smoking" signs with respect to fire damage) may reduce the aggregate losses an organization suffers over a period of time, but the size of individual losses is not likely to be reduced. Loss prevention measures that have no loss reduction effects, therefore, cannot justify lowering an organization's top limits of financial protection against accidental losses.

Most loss prevention measures go hand in hand with concepts of how losses are caused. In general, a loss prevention measure is an action taken or a physical safeguard installed before a loss occurs in order to break the chain of circumstances or causes that are thought to lead to the loss. Breaking the chain is supposed to stop the loss from happening, or at least make it less likely.

Because of the close link between loss causation and loss prevention, developing effective loss prevention measures usually requires a careful study of how particular losses are caused. For example, following H. W. Heinrich's theory of accident causation, most work injuries have traditionally been thought to result from a chain of events that includes an unsafe act or an unsafe condition. In this tradition, work safety efforts have focused on trying to eliminate specific, unsafe acts or unsafe conditions.[1] As another illustration, fire safety engineers speak of a "fire triangle"—the three elements of fuel, oxygen, and an ignition source, which all must be present in order for fire to occur. Consequently, preventing fire requires removing at least one of the three legs of the fire triangle.[2]

Common law holds that a person can be liable for negligent conduct only if four conditions occur together: (1) a duty owed to another, (2) a breach of that duty, (3) resulting harm to another, and (4) a sufficiently close or "proximate" causal connection between the breach and the harm. Therefore, efforts to prevent liability losses focus on removing at least one of these four necessary elements for liability, most frequently by trying to eliminate conduct that breaches duties owed to others.

Property Exposures. As with exposure avoidance, this discussion of loss prevention focuses on two exposures: fire damage to Promontory Point's headquarters and physical damage to Sheltering Arms' ambulances from highway accidents.

Fire Prevention. Fire prevention is an extensive specialty, requiring years of study. Below is a broad outline of this specialty and some of the preventive measures Promontory Point could apply to its headquarters:

A. Eliminating Potential Fuels
   1. Removing unnecessary flammables
   2. Safe storage of necessary flammables
   3. Good housekeeping to isolate potential fuels from ignition sources
B. Removal of Oxygen—storing highly flammable materials in oxygen-free (airtight) containers or environments
C. Removal of Ignition Sources
   1. Elimination of open flames and other heat sources (such as from the smoking of tobacco products)
   2. Compliance with the National Electrical Code to control electricity as a source of heat or flame
   3. Elimination or safe storage of reactive chemicals that, in particular situations, can cause flames to ignite
   4. Elimination of sources of spontaneous combustion
   5. Enforcement of "no smoking" regulations
   6. Screening of employees to identify those with poor fire safety records

This outline focuses only on ways of stopping fires from happening, not ways of extinguishing them or reducing the extent of damage they cause. For example, fire detection/suppression (alarm and sprinkler) systems are not listed because they do not prevent fires. As mentioned in the next section under "Loss Reduction," such systems only reduce fire loss once a fire has occurred.

Highway Accident Prevention. Most analyses of the causes of highway accidents focus on (1) defects in the overall highway system, including law enforcement; (2) shortcomings of the vehicle involved in an accident; and (3) shortcomings of the driver operating this vehicle. Efforts to prevent these accidents (as well as to reduce their severity—loss reduction) usually follow these analyses.

Within this framework, some loss prevention measures that Sheltering Arms could use to reduce the frequency of highway accidents causing physical damage to its ambulances include the following:

A. The Highway System
   1. Where possible, use the safest routes to and from hospital
   2. Urge authorities to keep roads in good condition and re-move traffic hazards
   3. Comply with applicable traffic laws in situations not involv-ing medical emergencies
B. Ambulance Vehicles
   1. Maintain these vehicles in good condition
   2. Forbid overloading or other uses of ambulances for which they were not designed
C. Ambulance Drivers
   1. Employ only competent drivers whose abilities, training, and attitudes qualify them for this stressful work
   2. Give drivers refresher training on a regular basis
   3. Make sure all drivers using ambulances are rested and in good physical condition

Net Income Exposures. The two net income loss exposures used as illustrations throughout this chapter are reduced revenues or increased expenses from, first, fire damage to Promontory Point's head-quarters building and, second, a strike of Sheltering Arms' unionized nurses.

From Fire Damage. Promontory Point is almost certain to suffer net income losses from any serious fire damage to its headquarters. Such damage will at least temporarily increase operating expenses, and if fire forces partial shutdown of some of the railroad's operations, revenues are also likely to decrease during the shutdown. Rental income would certainly be lost if fire rendered unusable the portion of the building that tenants occupy. Therefore, the only effective way to pre-vent any net income losses from such a fire is to prevent the fire itself. Fire prevention measures have already been outlined.

Promontory Point may be able to minimize these net income losses through sound contingency planning so that essentially normal opera-tions would continue despite a fire. If such planning is totally effective, the railroad would suffer no increases in expenses or decreases in reve-nue—these plans would have achieved loss prevention with respect to the net income loss exposure. A more likely result, however, is that these plans will only reduce the severity of the net income loss, making such planning an illustration of loss reduction rather than of loss prevention.

From Nurses' Strike. Similarly, any substantial strike of Sheltering Arms' nurses will almost certainly cause the hospital a net income loss by decreasing its revenues from patients it can no longer serve or by increasing its expenses when nonstriking administrative staff or other temporary personnel work long hours to complete the work the striking nurses would otherwise perform. Completely closing the hospital during the strike would probably not be feasible because of some patients' needs for continuous care. Shutting down would erase this net revenue, causing a net income loss.

The only clearly feasible way to prevent any net income loss caused by a nurses' strike is to prevent the strike itself by maintaining labor peace. Building good labor relations so that no strikes occur requires long-term senior management commitment to employees' concerns and to their equitable treatment. Therefore, preventing losses stemming from strikes is a responsibility that extends beyond the risk management professional. Labor relations typically is a personnel or senior management, rather than a risk management, responsibility. Nonetheless, labor union actions can cause losses that fall within the usual risk management realm: net income losses from extra expenses to continue operations or loss of revenues during partial shutdowns.

Liability Exposures. Preventing liability losses typically involves trying to avoid conduct for which liability may be imposed.

For Promontory Point's liability for damage or loss to passengers' luggage and Sheltering Arms' liability for medical malpractice growing out of open-heart surgery, the duties that must be carried out in order to prevent liability are reasonably clear. As a common carrier of passengers' luggage, Promontory Point is duty bound to deliver safely all luggage entrusted to it under virtually all conditions. A common carrier is a virtual guarantor of the safety of the cargo. Therefore, to prevent damage or loss for which passengers may bring claims, Promontory Point's baggage handlers and other personnel must exercise great care.

Health care facilities and personnel are generally not guarantors of the results of their work. They typically are held to a standard of care that courts deem reasonable under the individual circumstances. While the meaning of "reasonable" may differ from case to case and may change over time (generally in the direction of demanding more medical proficiency), the hospital can reduce the chance that a patient will bring a successful malpractice suit by taking such precautions as (1) informing the patient of the nature of the surgery and of the hazards it involves; (2) obtaining appropriate consents to surgery; (3) ensuring that all staff is competent; (4) effectively controlling operating room activities and conditions; and (5) providing good post-operative care.

Personnel Exposures. Preventing loss of key personnel through death, disability, retirement, or unemployment means reducing the likelihood of the events that would cause a key person to die, become disabled, retire prematurely, or otherwise become unemployed. In broad terms, personnel losses can be prevented by keeping key employees and family

FROM: MEDICAL & ACADEMIC AFFAIRS

2260

members healthy, safe, and happy in their currently productive roles. These general strategies, adapted to the particular persons and organizations involved, should be applied to the two personnel loss exposures upon which this chapter focuses: disability of Promontory Point's chief computer operator and death of Sheltering Arms' chief of staff and finance committee chairman.

Efforts to reduce the frequency of disability or premature death should focus on maintaining key persons' general good health and protecting them from manifestly dangerous situations. Appropriate measures to reduce the probability of resignation or other unemployment losses depend upon whether one takes the employer's or the employee's perspective. For an employer, preventing workers from resigning or retiring prematurely requires keeping employees content in their current jobs and sufficiently satisfied with their compensation, responsibilities, and working conditions so that they do not actively seek other employment or withdraw from the work force. An employee, on the other hand, can prevent resignation or premature retirement losses by seeking satisfying, stable employment.

Loss Reduction

Loss reduction measures reduce the severity of those losses that do occur. To analyze loss reduction opportunities, a risk management professional must assume that a loss has occurred and then ask what could have been done, either before or after the loss, to reduce its size or extent.

The two broad categories of loss reduction measures for any type of loss from any peril are (1) pre-loss measures, those which are applied before the loss occurs and (2) post-loss measures, those which are applied after the loss occurs. Pre-loss efforts to reduce loss severity may also reduce loss frequency—driving ambulances at lower speeds in nonemergency situations, for example. Pre-loss measures generally reduce the amount of property, the number of persons, or other things of value that may suffer loss from a single event. Post-loss measures typically focus on emergency procedures, salvage operations, rehabilitation activities, or legal defenses to halt the spread of loss or to counter its effects. Erecting firewalls to limit the amount of damage from any one fire is a pre-loss measure; an effective fire detection/suppression system is a post-loss measure.

Property Exposures. Of the two property loss exposures selected for this chapter, opportunities for loss reduction are somewhat greater for fire damage to Promontory Point's headquarters than for highway accident damage to Sheltering Arms' ambulances. The general location and nature of a fire can be more easily forecast than can a highway accident, making it easier to take pre-loss and plan post-loss actions to minimize building damage than ambulance damage.

Reducing Fire Losses. Before the outbreak of fire, Promontory Point could reduce the likely severity of fire loss at its headquarters by taking the following actions:

1. Erecting firewalls or otherwise establishing fire divisions so that spread of any fire which did strike a portion of the building would be confined
2. Reducing fire intensity by removing or storing in fire-resistive containers any flammable materials or building contents
3. Cooperating with the fire department to establish pre-fire plans for the actions the fire department should take in a fire emergency
4. Establishing a headquarters fire emergency plan for appropriate actions by Promontory Point personnel in the event of a fire
5. Installing and maintaining an appropriate fire detection/suppression system for the headquarters building (including any special fire protection needed for particular activities such as computer operations)

Immediately after a fire breaks out at Promontory Point's headquarters, appropriate post-loss measures would include the following:

1. Automatically activating of the fire detection/suppression system
2. Notifying public fire-fighting authorities (which may be a feature of the automatic fire detection/suppression system)
3. Implementing the headquarters fire emergency plan for Promontory Point personnel
4. Providing temporary physical protection against other perils for property undamaged by the fire
5. Salvaging fire-damaged property

Notice that the pre-loss and post-loss lists of loss reduction measures overlap because some (perhaps most) of the post-loss actions require pre-loss planning. This overlap is not a flaw in the analysis or ineffective risk management. It is merely good general management before loss occurs to achieve the post-loss goal of minimum damage. Efficient post-loss action does not occur automatically. It requires pre-loss planning, even practice drilling, for added assurance that plans will actually work in an emergency. Planning and execution are separate steps, and each is essential.

Highway Accident Reduction. Before any accidents involve Sheltering Arms' ambulances, the hospital could take the following measures to reduce the severity of damage to these vehicles:

1. Improve the crash resistance of these vehicles (both by strengthening their outer perimeters and by firmly attaching the ambulance's medical equipment to the inside of the vehicle so that the equipment will not be needlessly tossed about in an accident, perhaps causing further physical damage).
2. Operate the vehicles at the slowest speed consistent with their mission at any particular time.

After an accident, further physical damage to the ambulances can be prevented by properly protecting them and having them repaired as soon as possible. Rapid repairs also shorten the length of time a damaged ambulance is out of service, thus reducing net income loss to the hospital because of the unavailability of that particular ambulance.

Net Income Exposures. As detailed in Chapter 5, most net income losses stem from the loss of the use of property for a significant period of time. The severity of the net income loss suffered depends upon the extent to which the organization's revenues are decreased or expenses are increased during this time period until normal operations can be restored. It follows that reducing the severity of net income losses typically requires an organization to act, either before or after the use of any property is lost, to reduce, first, the time needed to resume normal operations or, second, the daily amounts by which its revenues are decreased or its expenses are increased until normalcy is again achieved.

From Fire Damage. For the net income exposure stemming from fire damage to Promontory Point's headquarters, the railroad could reduce the time required to resume normal operations by, for example, expediting repairs to the portion of the premises damaged by fire and, if feasible, finding temporary substitute facilities to use during the restoration. Finding such temporary facilities could be especially important for housing some of the railroad's most crucial operations and as temporary quarters for the tenants whose rents might otherwise be waived. Moreover, if doing so would reduce the railroad's operating costs without unduly reducing revenues, Promontory Point could discontinue any nonessential headquarters operations (or transfer some of these operations to other Promontory Point offices) and perhaps lay off some headquarters personnel.

From Nurses' Strike. For the net income exposure from a strike of Sheltering Arms' nurses, reducing the duration of the loss would entail ending the strike as soon as possible—consistent with the hospital's ability to meet the terms of any new labor contract. To maintain revenues and patient care during the strike, Sheltering Arms could, at least temporarily, rely more heavily on nonstriking personnel or could bring in new nurses to carry out the strikers' duties. However, protecting the hospital's net income during the strike would require restraint in acquiring temporary personnel lest the hospital incur substantial extra expense for this purpose.

Liability Exposures. With respect to liability losses, loss reduction comes into play after the occurrence of some conduct for which an organization may become liable. The objective of this loss reduction is to minimize the extent of the damage suffered by any potential claimant or to reduce the amount that the claimant may be able to collect because of having suffered loss for which the organization is legally responsible.

Liability loss reduction steps to minimize the harm done to any particular claimant include the following:

1. Appropriate first aid or other medical care to potential claimants suffering bodily injury
2. Measures to safeguard from further damage the property of others who may bring claims for property damage
3. Courteous treatment of potential claimants so that their actual or imagined injuries do not include undue mental distress, harassment, embarrassment, or the like

Minimizing the amounts for which claimants may be able to sue successfully involves establishing the strongest possible legal defense. The following are appropriate steps for this purpose:

1. Instructing employees not to admit guilt at the scene of an accident or take other action that may waive legal defenses
2. Gathering all possible evidence that may aid in defending a claim
3. Seeking competent legal counsel to defend the claim in question
4. Cooperating with defense counsel
5. Where appropriate and without admitting liability, offering to advance funds to a claimant for medical expenses or for other actions to mitigate the harm the claimant may suffer
6. Where appropriate, settling claims out of court in order to reduce legal expenses and to avoid uncertainties and delays in court procedures

Both Promontory Point's and Sheltering Arms' uses of these liability loss reduction strategies must be tailored to the particular exposures they each face. For dealing with liability for passengers' luggage that the railroad has damaged or lost, Promontory Point could take special care to preserve partially damaged luggage and to treat with special courtesy passengers who make claims for damaged or lost luggage.

Both these actions would tend to reduce the harm suffered by claimants. To strengthen its legal defenses, Promontory Point should investigate the circumstances surrounding claims to see if one of the exceptions to a common carrier's liability for damaged goods excuses it from legal responsibility. Furthermore, noting prior damage to luggage it accepts gives the railroad a basis for denying liability for pre-existing damage. In some cases, Promontory Point may choose to simply pay relatively small luggage claims without thorough investigation when the cost of paying the claim would be less than the cost of investigation and defense.

In contrast to the relatively frequent but typically small claims for luggage that Promontory Point may have lost or damaged, medical malpractice claims against Sheltering Arms Hospital are likely to be much more substantial and less frequent. The size of these malpractice claims and their adverse effects upon the hospital's reputation suggest more diligent efforts to reduce their severity by, for example, carefully documenting the treatment of all open-heart patients as evidence that the hospital exercised appropriate care in treating them, obtaining and cooperating with the best available legal counsel, and extending courteous treatment to potential claimants.

Personnel Exposures. The applications of loss reduction to personnel losses are somewhat limited. Reducing an organization's dependence upon any one key person by distributing his or her duties or skills among others is certainly sound risk management, but, technically, it is not loss reduction. As explained below, such spreading of responsibilities or skills is segregation of loss exposures. Similarly, subcontracting work to other organizations in order to call upon the special skills of their personnel is contractual transfer for risk control, the subject of which is treated below. Again, this is entirely proper risk management, but not loss reduction.

Applied to personnel loss exposures, loss reduction involves reducing the time an organization is without the services of the key person. For example, when someone like Promontory Point's computer operator is disabled, loss reduction involves rehabilitation to return the key person to work as soon as possible or, alternatively, hiring or promoting a replacement to carry on the disabled person's duties with as little disruption in normal operations as possible. Losses from the temporary absence of a disabled key person also may be reduced by returning him or her to part-time work as soon as possible (or perhaps consulting the disabled person to obtain his or her advice on special problems, which others can solve with this help. If loss of a key person is permanent, as when Sheltering Arms' chief of staff and chairman of its finance committee died, loss reduction requires promptly replacing this person with a competent successor.

Segregation of Exposure Units

The blanket term "segregation of exposure units" encompasses two distinct but closely related risk management techniques: *separation* of exposure units and *duplication* of exposure units. Both strive to reduce an organization's dependence upon any single asset, activity, or person, thus tending to make individual losses smaller and more predictable. The logic of segregation of exposure units is exemplified in the maxim, "Don't put all your eggs in one basket." When losses become smaller and more predictable, they become easier to manage and less disruptive.

Separation involves dividing an organization's own existing single asset or operation into two or more separate units. (Three examples are dividing an existing inventory between two warehouses, erecting fire walls to create separate fire divisions within a single building, and manufacturing in two plants a component part formerly produced in only one plant.) Separation is appropriate where an organization can meet its goals with only a portion of these separate units left intact. If total loss is suffered by any one unit, the portion of the assets or operations at the other location(s) is sufficient. With separation, all separated units are normally kept in daily use in the organization's operations.

Duplication involves complete reproduction of an organization's own "standby" asset or facility to be kept in reserve. This duplicate is not used unless the primary asset or activity is damaged or destroyed. Duplication is appropriate when an entire asset or activity is so important that the consequence of its loss justifies the expense and time of maintaining a duplicate. Two sets of accounting records or key items of equipment and back-up employees are examples of duplication of exposure units.

Separation and duplication are distinct from one another, and both are distinct from other means of loss reduction. Four points need to be noted. First, unlike other means of loss reduction, neither separation nor duplication of exposure units makes any special attempt to reduce the severity of loss to any one single unit. Second, both separation and duplication reduce the severity of an individual loss, but they may have differing effects on loss frequency. Using two distantly separated warehouses instead of one is likely to increase loss frequency because two units are now exposed to loss rather than just one. Duplication is not likely to increase loss frequency, presuming that the duplicated unit is kept in reserve and not used—is not as exposed to loss as is the primary unit put to daily use. (For example, a duplicate vehicle presumably is garaged and is not as vulnerable to highway accidents as is the primary vehicle.) Third, duplication is therefore likely to reduce the average, or "expected," annual loss from a given exposure because duplication reduces loss severity without increasing loss frequency. Fourth, separation may or may not decrease the average "expected" loss. Much depends on whether the reduction in loss severity from separation is more important than or is overshadowed by the increased loss frequency, which separation normally entails.

Both separation and duplication tend to be expensive, sometimes impractical risk management techniques. Separation, in particular, is seldom undertaken for its own sake but, instead, is a byproduct of other management decisions. For example, few organizations build and use a second warehouse simply to reduce the severity of losses to the former warehouse. However, if an organization is considering the construction of a second warehouse, the purchase of another vehicle, the hiring of another key computer operator, or other expansion, the risk management implications of creating these new, hopefully separate, exposure units may well be an additional argument in favor of the expansion.

In contrast, duplication—keeping a spare unit on standby for emergency use—often is primarily prompted by risk management considerations. Senior management recognizes the crucial nature of the duplicated operation or asset and is willing to invest in the duplicate as a safeguard against being without this essential element of its operations. Duplicate records, spare machinery parts, and cross-training employees to do several jobs within their department are typical risk management safeguards and are recognized and justified as such.

For cost reasons, separation of exposure units (and keeping all units in daily use) typically has more practical applications than does duplication (where standby units remain idle except during emergencies).

Segregating Property Exposures. Of the two property exposures examined in this chapter, Sheltering Arms' ambulances are likely to present more opportunities for segregation than does Promontory Point's headquarters. The railroad is not going to maintain two headquarters, although there may be certain key operations, such as adjusting train schedules or billing customers, for which the railroad would have contingency plans to conduct these activities at other Promontory Point facilities if necessary. For efficiency, these activities would normally be centralized in the headquarters office with the contingency facilities only being ready on a standby basis.

Separation could well be a vital risk management strategy for Sheltering Arms to minimize physical damage to ambulances involved in highway accidents. If the hospital's activities normally require an average outcome of, say, six ambulances in daily use, the hospital might consider operating with some "excess capacity" of seven or eight ambulances on a daily basis. Keeping all seven or eight units in daily use would be an example of separation. The hospital could "afford" to have one or two ambulances temporarily disabled and still have the necessary six to perform essential work. Alternatively, the hospital could practice duplication of exposure units by keeping one or two of its seven or eight ambulances permanently garaged, brought out only in emergency overload situations. Which of these two strategies would be more cost-effective depends upon the particular facts of the situation, but in either case, the hospital's risk management professional should recognize the value of this "excess capacity" as a way of segregating exposures.

Notice that the exposure here is physical damage to the ambulances in highway accidents. If the exposure were simply physical damage to the ambulance, including damage while garaged, an appropriate segregation of exposure units would avoid garaging all the ambulances in a single facility, lest they all be destroyed there. Many fire departments, ambulance services, and others whose activities revolve around emergency vehicles practice such segregation as a matter of course.

Segregating Net Income Exposures. When an organization owns, normally occupies, or otherwise has access to a number of locations among which it can shift its operations, it may have some opportunities to segregate its exposures to the net income loss that could result from substantial damage to any one of those locations. If one location is shut down (such as Promontory Point's headquarters after it is damaged by fire, or Sheltering Arms in the wake of a nurses' strike), the organization may be able to shift its operations to other facilities. Although this shifting will necessarily entail some extra expenses and probably a partial temporary reduction in revenue, the net income loss will not be as great as it would if the organization did not have alternative facilities.

The distinction between separation and duplication applies to alternative facilities as well as to other assets and operations. Separation occurs whenever an organization, following damage at one location, simply redirects work from that location to its other facilities, which must bear a temporary extra workload until the damaged facility is repaired. Promontory Point could probably shift some of its headquarters operations to other major facilities throughout the railroad's system until the building is repaired.

In contrast, Sheltering Arms, with only one major location, would not normally have other facilities of its own available for patient care and other activities. (Even if it did have such facilities, the nurses' strike would presumably extend to those facilities as well.) Neither separation nor duplication of exposure units may be a feasible way for the hospital to deal with its net income losses stemming from a nurses' strike.

Segregating Liability Exposures. For liability exposures, the applications of segregation of exposure units are somewhat limited.

Duplication, in the sense of "spare" or "back-up" parts or facilities, has little meaning here—an organization does not *want* to have more liability exposures. Separation, in the sense of creating smaller (and, incidentally, more numerous) loss exposures, is relevant to the control of some liability losses—especially where separation can decrease the numbers of persons or amounts of property that may be injured or damaged because of a negligent or other wrongful act for which an organization may be legally responsible. To illustrate from a case not involving Promontory Point or Sheltering Arms, the development of "jumbo" jets so substantially increased the potential severity of an airline's liability from the crash of a plane carrying several hundred people that insurance underwriters were, for a time, reluctant to offer limits of insurance that the airlines considered adequate. For smaller craft, however, the underwriters were not so reluctant because, in effect, smaller planes segregated the airlines' loss exposures by transporting passengers in a larger number of separate planes, each presenting an independent loss exposure.

Promontory Point might be able to separate its exposures to liability for damage to passengers' luggage by dispersing that luggage throughout the train. Such dispersion would reduce the amount of damage that would result from a derailment, overturn, or other accident affecting only one or a few cars because the luggage on the remaining cars would be safe. Without such dispersion, an accident involving the one baggage car could cause a total luggage loss on that train. For Sheltering Arms Hospital, however, such separation appears to offer no real opportunities to reduce the severity of its potential liability losses from open-heart surgery.

Segregating Personnel Exposures. Applied to loss of the services of key persons, segregation implies dividing one key person's activities among several persons so that the loss of any one person's talents does not have a potentially devastating effect. Within an organization, segregation can be achieved by cross-training a number of individuals in the same essential tasks so that, in an emergency, any one of them can continue the work. Duplication also can be achieved by training some on-call persons who could be summoned in an emergency. Promontory Point, for example, could employ this strategy with respect to its exposure to disability of its key computer operator.

Another opportunity to use segregation—specifically separation—in dealing with a personnel loss exposure is evident in the case of the death of Sheltering Arms' chief of staff and chairman of its finance committee. If, before death or other personnel loss occurred, these two sets of duties were divided between two executives or even between two assistants to the one executive holding both posts, then a personnel loss from whatever cause would not be such a major blow to the hospital.

Contractual Transfer for Risk Control

Contracts are an integral element of several risk management techniques. For example, if an organization decides it would rather use leased automobiles than purchase those vehicles, the lease contract leaves with the lessor many of the property loss exposures that would otherwise be associated with owning the cars. This arrangement is a contractual transfer for risk control. Again, one organization may agree to reimburse another for certain types of losses the other may suffer. This agreement is essentially an insurance contract except that, in this particular case, neither of these organizations is an insurer. Such an arrangement, often called a "hold-harmless agreement" or an "indemnity agreement," is a contractual transfer for risk financing.

The diverse contracts used in risk management have a variety of names. The fundamental distinction is between the following:

1. Contractual transfer for risk control—a contract that transfers to another entity the legal responsibility for performing a particular activity and for bearing specified types of losses that may grow out of that activity.

2. Contractual transfer for risk financing—a contract that transfers the financial burden of particular losses to another entity (not a commercial insurer) who acts as a transferee by agreeing to pay losses to or on behalf of the transferor. A contractual transfer for risk financing is conceptually equivalent to commercial insurance except that the transferee is not an insurer. Commercial insurance is a contract that transfers the financial burden of particular losses to a commercial insurer who acts as a transferee by agreeing to pay losses to or on behalf of the transferor [insured].

A *contractual transfer for risk control* is an agreement under which a transferor shifts to another (the transferee) the loss exposures associated with an asset or activity by requiring that transferee to perform certain activities and, as an element of those activities, to assume certain exposures and to bear any losses that arise out of those exposures. Under a contractual transfer for risk control, the transferor seeks no indemnity or other compensation from the transferee but, rather, expects the transferee to perform certain activities that the transferor deems unduly hazardous.

Under contractual transfers for risk financing, the transferee makes a financial promise to pay for particular losses but does not promise to perform any other activity (except perhaps safety inspections, accident investigations, or other activities tangential to that duty to pay). The transferor is entitled to financial payment for particular losses, making this transferor also an indemnitee. With contractual transfers for risk control, the transferor is entitled to the performance of a particular "risky" activity by the transferee. Here, the transferor does not expect an indemnity payment for any resulting losses because, under the contract, the transferee performing the risky activity is responsible for any losses that may result.

Exhibit 8-2 presents a simplified hypothetical example of the distinctions between these types of contractual transfer. This example shows that these distinctions rest on (1) which party is performing the "risky" activity, (2) whether the transferee's commitment is to perform an activity or to pay money, and (3) on whom any loss falls if the transferee fails to perform as promised.

Now consider the case in Exhibit 8-2 under a variety of circumstances. Assume that Digger Phelps' bulldozer slips beneath the quicksand of Baskerville's bog. If the bulldozer were lost during Phelps' first five minutes of work, before he amended the contract with a contractual transfer for risk financing protecting Phelps, the bulldozer risk would fall on Phelps. Baskerville's contractual transfer for risk control would have worked. Phelps, despite the loss of his bulldozer, would have been obligated to finish filling in the bog, and Baskerville's own bulldozer would have remained safe. As long as their contract was fairly bargained, Phelps could not hold Baskerville responsible for Phelps' loss of his bulldozer.

Alternatively, assume that Phelps' bulldozer is lost after the revised contract had been signed, with the contractual transfer for risk financing protecting Phelps. Under this amended contract, Baskerville would be obligated to pay Phelps 350 pounds to indemnify Phelps for loss of his bulldozer. Here, Phelps' contractual transfer for risk financing would seemingly have the upper hand because the financial burden of the loss of the bulldozer would fall on Baskerville. As before, however, Baskerville's own bulldozer would still be safe—to that extent, his contractual transfer for risk control would have worked. Phelps would remain obligated to complete the job, presumably with a replacement bulldozer.

Now assume a third, somewhat more complex scenario. Suppose the bulldozer slips beneath the quicksand after Phelps is well into his work and thinks that, as in the second case, he is protected by the contractual transfer for risk financing in his amended agreement with Baskerville. As before, he approaches Baskerville and asks for the 350 pounds as indemnity. But presume, as a complication, that Baskerville is suddenly deprived of his hereditary estate and, as a complete shock to both Baskerville and Phelps, Baskerville finds himself destitute and lacking any applicable insurance. In this case, the financial burden of the loss is very likely to fall on Phelps because, unless backed by insur-

Exhibit 8-2
Types of Contractual Transfer

The Ground of the Baskervilles

A Fanciful Adaptation from Sherlock Holmes to Illustrate
Contractual Transfers for
Risk Control and Risk Financing

Sir Henry Baskerville, wishing to remove from his property the quicksand bog that swallowed up so many characters in Sir Arthur Conan Doyle's famous saga of Sherlock Holmes, hires a landscaping engineer, Digger Phelps, to fill in Baskerville's famous bog using Phelps' bulldozer. (Sir Henry could have done this himself, using his own bulldozer, but he recognizes the hazards of the bog and does not want the Baskerville bulldozer to be lost in it.) The contract between Sir Henry and Digger specifies that Digger will use his own bulldozer and will assume all responsibility for damage to the bulldozer while on Baskerville's property. For Baskerville, this is a contractual transfer for risk control—by asking Digger Phelps to fill in the bog, Baskerville (as transferor) has transferred to Phelps (as transferee) responsibility for filling in the bog and for any related damage to Phelps' bulldozer.

Five minutes after Digger begins the work, the bulldozer almost slips beneath the quicksand of the bog. Recognizing this extreme hazard, Phelps refuses to continue unless Baskerville agrees to amend their contract with a provision that, should Phelps' bulldozer be lost in the quicksand, Baskerville will pay Phelps 350 pounds sterling, the agreed fair market value of a bulldozer comparable to the one Phelps is using. From Phelps' standpoint, this indemnification amendment to their agreement is a contractual transfer for risk financing under which Phelps, as transferor/indemnitee, is entitled to compensation from Baskerville, as transferee/indemnitor, should Phelps lose his bulldozer while filling in Baskerville's bog.

ance or some other independent guarantee, a contractual transfer for risk financing is only as good as the financial strength of the transferee/indemnitor. Baskerville's destitution makes Phelps' financial protection under the contractual transfer for risk financing virtually worthless. Despite this risk financing contract (or "hold-harmless" or "indemnity" agreement) supposedly benefiting Phelps, the financial burden of the loss still falls on him. (In contrast, in the first case where Baskerville was protected by the contractual transfer for risk control, Phelps' risk of his bulldozer falls on Phelps even though the bulldozer's destruction may impoverish Phelps. In this case, Baskerville would still have the legal right to force Phelps to fill in the bog. This absence of any expectation of indemnity distinguishes a contractual transfer for risk control from a contractual transfer for risk financing and from commercial insurance.)

Contractual transfer for risk control can easily be mistaken for exposure avoidance. Some have incorrectly said, for example, that one way to avoid the physical damage exposures inherent in operating a fireworks factory is to sell the factory to someone else so that the new buyer now faces these exposures. The seller, the former owner, is sometimes wrongly said to have avoided these exposures. This analysis is incorrect because it fails to recognize that the exposures inherent in operating the factory still exist. They have not been eliminated; they merely have been shifted to the new buyer through a contract of sale (from the seller's standpoint, a contractual transfer for risk control). True exposure avoidance requires eliminating the loss exposure for everyone, even for society as a whole, by using it for some other purpose, abandoning this factory, or not constructing it initially.

Transferring Property Exposures. Both Promontory Point and Sheltering Arms could contractually transfer to a lessor their respective property exposures to fire damage to the railroad's headquarters and highway accident damage to the hospital's ambulances. This transfer could be accomplished by leasing, instead of purchasing, the building and the ambulances. Since Promontory Point already owns the headquarters building and Sheltering Arms the ambulances, they could sell these properties to a third party and then lease them back from the new buyer. Through this lease arrangement, the owner/lessor would have the exposure to property damage to the headquarters building or ambulances it now owns. Presumably, the lease payments that Promontory Point and Sheltering Arms would make to the lessor would reflect the lessor's loss exposures to fire or highway accident damage to these properties.

Transferring Net Income Exposures. Few, if any, net income loss exposures lend themselves to risk control through contractual transfer. Most organizations derive their net income from activities, usually involving the use of tangible property. To induce some third-party transferee to undertake these activities, the transferor presumably would have to pay the transferee the same net income (revenues minus expenses) that the transferor now earns by using the same property for the same activity.

Sheltering Arms, however, may have one opportunity for contractual transfer for risk control. Several hospitals in the community may have mutually contracted with one another that, should any of them be shut down by a strike or other occurrence, the other hospitals entering into the contract would provide facilities for the affected hospital's patients and temporarily assume that hospital's administrative activities.

If the agreement called for the affected hospital to receive the revenue and to be charged with the expenses from the activities taken on by the other hospitals, the affected hospital, in essence, would be dealing with its net income loss exposure through contractual transfer. Having access to others' facilities would help the affected hospital control its net income loss on a temporary basis for the duration of the emergency. (Although this contract would allow each hospital to use a larger number of facilities in which to continue its operations, this contractual arrangement is not an example of segregation of exposure units. When an organization practices segregation, it spreads its operations among facilities that it owns or controls, not those of other organizations.)

The one net income exposure that Promontory Point may be able to transfer relates to its rental income from tenants in its headquarters building. The common law, together with typical lease provisions, provides that if a fire or other peril makes a premises untenantable, the tenants' obligations to pay rent are suspended until the premises are again made usable. Promontory Point *may* be able to insert into its leases a contrary provision stipulating that the tenants must continue to pay rent even if the premises are severely damaged by fire or some other peril. If its leases with its tenants are amended, and if the courts uphold this provision as being fairly bargained, then Promontory Point will have shifted to its tenants the railroad's exposure to loss of net income from fire damage to the rented premises. The railroad would be assured that its rental income would continue despite any fire damage.

Transferring Liability Exposures. The extent to which an organization can succeed in contractually transferring a liability loss exposure depends upon the courts' attitude toward the attempted transfer. Sheltering Arms could attempt to contract with a limousine company to supply drivers for the ambulances owned by Sheltering Arms and operated under its name. The contract between the hospital and the limousine organization might well specify that this livery firm and its drivers would be responsible for any liability growing out of highway accidents involving the ambulances. If Sheltering Arms assumes that the courts will uphold this attempted transfer of liability, then, from the hospital's point of view, it has contractually transferred to the livery firm the hospital's exposure to liability losses.

A more likely outcome, however, is that the courts would consider the livery firm and its drivers to be agents of Sheltering Arms. Therefore, under the general law of agency, the hospital would be legally responsible for the negligence or other fault of the ambulance drivers in causing highway accidents. The courts might impose the same agency-based liability on Sheltering Arms even if it were to subcontract its entire ambulance operations using both drivers and vehicles hired and owned by the subcontractor. This result would be especially likely if the hospital, rather than the subcontractor, were in the financially stronger position to pay adequate compensation for bodily injury or property damage in accidents involving these ambulances.

Thus, attempts to shift liability loss exposures contractually—completely ridding the transferor of any responsibility for the transferee's wrongdoing toward third parties—are not likely to succeed, largely for public policy reasons. The courts are reluctant to excuse from liability those parties for whose ultimate benefit the subcontracted activity is being conducted.

With respect to Promontory Point's liability as a common carrier for the safety of the luggage its passengers entrust to it, the courts are not likely to allow the railroad to "evade" this liability by subcontracting the transport of luggage to some other party. Similarly, in the medical malpractice context, courts—anxious to see patients adequately compensated for unfortunate medical results—are not likely to let the hospital shield itself from liability under contracts with operating surgeons specifying that the surgeons, and not the hospital, will be responsible for claims growing out of open-heart surgery.

Unlike contractual transfer for risk control, courts might uphold risk financing contractual transfers such as "hold-harmless" or "indemnity" agreements. For example, an agreement between Sheltering Arms and each of the surgeons who performs open-heart surgery at the hospital might well specify that the surgeon will "hold the hospital harmless from" or "indemnify the hospital for" liability claims brought against the hospital on account of the surgeon's acts of malpractice. This agreement between the physician and the hospital does not absolve the hospital from liability to third parties; it only provides the hospital with a possible source of indemnification if it must pay claims. Such an indemnification agreement between a surgeon and the hospital—or between any agent and its principal—does not run counter to, or even have any relevance for, the public policy reasons for holding the principal responsible for harm that an agent's conduct causes for third parties.

Transferring Personnel Exposures. Subcontracting crucial operations can be a very effective way for an organization to use contractual transfer for risk control in dealing with some personnel loss exposures. For example, if a firm finds itself especially dependent upon a key technician, such as Promontory Point's chief computer operator, the organization could hire a subcontractor to perform this function. The subcontractor is then obligated to complete the work regardless of the death, disability, resignation, or retirement of any one particular employee of the subcontractor on whose special talents the subcontractor relies to carry out the contract.

Such subcontracting, however, also creates some new uncertainties for the organization that relies on this contractual transfer for risk control. These uncertainties center around the reliability of the selected subcontractor. For example, as long as Promontory Point relies on its own employee to be the key computer operator, it knows and has faith in the individual. Relying upon a subcontractor can be equally effective only if Promontory Point has the same degree of confidence in the subcontracting firm.

Some key executive functions cannot, of course, be transferred to an outside organization. An example of such a nondelegable function is the work done by Sheltering Arms' chief of staff, who must be a hospital employee. This key executive currently has two roles—both chief of staff and chairman of the finance committee. It may be possible for the hospital to subcontract to a fund-raising organization or other firm many of the activities of the finance committee, thus reducing the hospital's dependence on this phase of this key executive's work.

RISK FINANCING TECHNIQUES

If risk control techniques do not treat a particular exposure adequately, the remaining alternatives are all risk financing techniques. Several risk financing techniques involve retention. An organization can retain loss exposures through current expensing of losses, through unfunded reserves, through funded reserves, through use of borrowed funds, or through an affiliated "captive" insurer. Contractual transfer provides another alternative for risk financing. The final alternative is commercial insurance.

Risk Financing Through Retention

All retention techniques for risk financing share the common characteristic that they draw upon funds originating within the organization suffering the loss or within that organization's economic family. The range of retention options can be arrayed, as in Exhibit 8-1, in increasing order of formality. These options are retention through current expensing of losses, retention through an unfunded reserve, retention through a funded reserve, retention through borrowed funds, and retention through an affiliated ("captive") insurer.

Retention Techniques. It is more efficient to define each of these five retention techniques before illustrating their appropriate uses. The following definitions of retention techniques, as well as of transfer techniques, are designed to serve the risk management professional in analyzing feasible risk financing options. Their focus is essentially managerial, and they should not be used for other (especially regulatory or other governmental) purposes. Specifically, it would be a misuse of the following definitions to cite them as evidence in a legal proceeding involving whether a particular risk financing arrangement is or is not retention or transfer. As a general rule, the federal Internal Revenue Code gives more favorable tax treatment to financing arrangements that are considered transfer than it does to financing arrangements that are considered retention. Because the tax status of risk financing arrangements is a public policy question, the following definitions may not apply in that context.

Retention Through Current Expensing of Losses. Retention through current expensing of losses involves paying losses as they occur, as normal, current business expenses. This financing technique is most appropriate for any losses to be paid from current revenues that will not disrupt unduly a given accounting period's financial results. For many organizations, the breaking of a windowpane or the puncturing of a single automobile tire routinely would be paid out of available cash. Depending on cash inflows and the other demands placed on those inflows, some organizations also would pay $2,500 of repairs resulting from an automobile accident as a current expense; still other organizations would consider a $25,000 or $50,000 fire loss one that could be easily absorbed with current cash flows without any special advance funding arrangements.

An organization's decision to pay losses as current expenses depends on its financial position, plans for future investment/expansion, seasonal fluctuations in cash flows, and debt commitments, as well as other factors. In evaluating these factors, the risk management professional should not attempt to make this or other financing decisions without consulting the organization's accounting and finance managers.

When determining the extent to which to treat losses as current expenses, the organization should be aware of the uncertainties that surround this technique. Specifically, current expensing may fail to provide anticipated cash sufficient to pay retained losses if any of the following is true:

- The organization has considered separately the exposures for which it wishes to retain some portion of resulting losses but has failed to consider the combined burden of paying losses arising out of several exposures, all of which may result within a short period.
- The organization's loss experience may be unexpectedly adverse. A single large loss, or a series of smaller losses in a short time,

may exceed the cash the organization can conveniently free from normal operations to restore losses.

- Anticipated cash flows from the organization's normal operations may unexpectedly decrease because of a downturn in its business. This decrease in anticipated cash flows could decrease the organization's ability to pay losses as current expenses.
- The organization's loss experience may not be sufficiently predictable for it to evaluate its ability to absorb losses as current expenses.
- The organization may face an inadequate spread of risk, creating potential catastrophe exposures. For example, one organization may reasonably believe it can retain as a current expense up to $300 physical damage to any one of its ten vehicles. However, this does not mean that it can retain $3,000 collective damage should all ten suffer loss while garaged at one location.

These sources of uncertainty, clearly evident when considering retention through current expensing of losses, also pervade, in differing degrees, other forms of retention. Therefore, in evaluating the extent to which it wishes to use any particular type of retention, an organization should examine its overall financial position rather than consider any one retention technique or any one loss exposure in isolation. It is the total amount of uncertainty in the organization's overall risk financing plan, as well as the uncertainty associated with any particular set of exposures, that should be the focus of the risk management professional's attention in making retention decisions, especially through current expensing.

Retention Through an Unfunded Reserve. An *unfunded reserve* is a bookkeeping account to which is charged each year (or other accounting period) the actual or anticipated losses from a particular exposure. Periodic additions to this reserve can be considered an expense for managerial purposes. The accumulated reserve, built up over a series of accounting periods, is equivalent to the nature of a liability that reduces the organization's retained earnings, accumulated surplus, or other owners' equity. For managerial purposes, this unfunded reserve recognizes the effects that actual or anticipated losses for which the reserve was established would have on the organization's current profits and accumulated earnings or surplus.

Most loss reserves, whether unfunded or funded, serve essentially a managerial function, helping executives to recognize the real financial impact that anticipated or actual losses may have on their organization's financial position. However, as the Internal Revenue Service currently interprets the federal Internal Revenue Code, additions to such loss reserves cannot usually be recognized as tax-deductible business expenses. A tax deduction is allowed only when the loss is paid from the reserve. Thus, unfunded reserves are not a specific source of funds except to the extent that these reserves enforce conservatism on the organization's management and forestall the organization's use of the funds for other purposes.

Unfunded reserves may fail to provide the cash the organization planned to have available to restore losses under either of the following circumstances:

1. A severe loss may occur before the reserve has been built to a sufficient level. Whether funded or unfunded, additions to re- serves typically are based on the average or "expected" value of losses, but actual losses may not conform to this expectation.
2. Because the reserve is unfunded, the organization may not have readily-available cash equal to the reserve balance. Because the reserve is an accounting entry without any earmarked cash, the unfunded reserve is subject to the same weaknesses as is retention through paying losses as current expenses.

Retention Through a Funded Reserve. With a *funded reserve*, the organization does set aside—usually as an investment in a stable finan- cial asset—cash equal to the periodic additions to the reserve in amounts that it anticipates will be sufficient to meet expected losses. The assets in a funded reserve should be liquid, that is, rapidly convertible into a highly predictable amount of cash when needed to pay losses. Even though a reserve is liquid, the cash it can provide may not be adequate under the following conditions:

1. A severe loss occurs before the fund is sufficient to meet it.
2. Some senior executives or others, viewing the funds in the re- serve as "idle," use the funds for purposes not related to risk financing. This use may leave the organization unprotected against losses for which its operating management thought it held adequate funds.
3. Due to difficulties in predicting the organization's loss experi- ence, the periodic contributions to the funded reserve (plus the investment earnings on those funds) may be too low, even in the long run, to pay for actual losses.

Funded loss reserves are relatively rare retention vehicles for at least two reasons. First, most organizations have better uses for their funds than merely to invest them in financial instruments in anticipation of future losses. Typically, an organization can earn more by devoting its funds to regular, productive operations. Second, seemingly idle reserve funds are, in most organizations, so attractive a "target" for competing managers seeking additional funding for their own operations that it is politically difficult for a risk management professional to defend these reserves.

Retention Through Borrowed Funds. In principle, there is no reason an organization cannot borrow funds to finance recovery from accidental losses. It could borrow funds through either (1) arranging, before a loss occurs, for a line of credit or other borrowing vehicle to be activated upon the borrower's request, after a loss; or (2) arranging, after a loss, to borrow the funds it needs to recover from that particular loss.

In practice, borrowing has not been widely used as a risk financing technique, perhaps because recovering from an "accidental" loss may not be viewed as a fully legitimate reason for going into debt. Moreover, relying on borrowed funds involves some significant uncertainties. First, if the borrowing arrangements are made before the loss occurs, the organization must estimate in advance the funds it will need to recover from the loss. If the loss exceeds these estimates, the borrowed funds, even if available, may not be adequate. Second, if the borrowing arrangements are made after the loss occurs, the organization may find that it is not able to borrow sufficient funds on the terms anticipated. (This may be because the loss has been so severe that the lender's confidence in the borrower's ability to repay the loan has been shaken.)

One may legitimately question why borrowing is considered risk retention rather than risk transfer. If borrowing is retention, and if all retention techniques involve use of funds that "originate" within the organization or its economic family, in what sense do the borrowed funds "originate" internally? The answer is that, when an organization borrows to restore accidental losses, it uses some part of its ability to borrow funds for other purposes. Since an organization's credit standing (its ability to borrow) is an asset to that organization, partial use of this borrowing capacity to pay for accidental losses diminishes this asset. In a real economic sense, borrowing constitutes retention.

Retention Through an Affiliated ("Captive") Insurer. Some large organizations or associations form subsidiaries through which to finance specified types of accidental losses the "parent(s)" may suffer. Just as a manufacturing firm may form a corporate subsidiary through which to purchase or manufacture a component or a service, so the parent of a "captive" insurer also can form a subsidiary through which to purchase "insurance." ("Insurance" is placed in quotation marks here because the Internal Revenue Service, in challenging or denying the tax deductibility to the parent of premiums paid to its captive, has questioned whether the transaction constitutes "insurance.") In economic reality, although not necessarily for tax purposes, the "captive" subsidiary of the organization thus becomes a highly formalized means of retention.

If a captive has only one parent, it is known as a "pure" or "traditional" captive. If it has several parents to which it offers financial protection, it is known as an "association" or "group" captive. In either case, the captive is designed to function as a regular insurance company—domiciled, regulated by, and paying taxes to the state in which it is headquartered. A captive often offers financial protection to other "outside" organizations beyond its parent(s) both so that it can more nearly achieve the spread of loss exposures underwritten by a typical commercial insurance company and also to enhance its independence from its parent(s).

The line between a captive insurer and a commercial insurer is not always clear. Many United States mutual insurance companies formed in the late nineteenth and early twentieth centuries specialized in offering coverages to firms in particular industries such as hardware stores, florists, or sawmills that felt they could not obtain adequate coverage at reasonable premiums from the existing insurers. In a sense, particularly in their earliest days, these specialized mutuals closely resembled some of today's association captives. The captive insurance arrangement, particularly with pure captives, closely resembles risk transfer through commercial insurance, demonstrating that the distinction between retention and transfer is not always clear.

While this lack of clarity does not pose serious difficulties for the internal operation of an organization's risk management program, it has generated some confusion in the application of tax laws based on the retention/transfer distinction. The Internal Revenue Service has challenged the status of premiums paid to a captive on the bases that the captive (1) was not managed by executives who were independent of the management of the parent(s); (2) did not write a sufficient portion of its "insurance" portfolio on exposures that were unrelated to the business of parent(s); and (3) did not reflect any valid business purpose of the parent(s) other than reducing income tax payments.

Appropriate Uses. An organization may retain losses for either of two reasons: (1) because retention is forced (there being no transfer options) or (2) because some form of retention is more cost-effective than any form of transfer. These two types of retention may be called *forced retention* and *optional retention*, respectively. (A possible third reason for retaining losses from a particular exposure is that the organization has not recognized the exposure and therefore has made no funding arrangements. One of the most fundamental objectives of risk management is to recognize as many loss exposures as possible, thus minimizing retention through ignorance.)

Forced retention may result from a number of causes, including the following:

1. The peril that caused the loss was uninsurable (such as wear and tear or nuclear damage to property) or otherwise nontransferable.
2. The loss was not within the scope of the organization's commercial insurance or other contractual transfer for risk financing. (Extra expenses were retained because no coverage for them was specified.)
3. All or some portion of a loss fell within a deductible that the insurer required in order to exclude coverage of relatively small, insured losses.
4. The size of the loss was such that:
   (a) it exceeded the limits of the organization's insurance, and the excess had to be paid directly by the organization, or
   (b) the insurer or other transferee was unwilling, or did not have the financial capacity, to pay the loss.

Similarly, optional (presumably informed and conscious) retention may be the result of any of several factors, including the following:

1. The loss resulted from an exposure that the organization decided to fully retain such as flood damage in a flood-prone area, through any one or a combination of the retention options described earlier.
2. The size of the loss was such that only a portion of it fell within a deductible or other retention in the organization's program of insurance or other contractual transfer for risk financing.
3. The organization chose a deductible that excluded all or some portion of a loss that could have been fully insured.

Before choosing what, if any, optional retention an organization should undertake, its risk management professional, key financial executives, and perhaps other managers need to take cognizance of the extent of the organization's forced retention. Since any organization, at any given time, has only a given capacity to retain losses safely and cost-effectively, and because the organization has no choice with respect to its forced retentions, its optional retentions should be regarded as a residual. That is, it should consider optional retentions only after it has dealt with its forced retentions for all loss exposures considered collectively, not just for each one separately.

Within its area of optional retention, an organization's decision to retain or to transfer a given exposure depends largely on the characteristics of both the losses and the organization. As a general rule, an organization can more safely and more cost-effectively retain exposures that generate losses that meet the following criteria:

1. Are limited in the size of an individual loss to an amount clearly within the organization's retention capacity
2. Are unlikely to cause a large number of losses within a short period, lest the aggregate of retained losses be beyond the organization's retention capacity for that period
3. Are sufficiently frequent to be routinely budgeted.

While perhaps no loss exposure ideally fulfills all three of these criteria, those that more nearly meet them tend to be the better candidates for retention. Further, an organization's retention options are not limited to the simple choice of fully retaining versus fully transferring all losses from a given exposure. Between these two extremes, a wide range of possible levels of retention—through deductibles or "self-insured" retentions (SIRs)—can be combined with commercial insurance or some other transfer technique to finance losses above these levels. Small amounts of loss, within the limits many organizations are likely to choose as their deductibles, meet these three criteria more fully than do the less predictable extremes of more severe, higher levels of loss. Thus, by choosing its deductibles and SIRs carefully, an organization can limit retention to the losses that meet these criteria.

The financial and managerial characteristics of an organization also affect the types and amounts of optional retentions that the organization should choose. More specifically, an organization's capacity to retain loss exposures is increased when one or more of the following is true:

1. The organization has the assured financial capability, both currently and in the foreseeable future, to generate funds sufficient to pay losses within its chosen retentions without unduly disrupting the organization's normal productive activities. (This financial capacity can be based on past accumulations of retained earnings or on current earnings. In either case, the organization's senior management must devote appropriate portions of accumulated or current earnings to finance recovery from accidental losses.)
2. The organization's senior management (and owners in small or medium-sized organizations) are psychologically comfortable with the levels of retention the organization adopts.

There is no one "right" set of retention levels for all organizations facing a particular set of loss exposures. The characteristics of the exposures do not wholly determine the appropriate retention choices— some characteristics of the organization also are important. When the characteristics of an organization change—as when its financial strength is affected by swings in economic cycles or long-term persistent trends of growth or decline, when its managers' philosophies change, or when the relative costs of retention and transfer change—the uses of retention that are appropriate for that organization are also likely to change. Thus, there are no uses of retention that, even for one organization, are fully appropriate for "all time."

Property Exposures. Sheltering Arms' ambulances, which may suffer highway physical damage, appear to offer more opportunities for complete retention than does Promontory Point's headquarters building, which may suffer fire losses. There are two reasons for this result. First, while the total value of each property (building or vehicle) sets a limit on each exposure to loss, the value of one ambulance is more likely to be within Sheltering Arms' retention capacity than the value of the headquarters building is likely to be for Promontory Point. Second, Sheltering Arms has a number of ambulances, giving it a greater spread of exposure and greater predictability of losses than Promontory Point enjoys with its headquarters building. This greater predictability is enhanced by the fact that highway accidents are more frequent than fires, making their resulting physical damage easier to budget.

To whatever extent these two organizations retain these exposures, they are likely to pay for retained losses through relatively informal means of retention, such as current expensing of losses or use of a funded or unfunded reserve. Both organizations could practice *partial* retention of these respective exposures—selecting appropriate deductibles on their fire and vehicle damage insurance—and transferring to the insurer exposures to losses that may exceed these deductibles.

Net Income Exposures. Net income exposures are generally less amenable to full retention than are property exposures because net income losses are not as self-limiting. There is no upper limit, short of bankruptcy, on the maximum probable loss. Many organizations do, however, practice partial net income retention through deductibles in their business interruption, extra expense, or other insurance coverages. Promontory Point might well have such a deductible included in its business interruption policy covering losses stemming from physical damage to its headquarters building.

Sheltering Arms' exposure to net income loss from a nurses' strike poses a significantly different situation—forced retention. Net income losses stemming from actions of unionized employees typically are not insurable (or otherwise transferable) because, first, the loss tends to be within the insured's control and, second, there is often an incalculable probability of a catastrophe loss from widespread strikes throughout the economy. Therefore, Sheltering Arms must fully retain this exposure. Among its retention options may be an association captive, through which a number of hospitals could perhaps mutually insure one another against strike-related losses of income, much as some newspapers have done in the past.

Liability Exposures. With relatively rare exceptions, liability exposures do not lend themselves to full retention for two reasons. First, most liability losses are not self-limiting and can reach or exceed an organization's net worth, thus bankrupting it. Second, beyond payments to claimants, liability exposures also entail outlays for legal defense. Few organizations possess sufficient legal staff among their personnel but must acquire it through insurance. (Insurance typically covers investigative and courtroom costs related to insured claims.) For both of these reasons, Sheltering Arms is likely to fully insure its medical malpractice exposures growing out of open-heart surgery. Some hospitals, however, have joined together through association captives to manage medical malpractice claims, especially at times when medical malpractice insurance has not been widely available from commercial insurers at premium rates hospitals have considered appropriate.

An example of the unusual liability exposure that does tend to be self-limiting is Promontory Point's exposure as a common carrier for damage to or loss of passengers' luggage. With respect to individual items of luggage, the value of the potential loss typically is quite small (say, not more than $1,000) relative to the railroad's financial resources. Furthermore, given the railroad's common carrier status, Promontory Point can expect to settle most claims routinely, without many legal complications. In fact, the railroad's personnel, with their transport expertise, may be better able to investigate and manage luggage claims than could a typical insurer or other transferee. However, this reasoning applies more to individual loss of one particular passenger's luggage than to complete destruction of all luggage in the several cars that may constitute a derailed or demolished train. To finance such potential aggregate losses to passengers' luggage in a single event, Promontory Point may wish to purchase insurance with a large deductible.

Personnel Exposures. Most organizations routinely retain exposures to loss of the services of a key person who dies, becomes disabled, resigns, or retires. With respect to retirement, resignation, and disability, this retention is often forced because few insurers or other transferees are willing to accept these exposures, many of which can be anticipated and are clearly within the organization's control. With respect to the loss of the services of a key person who dies, "key person" insurance is widely available. However, because life insurance policies pay a fixed amount for the death of the person whose life is insured, these insurance proceeds may fall short of the organization's true economic loss from the death of a particular key person. To the extent of any shortfall, the organization again retains the key person exposure.

Promontory Point probably will be forced to retain the losses it can expect to suffer from the disability of its key computer manager. Sheltering Arms may or may not choose to obtain a life insurance policy on its chief of staff and chairman of its finance committee.

Contractual Transfer for Risk Financing

In addition to the various forms of retention, the other risk financing options consist of some form of transfer. As shown in Exhibit 8-1, the two major risk transferring options are contractual transfer for risk financing and commercial insurance. The two forms of risk transfer are quite similar except for the nature of the transferees. Under contractual transfer for risk financing, the transferee is some organization, individual, or entity other than a commercial insurer. Therefore, the contract is not an insurance contract and the transferee is not regulated as an insurer. Under commercial insurance, the transferee is an insurer.

Definition. A contractual transfer for risk financing is a contract under which one party, the transferee/indemnitor, agrees to pay for specified types of losses for which, in the absence of that contract, the financial burden would otherwise fall upon the transferor/indemnitee. The transferee may agree to reimburse the transferor directly, in which case the contract is often called an *indemnity* contract or clause. Alternatively, the transferee may agree to pay losses on behalf of the transferor, in which case the contract of transfer is often called a *hold-harmless* agreement or clause because the transferee holds the transferor harmless from financial responsibility for the loss—typically a claim that a third party brings against the transferor—that is the subject of the transfer contract. The contractual transfer specifies the types of loss for which the transferee agrees to be financially responsible. The agreement also may or may not require the transferee to maintain and give evidence of insurance adequate to fulfill its obligations under the contractual transfer for risk financing.

The example in Exhibit 8-2, "The Ground of the Baskervilles," illustrates the difference between contractual transfer for risk control and contractual transfer for risk financing. In that case, the contractual provision under which Sir Henry Baskerville agrees to indemnify Digger Phelps if Digger's bulldozer is lost in the bog is a contractual transfer for risk financing. Baskerville's only obligation under that provision is to pay Phelps the specified 350 pounds if the bulldozer is lost in the bog. Beyond this, Baskerville has no obligations to perform any other activities or to pay any other losses. In this example, only property loss exposures were involved.

In practice, many contractual transfers for risk financing deal with the transferor's potential liability to third parties or to the general public. To illustrate in terms of Baskerville's bog, Sir Henry might have required Phelps to hold Baskerville harmless from any liability claims that others might bring against Baskerville, as the landowner responsible for the bog, growing out of any work that Phelps did there. Phelps would have been the transferee/indemnitor with respect to the public liability exposure of Baskerville, the transferor/indemnitee. Their contractual transfer for risk financing (or hold-harmless clause) might have read as follows:

> The Contractor (Phelps) shall indemnify and hold harmless the Owner (Baskerville) and his agents and employees from and against all claims, damages, losses, and expenses—including attorneys' fees—arising out of and resulting from the performance of the work (on the bog), of every nature and description brought or recoverable against the Owner or his employees or agents.

While this is a relatively broad grant of seeming protection to Baskerville, apparently covering all claims without financial limit, Baskerville's protection is, in reality, only as sound as Phelps' financial strength. For this reason, Baskerville might also have required Phelps to purchase insurance to cover Phelps' obligation to indemnify Baskerville. In fact, Baskerville might even have required that Phelps pay for such insurance, with Baskerville purchasing it in Phelps' name.

Contractual transfers for risk financing usually alter the rules of common law that would otherwise apply in allocating losses. The wording and apparent meaning of these transfers are limited only by the ingenuity of the legal profession, provided courts are willing to enforce these contractual transfers as written. Moreover, some state statutes limit the extent to which parties may shift financial responsibility for loss. In general, court decisions and statutes render ineffective attempted contractual transfers for risk financing that, at face value, are either unfairly bargained and unconscionable or act to deprive the public of adequate compensation for injuries. For example, if Sir Henry Baskerville was very rich and in a much better position than Digger Phelps to control the safety of the bog, the courts (or an applicable statute) might disregard Baskerville's attempt to shift financial responsibility to Phelps.

Consequently, the financial protection that a transferor/indemnitee gains under a contractual transfer for risk financing is subject to the following uncertainties:

1. The transferee/indemnitor may not have insurance or other financial resources to meet its obligations to the transferor/indemnitee.
2. A court may find that the transfer agreement does not ade-

quately define the transferred exposure as the parties had intended. (For example, does the above quoted agreement apply if one of Sir Henry Baskerville's employees, entitled to workers compensation benefits from Sir Henry, falls into the bog while Phelps is working on it?)

3. A court or a statute may declare that the contractual transfer is unenforceable because it is unconscionably harsh on the transferee.

Appropriate Uses. As with contractual transfer for risk control, contractual transfer for risk financing is appropriate only when a party wishing to transfer the financial burden of a potential loss can find an appropriate, financially responsible, willing transferee. Among the property, net income, liability, and personnel loss exposures examined in this chapter, only two—both involving liability to third parties—appear to meet these conditions even approximately. With respect to the first of these exposures, Promontory Point might subcontract its baggage-handling operations to another organization (an attempted contractual transfer for risk control of the exposures associated with the baggage operation). However, given the railroad's status as a common carrier, its management would realize that a court would probably allow the railroad to still be sued for loss or damage to luggage caused by the subcontractor. Therefore, as part of the subcontracting agreement, Promontory Point might also require the subcontractor to hold Promontory Point harmless from any baggage-related claims. This hold-harmless provision would serve as a contractual transfer for risk financing if the courts did not allow the underlying subcontract to shield Promontory Point from liability. However, this attempted contractual transfer for risk financing might also fail, depending upon whether or not the provision appeared to be reasonably bargained and whether or not the passengers received adequate compensation from the subcontractor for their baggage losses.

Sheltering Arms also has an opportunity for contractual transfer for risk financing. Sheltering Arms might attempt to require that, as a condition for having surgical privileges to use the hospital's facilities, all surgeons agree to hold the hospital harmless from medical malpractice claims related to open-heart surgery. The security of the hospital's financial protection from such provisions would be subject to each of the three limitations listed above for all contractual transfers for risk financing. Therefore, prudent risk financing by the hospital would require that it, too, be prepared to meet medical malpractice claims brought against it from open-heart surgery in the event that the financial protection expected under the agreements with the surgeons did not materialize.

Commercial Insurance

While commercial insurance is perhaps the most evident, most widely used of all risk management techniques, it is the last technique described in this chapter because commercial insurance should be the "last resort" in a sound risk management program. It should be the alternative used when no other technique or combination of techniques is sufficient. When properly used in combination with other risk management techniques, commercial insurance fulfills its intended role of providing truly needed protection and thus both better serves the insured and generates a more reliable underwriting profit for the insurer.

Definition. As usually defined, commercial insurance is a contract under which one party, the insurer, agrees—in exchange for the payment of a (usually) periodic premium—to pay for specified losses the insured may suffer, up to (usually) specified amounts, under conditions specified in the insurance contract. Other than incidental duties tangential to paying insured losses, a commercial insurer typically has few duties under the contract.

Purchasing commercial insurance is generally the most reliable form of risk financing. The only significant uncertainties facing an insured under a commercial insurance contract are the following possibilities:

1. The commercial insurer may become insolvent or refuse to meet its policy obligations for some other reason.
2. The insurer and the insured may disagree as to whether a loss is insured or as to the amount of the loss.
3. The amount of the loss may be so large that some portion of it exceeds the applicable limit of the commercial insurance.

The first of these three sources of uncertainty can be reduced through careful selection of financially sound insurers. In addition, most states have guarantee funds designed to meet policy obligations of insolvent insurers. The second uncertainty, relating to the scope and limits of coverage, can be minimized through insurer/insured discussions of the meaning of the insurance contract in particular situations (or, if necessary, through litigation after a loss occurs). The third potential difficulty, inadequate limits, can be forestalled through the insured's proper selection of coverage limits. Despite these precautions, some residual elements of uncertainty may linger in a commercial insurance transaction. Nonetheless, if anything can be taken as "given" in risk financing, it is that, by and large, a commercial insurer will pay an insured loss.

Appropriate Uses. In order for an organization to insure against the financial consequences of a particular loss exposure, that exposure must meet, to at least a reasonable degree, the traditional "requirements" of an insurable exposure. As generally recognized in the insurance industry, these requirements are as follows:

1. Many persons exposed independently to the loss will purchase the insurance.
2. The exposures will not be too heterogeneous.
3. The losses will be definite as to cause, time, place, and amount.
4. The expected loss for each insured during the policy period will be calculable.
5. The loss will be accidental from the viewpoint of the insured.[3]

The fact that an exposure is commercially insurable does not mean that a particular organization should choose to purchase the available insurance. Other risk financing techniques, used alone or in conjunction with insurance, may be more cost-effective and provide substantially comparable financial protection. Chapters 11 and 12 of this text present general guidelines for making decisions about when to purchase commercial insurance. The ARM 56 text, *Essentials of Risk Financing,* explores the complexities of making appropriate insurance and other transfer/retention risk financing decisions.

SUMMARY

This chapter focuses on the second step of the risk management process, examining alternative risk management techniques that may be applied, individually or in combination, to property, net income, liability, and personnel loss exposures. The various techniques, charted in Exhibit 8-1, fall into two broad categories: risk control techniques to prevent losses from occurring (or to minimize their size) and risk financing techniques to pay for those losses that, despite even the best risk control efforts, inevitably occur.

Except where exposure avoidance completely eliminates any possibility of loss, sound risk management calls for combining some risk control technique(s) with some risk financing technique(s) for each significant loss exposure an organization may face. Without risk financing, risk control techniques are not sufficient because some losses are almost bound to occur, and recovery from these losses must be financed. Without effective risk control, risk financing techniques typically do not constitute effective risk management. Merely paying for losses as they occur, rather than trying to stop them or minimize their size, is wasteful, both of an organization's funds and of the entire economy's overall resources.

With alternative risk management techniques and their possible applications clearly in mind, risk management professionals should turn to the next step in the risk management decision process: selecting the most cost-effective technique or combination of techniques. This third step is the focus of Chapters 9 through 12 of this text.

Chapter Notes

---

1. H. W. Heinrich, Dan Petersen, and Nestor Roos, *Industrial Accident Prevention*, 5th ed. (New York, NY: McGraw-Hill Book Company, 1980), pp. 20–31.
2. Gordon P. McKinnon (ed.), *Fire Protection Handbook*, 16th ed. (Boston, MA: National Fire Protection Association, 1986), pp. 4-42 to 4-47.
3. C. Arthur Williams, Jr., George L. Head, Ronald C. Horn, and G. William Glendenning, *Principles of Risk Management and Insurance*, 2nd ed. (Malvern, PA: American Institute, 1981), p. 233.

CHAPTER 9

Forecasting—The First Basis for Risk Management Decisions

Risk management decisions rest on forecasts of future losses. These forecasts help determine the demands that will be placed on the risk management department as it works to protect the organization against accidental losses. As a foundation for the description in subsequent chapters of proper procedures for selecting risk management techniques, this chapter uses arithmetic and common-sense explanations of loss forecasting techniques that should help the risk management professional accomplish the following:

- Gather and organize the data on past losses needed to make forecasts of future losses. Forecasts are the basis of the third step of the risk management process, decision making.
- Describe and apply in intuitive, common-sense ways the two most widely used types of forecasting tools—probability analysis and trend analysis—to develop tables and charts for forecasting accidental losses.
- Decide when it is better to use probability analysis and when it is better to use trend analysis for loss forecasting.
- Understand the limitations of loss forecasts—whether based on probability analysis or trend analysis—and avoid their pitfalls by minimizing their limitations.

The unpredictability of accidental losses—the mere fact that they are accidental—has been said to be the most challenging part of risk management. Many say that, if an organization's property, net income, liability, and personnel losses were as predictable as its sales or production costs, then risk management would be no different than any other specialty within general management. They claim that cost-effective risk management decisions would then be made like any other type of business decision—by finding the presumably known benefits and costs of each alternative and then choosing the option whose benefits most exceed its costs.

However, those experienced in forecasting an organization's sales, costs, or profits face uncertainty at least as great as those who would forecast future losses. The same forecasting techniques applied throughout general management are equally valid for projecting future accidental losses. In the aggregate, over a substantial period, these losses are as predictable as many other costs.

DEVELOPING DATA ON PAST LOSSES

Forecasting accidental losses, like any other future event, requires detecting patterns in the past and projecting them into the future. These patterns may be as simple as "no change." More often than not, tomorrow's weather will be the same as today's. There also may be much truth in saying that this year's accidental losses for a particular organization will be about the same as last year's.

Alternatively, a pattern for the future may be one of change. The advance of a cold front may signal more severe weather tomorrow. Plans to increase factory output may foretell a greater number of injuries to employees. Furthermore, if inflation is projected to continue, each of these employee injuries may be more costly next year. Even when the pattern is one of change, there are some elements of constancy: the frequency of work injuries may be predictably related to output levels, and the rate at which inflation increases the financial impact of a given injury or property loss may be a continuation of past inflationary trends.

Thus, forecasting future accidental losses by finding these patterns begins with deciding which of two basic patterns, "no change" or "change in a predictable way," applies. Finding these patterns requires careful study of data on past losses. With adequate data in hand, a risk management professional can then look for patterns.

To find patterns that may be discovered in past losses, a risk management professional should attempt to find data that is (1) complete, (2) consistent, (3) relevant, and (4) organized. This data should be obtained by a reasonable expenditure of money, effort, and time.

Consider, for example, the situation facing Promontory Point's risk management professional when he joined the company in early 19X5. Because train derailments had been a major concern of the railroad's senior management, one of the first records the new risk management professional received was a listing, prepared by the accounting department, of the dates and historical dollar amounts (unadjusted for inflation) of the losses from derailments the railroad suffered from 19X1 through 19X4.

Complete Data

Since risk management professionals must rely upon others to gather much, perhaps most, of the information for making risk management decisions, Promontory Point's risk management professional was thankful to have this data from the accounting department. He knew that he would have to gather from others not only the amounts of losses, such as data in Exhibit 9-1, but also information on the circumstances surrounding each loss. Factors such as the location of each derailment, the time of day it occurred, the members of the train's crew at the time of the derailment, and the cargo being carried in the derailed cars might be helpful in isolating and correcting the precise causes of particularly frequent or severe losses.

A risk management professional must rely upon personal insight and judgment to recognize when crucial data may be missing. For example, when Promontory Point's risk management professional first examined the accounting department's report, it did not show any losses for 19X2. The losses whose amounts are marked with a single dagger in Exhibit 9-1 were omitted from the original report. Since derailments had occurred in each of the other three years, it seemed reasonable to ask accounting to verify that there had been no 19X2 derailments.

After checking, accounting found that the clerk who had been recording these losses during 19X1 had been replaced in 19X2 with a new clerk who had not been aware of the need to post losses to the summary account from which the report to the risk management professional had been prepared. Through insight and a cooperative spirit, needed data were obtained.

Consistent Data

To reflect past patterns, loss data must be consistent in at least two respects. First, the loss data must be collected on a consistent basis for all recorded losses. Second, to adjust for differences in price levels, all losses must be expressed in constant dollars, which, for Promontory Point in early 19X5, might well have been 19X4 dollars.

Consistent Basis for Data Collection. Loss data may hide patterns useful in forecasting future losses. If collected from different sources using different techniques, the possible sources of inconsistency are numerous. For example, in examining the amounts in the "Historical Amount" column of Exhibit 9-1, Promontory Point's risk management

Exhibit 9-1
Calendar of Historical Losses

Date	Historical Amount
19X1	
April 21	$ 1,008
May 3	4,651
September 29	155
December 4	1,783
19X2	
March 18	$ 1,271[†]
July 12	6,271[†]
August 15	7,119[†]
November 1	13,208[†]
19X3	
February 8	$ 5,189
May 17	7,834
July 27	2,100[††]
August 4	15,000[††]
December 19	12,830
19X4	
January 2	$ 6,782
January 9	21,425
April 22	4,483
June 10	9,059
June 14	4,224
October 23	35,508

[†] Originally omitted from listing by Accounting Department
[††] Upon further inquiry, these two reported amounts proved to be estimates which should have been $3,774 and $12,925 repectively.

professional noticed that two losses, those whose amounts are marked with double daggers, were reported in even hundreds of dollars.

While a dollar amount ending in "00" or "000" is just as likely as an amount ending in any other two or three digits, a risk management professional should be aware of the common tendency to use approximate, round numbers—numbers that may not be as accurate as others. An inquiry to accounting revealed that these double-daggered amounts were estimates, made either by the engineer of the train that derailed or by his supervisor. Therefore, while not to be ignored, these amounts are likely to be less credible than the other loss figures in Exhibit 9-1.

To make these two estimates more useful in forecasting future losses, Promontory Point's risk management professional asked for the bills resulting directly from these two losses. Thus reconstructed to be consistent with the other data, these amounts were changed from $2,100 to $3,774 and from $15,000 to $12,925. These revised figures are used in all subsequent calculations.

Amounts of Loss Adjusted for Price Level Changes. Losses expressed in historical amounts should be adjusted for price level changes. Otherwise, two identical losses occurring in different years will be reported as differing in amount. Inflation will make the later loss appear larger because it is measured in less valuable dollars. To avoid this distortion, all losses must be expressed in constant dollars. Following standard practice, the price level for the most recent complete year— here, 19X4—is used for expressing all losses in constant dollars.

For example, the value of a 19X1 loss would have to be increased to reflect the change in the relevant price index since 19X1. It is necessary to "inflate" the historical amounts of all past losses to current (19X4) levels by multiplying the historical amount of each loss in a given year by an inflator appropriate for that year. For instance, the inflator to bring 19X1 losses up to 19X4 price levels is computed as follows:

$$\text{Inflator (19X4)} = \frac{\text{Current (19X4) price index}}{\text{Price index for a given year (19X1)}}$$

The best approach to inflating ("indexing") past losses is to apply separate inflators to each element of cost in each loss—for example, separate inflators for property damage and liability claims. However, because of the difficulty of getting such specific price indexes, Promontory Point's risk management professional decided to use an index that combined changes in (1) the costs of railcar construction, representing the costs of repairing/replacing damaged railcars and (2) the cost of medical care, on the assumption that these two types of cost are the major elements in most derailment losses.

Given a suitable price index, indexing mechanics are straightforward. Exhibit 9-2 shows how appropriate inflators for each year should be computed. Since the price index stood at 115.2 in 19X1 and at 148.6 in 19X4, 19X1 losses should be multiplied by the ratio of 148.6/115.2 (yielding an inflator of 1.29). Similarly, computing the inflators for other years involves dividing the 19X4 price index by the price index for each year (shown in the second column of Exhibit 9-2). This results in inflators of 1.18 for 19X2 losses, 1.06 for 19X3 losses, and 1.00 for 19X4 losses (historical and constant dollars being the same in 19X4).

Exhibit 9-3 shows both the historical and adjusted amounts for each loss. The adjusted amount of each loss has been computed by a two-step

Exhibit 9-2
Inflators for Losses to 19X4 "Current Dollars"

Year	Price Index (P 19X0 = 100)	Inflators Computed as	Figure
19X1	115.2	P_{X4}/P_{X1}	1.29
19X2	125.9	P_{X4}/P_{X2}	1.18
19X3	140.2	P_{X4}/P_{X3}	1.06
19X4	148.6	P_{X4}/P_{X4}	1.00

process: (1) multiply each loss by the inflator for the year in which the loss occurred and (2) round the result to the nearest $100 to simplify later calculations. The gain in simplicity is well worth the slight loss of precision through rounding.

To illustrate, the first loss in Exhibit 9-3 (or in Exhibit 9-1), had a historical value of $1,008 on April 21, 19X1. When multiplied by the 19X1 inflator of 1.29, the adjusted amount of this loss becomes $1,300.32. After rounding to the nearest $100, the loss becomes $1,300, shown in the "Adjusted Amount" column of Exhibit 9-3. Similarly, the November 1, 19X2 loss, with a historical value of $13,208, adjusts to $15,600.

These calculations involve some assumptions about the timing of losses, which, while customary, are somewhat arbitrary, and thus should be carefully noted. For the year in which a loss occurs, adjusting its historical amount by the full rate of inflation during that year is technically correct only if it is assumed the loss occurred on the last day of the year. Otherwise, if the loss is assumed to have occurred sometime earlier during that year, only a portion of the entire price level change during that year should be used to adjust the historical loss figure to inflate it to the price level existing at the end of the year the loss occurred.

A reasonable, somewhat more realistic assumption would be that all losses occurred in the middle of the year and that only half of that year's inflation rate would bring those losses to year-end price levels. Even this assumption is realistic only if it can be further assumed that the rate of increase in prices was uniform throughout the year. Thus, if the inflation rate during 19X3 were 6 percent, some additional accuracy could be gained by inflating these losses by only 3 percent (instead of 6 percent) to bring losses up to price levels existing at the beginning of 19X4 on the assumption that these losses presumably occurred in mid-19X3.

However, because additional accuracy is gained only if the rate of

Exhibit 9-3

Adjustment of Historical Losses to 19X4 Price Levels

Date	Historical Amount	Adjusted Amount	Annual Total	Annual Number
		19X1		
April 21	$ 1,008	$ 1,300		
May 3	4,651	6,000		
September 29	155	200		
December 4	1,783	2,300	$ 9,800	4
		19X2		
March 18	$ 1,271	$ 1,500		
July 12	6,271	7,400		
August 15	7,119	8,400		
November 1	13,208	15,600	$32,900	4
		19X3		
February 8	$ 5,189	$ 5,500		
May 17	7,834	8,300		
July 27	3,774	4,000		
August 4	12,925	13,700		
December 19	12,830	13,600	$45,100	5
		19X4		
January 2	$ 6,782	$ 6,800		
January 9	21,425	21,400		
April 22	4,483	4,500		
June 10	9,059	9,100		
June 14	4,224	4,200		
October 23	35,508	35,500	$ 81,500	6
			Total	$169,300
Arithmetic Mean (Total/19)				$ 8,911

price increase was uniform throughout the year (for example, one-half of one percent during each month of 19X3) and because this approach is rarely used when only annual price index figures are available, this discussion follows the more usual practice of applying all inflators on an annual, rather than a semi-annual, basis. If monthly price index figures are available, improved accuracy could be gained by applying this indexing procedure on a monthly basis, starting with the month in which each loss occurred.

Relevant Data

The amounts of past losses should be valued on the basis most relevant to risk management—usually the cost to the organization of restoring the loss. For property losses, this is the repair or replacement cost of the property at the time it is to be restored, not the property's historical "book" value. For liability losses, the loss should include not only any claims paid but also the cost of investigating and defending or settling the claim. Business interruption losses must include not only losses of revenue from the shutdown of operations but also any additional expenses an organization incurs while trying to return business to normalcy.

For Promontory Point's derailment losses, the risk management professional was happy to learn that the values reported by accounting included the full amounts of these losses at the time each derailment occurred. These values included the then replacement cost of railroad property damaged, the amounts paid to shippers for damage to their cargoes, and the railroad's revenue and extra expense losses stemming from these derailments (again, expressed in historical dollars). Thus, once adjusted for inflation, the amounts provided by accounting were, in this fortunate case, appropriate for risk management. Had the data not been appropriate, the risk management professional would have had to confer with experts in accounting statistics and valuation techniques to value these losses properly or to make adjustments for any losses that had to be omitted because they could not be properly valued.

Organized Data

Listing losses by calendar dates, as in Exhibits 9-1 and 9-3, may fail to disclose patterns that could be revealed by listing losses by size. An array of losses—amounts of losses listed in increasing or decreasing value—may reveal clusterings of losses by severity and may also focus attention on large losses, which are often the most important in making risk management decisions. Organizing losses is the first step in charting losses by size to develop probability distributions or loss trends.

An array of the nineteen derailment losses Promontory Point suffered in 19X1 through 19X4 appears in Exhibit 9-4. The third column from the left is the adjusted amounts, with the other columns showing the dates, historical (unadjusted) amounts, and the rank of each arrayed loss. Notice that the numbers in the far right-hand column of Exhibit 9-4, "Rank," are arranged so that the largest loss, presumably the most important, has a ranking of "1," while the smallest loss ranks "19" (last). Finally, notice that ranking losses by adjusted amounts rather than historical amounts eliminates distortions caused by mere price level

Exhibit 9-4

Array of Historical and Adjusted Losses

Date	Historical Amount	Adjusted Amount	Rank in Array
September 29, 19X1	$ 155	$ 200	19
April 21, 19X1	1,008	1,300	18
March 18, 19X2	1,271	1,500	17
December 4,19X1	1,783	2,300	16
July 27, 19X3	3,774	4,000	15
June 14, 19X4	4,224	4,200	14
April 22,19X4	4,483	4,500	13
February 8, 19X3	5,189†	5,500	12
May 3, 19X1	4,651	6,000	11
January 2, 19X4	6,782†	6,800	10
July 12, 19X2	6,271†	7,400	9
May 17, 19X3	7,834†	8,300	8
August 15, 19X2	7,119	8,400	7
June 10, 19X4	9,059	9,100	6
December 19, 19X3	12,830	13,600	5
August 4, 19X3	12,925	13,700	4
November 1, 19X2	13,208	15,600	3
January 9, 19X4	21,425	21,400	2
October 23, 19X4	35,508	35,500	1

† Loss for which adjustment of historical amount to 19X4 constant
dollars changes ranking in array

changes and is therefore more useful in identifying the true impact of each loss.

Thus adjusted and organized, historical loss data provide an important basis for forecasting future losses. The following discussion explains how to make such forecasts, first by using probability analysis (of a presumably unchanging world) and then by using trend analysis (of a presumably changing world, but changing in a predictable manner).

PROBABILITY ANALYSIS

Probability analysis is particularly effective for predicting future accidental losses in organizations that (1) have a substantial volume of data on past losses and (2) have fairly stable operations so that (except for price level changes) patterns of past losses presumably will continue in the future. In such an unchanging environment, past losses may be viewed as a sample of all possible losses that the organization may suffer in the future. The larger this sample of losses and the more stable the environment that produces those losses, the more reliable will be the forecasts of future losses.

The Nature of Probability

Probability is the relative frequency with which an event can be expected to occur in the long run in a stable environment. For example, given many tosses, a coin can be expected to come up "heads" as often as it comes up "tails." Given many rolls of one die from a pair of dice, a "4" can be expected to come up one-sixth of the time. According to one standard mortality table, slightly over 2 percent of males aged sixty-two can be expected to die before reaching age sixty-three.[1] Finally, of the many automobiles now on the road, insurance company statistics in 1988 indicated that 1 out of every 132 could be expected to be stolen within the year.[2]

Any probability can be expressed as a fraction. The probability of a "head" on a coin toss can be expressed as 1/2, or 50 percent, or 0.50. The probability of a "4" on one roll of one die can be written as 1/6, 16.66 percent, or 0.167. Similarly, 1/132, 0.758 percent, and 0.00758 are all proper ways of indicating the probability that a particular automobile would be stolen during 1981.

The probability of an event that is totally impossible is 0, the probability of an absolutely certain event is 1.0, and the probabilities of all events that are neither totally impossible nor absolutely certain are greater than 0 but less than 1.0.

Probabilities can be developed either from historical data or from theoretical considerations. Probabilities associated with coin tosses or dice throws can be developed theoretically and are totally unchanging. From a description of a fair coin or die, a person who has never seen either of them could calculate the probability of, say, a "head" or a "4." Some writers label such theoretical probabilities as "prior to experience" or "*a priori.*"

In contrast, the probability that a sixty-two-year-old male will die or that a particular car will be stolen during the year cannot be deduced theoretically but must be estimated by studying the loss experience of a sample of men aged sixty-two or a sample of cars. The empirical or experiential probabilities deduced solely from historical data may change as new data is discovered or as the environment that produces these events changes. In contrast to *a priori* probabilities, empirical probabilities are only estimates whose accuracy depends upon the size and representativeness of the group of samples being studied. Moreover, empirical probabilities may change, whereas *a priori* probabilities are constant as long as the physical conditions that generate them remain unchanged. For example, the same source cited above indicating that in 1988, 1 vehicle in 132 could expect to be stolen within the year also reported that in 1970, this ratio was 1 in 121.

Sources of Probability Data

Risk management professionals often have significant difficulty developing data for probability distributions of accidental losses. The organization's own loss data often is not substantial enough to be reliable, and the data on the combined experience of other organizations, if available at all, frequently is not sufficiently specific or current to be particularly useful.

Therefore, while probability analysis is an important forecasting tool, most probabilities of particular types of losses are, at best, estimates compounded from a number of sources: the organization's own loss experience, that of similar organizations, and perhaps nationwide data from insurance companies, insurance rating organizations, or such organizations as the National Safety Council or the National Fire Protection Association. Because the underlying chances of loss are empirical probabilities that must be estimated and are subject to change, a risk management professional must pay close attention to the sources of loss data.

Constructing Probability Distributions

A probability distribution is a presentation, in a table or in a graph, of all possible outcomes of a particular set of circumstances and of the probability of each possible outcome. Because every such distribution includes the probability of every possible outcome, making it certain that one of these outcomes—and only one—will occur, the sum of the probabilities in a probability distribution *must* be 1.0.

This definition of a probability distribution applies to both *a priori* probabilities (such as those involved in tossing coins or rolling dice) and empirical probabilities (such as of the number or size of accidental losses). For example, in the flipping of a fair coin, each of the two possible outcomes, "heads" or "tails," has an equal probability of one-half, or 50 percent. Since, on a particular flip of a coin, only one outcome is possible, these outcomes are described as "mutually exclusive." Similarly, since these two outcomes are the only possible results and therefore exhaust all possibilities, they are said to be "collectively exhaustive." A properly

Exhibit 9-5
Probability Distribution for One Coin Toss

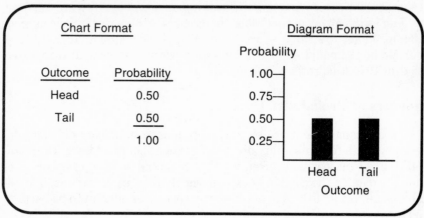

constructed probability distribution always contains outcomes that are both mutually exclusive and collectively exhaustive.

A chart and diagram of the probability distribution of the outcomes of a single flip of a fair coin appear in Exhibit 9-5. Observe that the sum of the probabilities, in both the chart and the diagram, is 1.0, and that both the chart and the diagram include all possible outcomes. By using these formats and by keeping in mind that all valid probability distributions contain events that are mutually exclusive and collectively exhaustive, one can chart and diagram other probability distributions.

Consider now a slightly more complex probability distribution: a distribution of the total number of points on one throw of two dice, one red and one green. The 36 equally likely outcomes (green 1, red 1; green 1, red 2; ... green 6, red 6) are shown in Exhibit 9-6. There are eleven possible outcomes (ranging from a total of 2 points to a total of 12 points) and the probability of each of these eleven possible outcomes is proportional to the number of times each point value appears in the table of outcomes. As the chart indicates, the probability of a total of 2 points is 1/36 because only one of the 36 possible ways the dice may fall (green 1, red 1) produces a total of 2 points. Similarly, 1/36 is the probability of a total of 12 points. The most likely total point value, 7 points, has a probability of 6/36, represented in the table of outcomes by the diagonal southwest-northeast row of sevens.

In the diagram showing each possible outcome, the height of the vertical line above each outcome is proportional to the probability of that outcome. Exhibit 9-6 presents three views of a complete probability distribution: all possible outcomes are accounted for (they are collectively exhaustive), and the occurrence of any possible outcome (such as

Exhibit 9-6
Probability Distribution of Total Points on One Roll of Two Dice

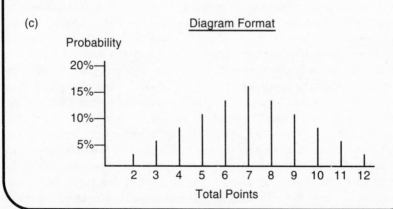

(a)

Table of Outcomes

Red Die

G r e e n D i e		1	2	3	4	5	6
	1	2	3	4	5	6	7
	2	3	4	5	6	7	8
	3	4	5	6	7	8	9
	4	5	6	7	8	9	10
	5	6	7	8	9	10	11
	6	7	8	9	10	11	12

(b)   Chart Format

Total Points— Both Dice	Probability				
2	1/36	or	0.028	or	2.8%
3	2/36	or	0.056	or	5.6%
4	3/36	or	0.083	or	8.3%
5	4/36	or	0.111	or	11.1%
6	5/36	or	0.139	or	13.9%
7	6/36	or	0.167	or	16.7%
8	5/36	or	0.139	or	13.9%
9	4/36	or	0.111	or	11.1%
10	3/36	or	0.083	or	8.3%
11	2/36	or	0.056	or	5.6%
12	1/36	or	0.028	or	2.8%
Total	36/36	or	1.001[†]	or	100.1%[†]

[†] Separate probabilities do not add to 1.000 or 100.0% because of rounding

(c)   Diagram Format

Probability

Exhibit 9-7

Probability Distribution of Loss Severity Developed from
Promontory Point's 19X1-19X4 Derailment Losses

(1) Size Category	(2) Number of Losses	(3) Percent of Number of Losses	(4) Amount of Losses (X 1,000)	(5) Percent of Dollars of in Category
>$0 but not > $1,000	1	5.26	$ 0.2	0.12
>$1,000 but not > $5,000	6	31.58	17.8	10.51
>$5,000 but not > $10,000	7	36.84	51.5	30.42
>$10,000 but not > $20,000	3	15.79	42.9	25.34
>$20,000 but not > $30,000	1	5.26	21.4	12.64
>$30,000	1	5.26	35.5	20.97
	19	100.00	$169.3[†]	100.00

[†] This total, $169,300, is also the sum of the four amounts shown in the "Annual Total" column of Exhibit 9-3.

green 1, red 1, or alternatively, a point total of 4) makes impossible (or excludes) any other outcome.

Tossing coins and rolling dice involve *a priori* probabilities easily demonstrated to common sense. Empirical probability distributions generated from loss experience follow the same rules as the distributions of *a priori* probabilities. For example, the data on loss size in Exhibit 9-7 include in Column 3 a probability distribution of the sizes of Promontory Point's derailment losses based on its 19X1-19X4 loss experience. Given the array of losses by size in Exhibit 9-4, it is possible to group these losses into the size categories presented in Column 1 of Exhibit 9-7 (or into any other convenient size categories), and to determine by count, shown in Column 2, how many losses fall into each category. Given 19 losses over four years, the probability of losses in each category is computed by dividing the number of losses in that category by 19. The sum of the resulting decimal fractions is 1.000, with any given loss falling into only one category. Thus, the probability distribution in Column 3 of Exhibit 9-7 meets the requirements of including outcomes that are both mutually exclusive and collectively exhaustive.

Columns 4 and 5 of Exhibit 9-7 present some additional information a risk management professional may develop to supplement the probability distribution in Column 3. Each dollar amount in Column 4 shows the total of the losses in the size category in Column 1. The adjusted amounts of these losses, which total $169,300, are taken from Exhibit 9-3. Column 5 of Exhibit 9-7 expresses the dollar amounts in Column 4 as percentages of this $169,300 total.

Columns 4 and 5 show that, while large dollar losses are individually quite infrequent, they usually account for the bulk of the dollar total of losses. For example, the three losses that are greater than $10,000 but less than $20,000 total $42,900, or about 25 percent of the total dollar amount of losses. The five losses that exceed $10,000 total $99,800, about 59 percent of the total dollar volume of derailment losses.

The probability distribution of derailment loss sizes in Column 3 differs in two ways from the probability distributions of coin tosses and dice rolls developed earlier. First, the outcomes shown in Column 1, size categories of losses, are somewhat arbitrary and are not as self-evident as the heads/tails outcomes in tossing coins or the 2 through 12 total point scores in rolling two dice. Second, the highest possible dice total clearly is 12, while the highest size category of derailment losses, " > $30,000," is open-ended, with no evident upper limit.

Having more losses generates a more complete and reliable probability distribution only if these added losses permit better use of the law of large numbers. Developed by eighteenth century mathematicians and perhaps more aptly labeled "the stability of statistical frequencies" by the British economist John Maynard Keynes, the law of large numbers applies, under certain circumstances, to events that may have a variety of outcomes. The law states the following:

> As the number of independent events increases, the actual relative frequency (percentage) of each of the possible outcomes more nearly approaches the theoretically expected relative frequency (percentage) of that outcome.

The law of large numbers applies to forecasts of future events only when the events whose outcomes are being forecast meet the following criteria:

1. The events have taken place in the past under substantially identical conditions and have resulted from unchanging basic causal forces.
2. The events can be expected to occur in the future under the same, unchanging conditions.
3. The events have been, and will continue to be, both independent of one another and sufficiently numerous.

With accidental losses, the law of large numbers—when it can be applied—implies that, as the number of losses increases, the actual relative frequency of losses (as a percentage of units exposed to loss) more nearly approaches the theoretically expected relative frequency of losses. Similarly, the distribution of the size of losses also more nearly approaches the theoretically expected loss severity distribution. For the law to apply to forecasts of future losses, both the past losses upon which the forecast is based and the future losses that it projects must have struck exposure units that *have been* and *will remain* (1) essentially identical, involving comparable values exposed to comparable hazards and (2) numerous and independent, so that no one occurrence of a peril can simultaneously strike a substantial percentage of exposure units.

The real world meets these conditions only in degree, usually partially, but rarely wholly. When gathering data on past losses to use in forecasting future losses, it is desirable to have data that closely approach these two conditions. In short, the more losses that enter into a forecast—if drawn from a large number of substantially identical, independent exposures comparable to future exposures—the more reliable is the resulting forecast of future losses.

Characteristics of Probability Distributions

One important characteristic of all probability distributions has already been noted: every distribution must assign relative frequencies to all possible outcomes of a particular event. That is, the probabilities in a valid probability distribution must be mutually exclusive and collectively exhaustive.

Probability distributions also are described in terms of three additional characteristics: skewness, central tendency, and dispersion.

Skewness. Skewness pertains to whether a probability distribution is "balanced," or symmetrical, with a hump in the center, or whether the hump is to one side (left or right) with a long, thin tail extending to the other side.

The Three General Possibilities. There are three general possibilities with respect to skewness. First, a "balanced," or symmetrical, distribution has no skewness. The hump in such a distribution, showing the most likely outcomes, is in the center. Therefore, the probabilities of less likely outcomes decline at the same rate on both sides of this central value in the distribution. The diagram in Exhibit 9-6 of a probability distribution of the total points on a single roll of two dice illustrates such a symmetrical distribution. This symmetrical distribution is one of the three general possibilities shown in Exhibit 9-8.

Notice the curves shown in Exhibit 9-8 differ from the vertical lines depicted in Exhibit 9-6. These curves are created by joining with a smooth line the tops of the vertical lines in the earlier exhibits so that the height of the curve indicates the probabilities of various outcomes. In this

Exhibit 9-8

Typical Shapes of Symmetrical and Skewed Distributions
Showing Relative Locations of Mean, Median, and Mode

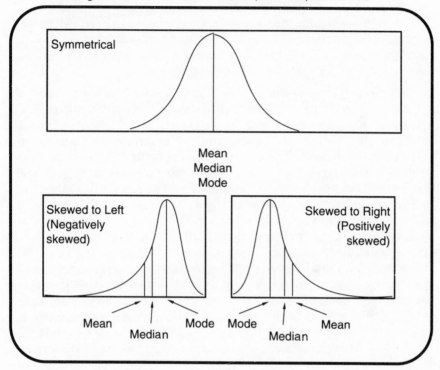

format, the area under the probability curve, representing a summation of all the probabilities of all the possible outcomes, totals 1.0.

The second general possibility is negative skewness. In a negatively skewed probability distribution, the outcome with the highest probability is above the center of the range of outcomes covered in that distribution, and the thin tail of low probability outcomes extends to the left. Although relatively rare in risk management, such distributions may apply to unprotected properties where, for example, most losses caused by fire, explosion, or flood are generally presumed to be total rather than partial. In such a case, a probability distribution of loss size to an unprotected property might well follow the general shape of the negatively skewed distribution in Exhibit 9-8.

The third general possibility is a positively skewed distribution, in which the most frequent outcome is below (to the left of) the center of the range of the distribution, and the relatively long tail (indicating low probabilities) extends to the high values in the distribution. For example, with protected properties, a distribution of loss size by fire, theft, or flood is generally presumed to follow the shape of the positively skewed distribution in Exhibit 9-8 because small losses tend to be more frequent than large ones.

Skewed probability distributions are sometimes described by the direction in which their tails point. Thus, a distribution that is "skewed right" is a positively skewed distribution, while a distribution that is "skewed left" is a negatively skewed distribution.

The Special Case of the "Normal" Distribution. A special kind of symmetrical distribution is often called the "normal distribution." This particular probability distribution applies to a very wide variety of physical phenonema that involve chance variations around some central, average, or expected value. The normal distribution applies to many real-world situations when the number of separate events is quite large and the factors that influence each separate outcome remain unchanged.

To cite an illustration that would apply to Promontory Point's efforts to prevent derailment losses, the railroad's management has installed electrical signs along its tracks to warn engineers of dangerous conditions at night. Each sign can be equipped with only one bulb. The useful life of the light bulbs in these signs is governed by a normal probability distribution. That is, each light bulb has the same average or expected life before burnout, but the variability around this average from light to light is described by the normal distribution. To warn train engineers, maintenance crews need to replace lights often enough that the probability of a sign being unlit (and, therefore, perhaps causing a train to be derailed) is sufficiently small.

Suppose, for example, that the average life of such an electric bulb is 5,000 hours. While 5,000 may be a valid average, some bulbs will burn out at 4,500 hours, some at 5,500 hours, and still others will burn out earlier or later. Because a normal probability distribution applies, however, the deviations around the 5,000-hour average life will be symmetrical.

In more precise terminology, the actual life of a given electric bulb is "normally distributed" around the 5,000-hour average or expected value. Fortunately for the safety of the railroad, the characteristics of the normal probability distribution provide a way of scheduling maintenance so that the likelihood of a bulb burning out before it is replaced can be kept below any margin of safety Promontory Point's management wishes to specify. To see how this can be done, one must first understand more about the other two characteristics of all probability distributions: central tendency and dispersion.

Central Tendency. The central tendency of a probability distribution is the single outcome within the distribution that, in some sense, is the "most representative" of all possible outcomes. Many probability distributions cluster around a particular value, which may or may not be in the exact center of the range of the distribution. This value is often used as the most representative of the outcomes included within the distribution. The three most widely accepted ways of identifying this most representative outcome are the arithmetic mean, the median, and the mode. For any particular distribution, the relationship of these points to one another and to the hump of the distribution depends on its skewness.

The Arithmetic Mean. The arithmetic mean of a distribution is a more precise name for the common "average," which is the sum of the items in the distribution divided by the number of items. For example, the arithmetic mean for the annual number of derailment losses Promontory Point suffered between 19X1 and 19X4 is the sum of 4 losses in 19X1 plus 4 losses in 19X2 plus 5 losses in 19X3 plus 6 losses in 19X4—the entire total of 19 being divided by 4 to compute the arithmetic mean of 4.75 losses per year. Most authors use the term "mean" by itself as shorthand for "arithmetic mean." (An equivalent term is "expected value.")

Any series of numbers can be averaged. For example, the data in Exhibit 9-3 shows that the average adjusted dollar amount of the 5 derailment losses Promontory Point suffered in 19X3 was $9,020 ($5,500 + $8,300 + $4,000 + $13,700 + $13,600 = $45,100/5 = $9,020). Similarly, the average adjusted amount of each derailment loss over all four years was, to the nearest dollar, $8,911 (computed as $9,800 + $32,900 + $45,100 + $81,500 = $169,300/19 = $8,911).

The procedure for calculating the arithmetic mean of a probability distribution is only slightly more complex than the above procedure for calculating the arithmetic mean of any series of numbers. For a probability distribution, the only difference is that, instead of dividing by the number of items, each value in the distribution is multiplied by its respective probability, and the sum of these products is the mean of the distribution. In other words, each value in the distribution is weighted by its probability, and the arithmetic mean of the distribution is the weighted average.

Thus, if the values in the probability distribution are symbolized X_1, X_2, X_3, ... X_n, each having respective probabilities of p_1, p_2, p_3 ... p_n, the arithmetic mean, or expected value, of the distribution is the sum of $(p_1 X_1) + (p_2 X_2) + (p_3 X_3) + ... (p_n X_n)$. For the dice example, the arithmetic mean of the distribution could be computed as shown in Exhibit 9-9. This procedure for calculating an arithmetic mean applies to all probability distributions regardless of their skewness or dispersion.

Median and Cumulative Probabilities. The median of a series of

Exhibit 9-9

Computing the Mean (Expected Value) of a Probability Distribution—
The Example of Two Dice

(1) Points (X)	(2) Probability (p)	(3) Col. (1) x Col. (2) (pX)
2	1/36	2/36
3	2/36	6/36
4	3/36	12/36
5	4/36	20/36
6	5/36	30/36
7	6/36	42/36
8	5/36	40/36
9	4/36	36/36
10	3/36	30/36
11	2/36	22/36
12	1/36	12/36
Totals:	36/36	252/36

Arithmetic Mean = 252/36 = 7.0

numbers or of a probability distribution is the "value in the middle," the value for which the number of lower observations or outcomes equals the number of higher observations or outcomes. Thus, in the array of nineteen losses in Exhibit 9-4, the median loss has an adjusted amount of $6,800. This tenth loss (counting from either the top or the bottom of the array) is the median because there are nine losses smaller and nine losses larger. For the five 19X3 losses in Exhibit 9-3, the median loss is $8,300. Inspection of the exhibit shows that two losses are smaller and two are larger.

When the number of observations or outcomes is an even number, the median is the arithmetic average of the middle two. Thus, among the four 19X2 losses in Exhibit 9-3, the median is the mean of $7,400 and $8,400 or $7,900.

The median of a probability distribution is again the "value in the middle," the value for which the probability of higher observations is equal to the probability of lower observations. This median value can be found by summing the cumulative probabilities in the distribution to find the value for which a cumulative probability of 50 percent is reached. For example, 7 is the median of the probability distribution of points in rolling two dice because 7 is the only number of points for which the

Exhibit 9-10
Cumulative Probability Distribution of Total Points in Rolling Two Dice

(1) Number of Points (X)	(2) Probability (p)	(3) Cumulative Probability (sum of p's)
2	1/36	1/36
3	2/36	3/36
4	3/36	6/36
5	4/36	10/36
6	5/36	15/36
7	6/36	21/36
8	5/36	26/36
9	4/36	30/36
10	3/36	33/36
11	2/36	35/36
12	1/36	36/36

probability of higher observations (15/36) is equal to the probability of lower observations. That is, there are 15 equally probable ways of getting a result higher than 7 and 15 equally probable ways of getting a result lower than 7.

This same result can be confirmed by cumulating the probabilities of outcomes equal to or less than a given number of points in rolling two dice, as in Exhibit 9-10. The cumulative 50 percent probability (18/36) is reached with 7 points (actually, in the middle of the 7-point class of results). Therefore, 7 is the median of this distribution.

The cumulative probabilities in Column 3 of Exhibit 9-10 indicate the probability of a roll yielding a certain number of points or less. For example, the probability of rolling a 3 or less is 3/36 (or the sum of 1/36 for rolling a 2 plus 2/36 for rolling a 3). Similarly, the probability of rolling a 10 or less is 33/36, computed by adding the individual Column 2 probabilities of outcomes of 10 points or less. When working with probability distributions of losses, computing probabilities of losses equal to or less than a given number or dollar amount can be helpful in selecting retention levels.

Exhibit 9-11 shows how to derive a cumulative probability distribution of loss sizes from the individual probabilities of loss size in Exhibit 9-7. Column 3 indicates that, on the basis of the available data, 5.26

percent of all losses are less than $1,000 and another 31.58 percent are greater than $1,000 but less than $5,000. Thus, the probabilities of a loss being $5,000 or less is the sum of these two probabilities, or 36.84 percent as shown in Column 3. Similarly, as shown in Column 5, losses of $5,000 or less can be expected to account for 10.63 percent of the total dollar amount of all losses.

The cumulated probabilities in Column 3 indicate that the median individual loss is between $5,000 and $10,000, the class in which the 50 percent cumulative probability is reached. This result is consistent with the $6,800 median loss found earlier by inspection of Exhibit 9-4.

Beyond locating the median loss, Exhibit 9-7 and Exhibit 9-11 have some implications for risk management decisions. For example, if Promontory Point were to insure its derailment losses subject to a $5,000 per accident deductible, the railroad could expect to retain the full amount of more than one out of every three losses (36.84 percent of the number of losses in Column 3 of Exhibit 9-11). It would also retain the first $5,000 of every larger loss (an additional $60,000 for the twelve losses in Column 2 of Exhibit 9-7 that exceed $5,000). Thus, Promontory Point's total expected annual retention with a $5,000 deductible would be the expected value of the full amount of all losses not exceeding $5,000 ($18,000, computed as $0.2 + $17.8, from Exhibit 9-7, Column 4, × 1,000) plus $60,000 ($5,000 × 12, the number of such larger losses from Exhibit 9-7, Column 2). This makes a grand total of $78,000. This expected retention would be about 46 percent of the $169,300 total of all expected derailment losses. This is the amount that Promontory Point might well budget annually for retained derailment losses or use as a comparison against an insurance premium credit for a $5,000 deductible.

If, on the other hand, Promontory Point were to adopt a $10,000 deductible, it could expect to retain the full amount of more than seven out of every ten losses (73.68 percent of the number of losses in Exhibit 9-11, Column 3), or from Exhibit 9-7, $119,500 of annual losses (consisting of the $69,500 full expected value of losses not exceeding $10,000 plus $10,000 for each of the five expected larger losses). This expected retention would be approximately 74 percent of the total amount of all expected losses.

Mode. The mode of a distribution is the single value that is most likely to occur. With a distribution that has a single hump, the mode is the value of the outcome directly beneath the peak of that hump. In the distribution of total points of throws of two dice, the mode is seven points. In the distribution of the sizes of derailment losses, the mode falls within the most populous size class (in Exhibit 9-7, Column 2, $5,000-$10,000, with 7 losses). The fact that both the mode and the

Exhibit 9-11

Cumulative Probabilities That Derailment Losses Will Not Exceed
Specified Amounts

(1) Size Category	(2) Percent of Number in Category	(3) Cumulative Percent of Number of Losses not Exceeding Category	(4) Percent of Value in Category	(5) Cumulative Percent of Dollars of Loss Not Exceeding Category
> $0 but not > $1,000	5.26	5.26	0.12	0.12
> $1,000 but not > $5,000	31.58	36.84	10.51	10.63
> $5,000 but not > $10,000	36.84	73.68	30.42	41.05
> $10,000 but not > $20,000	15.79	89.47	25.34	66.39
> $20,000 but not > $30,000	5.26	94.73	12.64	79.03
> $30,000	5.26	100.00	20.97	100.00
	100.00		100.00	

median fall in the same class does *not* imply that the mode and the
median are the same dollar amount.

The actual array of adjusted loss sizes (Exhibit 9-4) shows that,
because no particular dollar amount of loss occurred more than once, no
specific dollar amount can be said to be the mode. However, it is reasonable to assume that losses will occur more frequently in the $5,000-
$10,000 size category. That is, this category will have more losses than
will any other category.

In one sense, $0 or "no loss" is the most frequent *outcome* sug-
gested by the four years' data on Promontory Point's derailment losses.
For any particular day, week, or month, the most frequent outcome is
that there were no derailment losses. This is true in many risk management situations—"no loss" is the most frequent outcome. The mode, the
mean, and the median of the derailment loss distribution are actually
measures of the central tendency of *losses* rather than outcomes. Yet,
risk management focuses on accidental losses and how best to cope with
them. Therefore, despite the fact that "no loss" is often the most likely
single outcome, planning for no loss is poor risk management.

Relationships of Mean, Median, and Mode to Skewness. In a distribution that has only one hump (technically, a unimodal distribution), the
direction of skewness typically determines the relative locations of its
mean, median, and mode.

In a negatively skewed distribution, the median tends to be smaller than the mode, and the mean smaller than the median. As shown for the negatively skewed distribution in Exhibit 9-8, they appear from left to right as mean, median, mode. In a positively skewed distribution, the median tends to be larger than the mode, and the mean larger than the median. From left to right, they fall in mode-median-mean order.

In general, the mode of a skewed unimodal distribution is at the hump of the distribution, the mean is the measure of central tendency most polled by extremely high or low values toward the tail of the distribution, and the median typically falls between the mode and the mean.

In a symmetrical distribution, the mean, median, and mode typically have the same value.

Dispersion (Variability). Dispersion describes the extent to which the distribution is spread out rather than concentrated around a single outcome. It is the degree of variability from the mean of the distribution. The less the dispersion around the mean of a distribution, the greater the likelihood that actual results will fall within a given range of that mean. With less dispersion, there is less uncertainty involved in predicting that a result close to the mean actually will materialize.

There are two widely used measures of dispersion. One is the standard deviation of a distribution; the other is its coefficient of variation.

Standard Deviation. A standard deviation of a set of items is the square root of the average of the squared deviation of each item from the arithmetic mean of those items. It is a special kind of average, an average of deviations (or differences) between individual, varied values and the arithmetic mean of those values.

The precise method for computing a standard deviation depends on whether the items are individual observations (such as the amounts of individual losses) or are the values within a probability distribution (like the probabilities of points in throwing two dice).

The following is the procedure for calculating the standard deviation of a set of individual observations not involving probabilities:

1. Find the arithmetic mean of the observations (the sum of the observations divided by the number of observations).
2. Subtract the mean from each of the observations (with the result being positive for each observation larger than the mean, and negative for each observation smaller than the mean).
3. Square each of the resulting differences (the rules of algebra making all resulting squares positive).
4. Find the sum of these squares.
5. Divide this sum by the number of observations minus one.
6. Find the square root of the resulting quotient.

Exhibit 9-12

Computing a Standard Deviation—Individual Observations

(1) Loss (x 1,000)	(2) Deviation From Mean (X – M)	(3) Squared Deviation (X – M)^2
1.5	– 6.7	44.89
7.4	– 0.8	0.64
8.4	0.2	0.04
15.6	7.4	54.76
32.9		100.33

(n = 4)

Mean = M = 32.9 ÷ 4 = 8.225, rounded to 8.2

S.D. = $\sqrt{\text{sum } (X - M)^2 / N - 1}$

= $\sqrt{100.33/3}$, or $\sqrt{33.44}$

= 5.78

Exhibit 9-12 shows how to apply this procedure to the adjusted dollar amounts of the 4 losses Promontory Point suffered in 19X2, with the amount of each loss being expressed in thousands of dollars. This brief example demonstrates the procedure for computing the standard deviation of any number of observations of any size.

In Exhibit 9-12, Step 1 of the procedure outlined above requires dividing the total amount of the 4 losses in Column 1 by 4 to find the arithmetic mean loss, which, rounded, is 8.2. Step 2 is done in Column 2, which shows the result of subtracting this mean from each loss. Step 3, shown in Column 3, involves squaring each number in Column 2. Step 4 requires finding the total, 100.33, of the squared values in Column 3. Steps 4 and 5 appear at the bottom of the exhibit, where the standard deviation (S.D.) is computed by first dividing 100.33 by 3 (the number of observations, N, minus 1) to find the quotient (33.44) and then extracting the square root of this quotient.

For a probability distribution, in contrast to a set of observations, the comparable procedure for finding the standard deviation is as follows:

1. Find the expected value (or mean) of the distribution.
2. Subtract this expected value from each outcome included in the distribution.
3. Square each of the resulting differences.

Exhibit 9-13

Computation of the Standard Deviation of a Probability Distribution—
The Example of Two Dice

(1) Points (X)	(2) Probability (p)	(3) (X − M)	(4) (X − M)²	(5) p(X − M)²		
2	1/36	− 5	25	(1/36)(25)	=	25/36
3	2/36	− 4	16	(2/36)(16)	=	32/36
4	3/36	− 3	9	(3/36)(9)	=	27/36
5	4/36	− 2	4	(4/36)(4)	=	16/36
6	5/36	− 1	1	(5/36)(1)	=	5/36
7	6/36	0	0	(6/36)(0)	=	0
8	5/36	+ 1	1	(5/36)(1)	=	5/36
9	4/36	+ 2	4	(4/36)(4)	=	16/36
10	3/36	+ 3	9	(3/36)(9)	=	27/36
11	2/36	+ 4	16	(2/36)(16)	=	32/36
12	1/36	+ 5	25	(1/36)(25)	=	25/36
						210/36

M = mean of distribution = 7, previously computed

S.D. = $\sqrt{210/36}$

= $\sqrt{5.83}$

= 2.4 approximately

4. Multiply each resulting square by the probability associated with
   the outcome for which the squared difference was computed in
   step 3.
5. Sum the resulting products.
6. Find the square root of the resulting sum.

Exhibit 9-13 shows this procedure for the standard deviation of the
points in rolling two dice. M, the mean of this distribution, was computed
in Exhibit 9-9 to be 7 points. Column 3 of Exhibit 9-13 subtracts 7 from
the point values arrayed in Column 1, Column 4 squares the differences
shown in Column 3, and Column 5 multiplies each of these differences
by the probability of the respective number of points. The sum of the
products in Column 5, 210/36, or 5.83, is the square of the standard
deviation. Therefore, the standard deviation is approximately 2.4 points.

Exhibit 9-15 applies this same general procedure for computing a
standard deviation to the probability distribution of the dollar amounts
of Promontory Point's derailment losses for 19X1 through 19X4. To

Exhibit 9-14

Calculation of Expected Value (Mean) of Probability Distribution
of the Size of a Derailment Loss

Size Category (x 1,000)	Midpoint X(x 1,000)	Probability (p)	(p)X
> $0 but not > $1	0.5	0.0526	0.0263
> $1 but not > $5	3.0	0.3158	0.9474
> $5 but not >$10	7.5	0.3684	2.7630
> $10 but not > $20	15.0	0.1579	2.3680
> $20 but not > $30	25.0	0.0526	1.3150
> $30	35.5[†]	0.0526	1.8673
			9.2870

Mean X = 9.287 (rounded)

[†] Note: For an open-ended class, the class midpoint is assumed to be
the mean of the actual observations in this class.

compute this standard deviation, however, it is necessary to know the
mean of the probability distribution of derailment losses, which is computed in Exhibit 9-14. Given that a derailment has occurred, Exhibit 9-14
indicates the respective probabilities of the various sizes of loss. The
procedures in Exhibits 9-15 (losses) and 9-13 (dice) are identical. However, the possible dollar amounts of derailment losses are much more
numerous (potentially unlimited) than the point values on two dice, and
the probability distribution is expressed in terms of categories of loss
size, not precise dollar amounts.

Exhibits 9-14 and 9-15 make two adjustments for differences in the
underlying data: (1) all the losses in a given size class are assumed to
equal the midpoint (x) of that class (for example, all losses greater than
$1,000 up to $5,000 are assumed to be $3,000 in this calculation) and
(2) the arithmetic mean of all the actual losses in the open-ended size
category of > $30,000 is used to represent the value of all these losses.
Exhibits 9-14 and 9-15 express all losses in thousands of dollars to simplify the calculations (for example, a $500 loss is expressed as $0.5).

With the adjustments just mentioned, Exhibit 9-15 computes the
standard deviation of the size of derailment losses by the same procedure
as in Exhibit 9-13 to be approximately $8,494. The mean and standard
deviation computed from the nineteen individual losses differ from the
mean and standard deviation derived from the probability distribution

Exhibit 9-15
Calculation of Standard Deviation of Probability Distribution of the Size of Derailment Losses

Size Category (X 1,000)	Midpoint (x)	Probability (p)	(X – M)	(X - M)²	p(X – M)²
> $0	0.5	0.0526	– 8.4	70.56	3.711
> $1.0	3.0	0.3158	– 5.9	34.81	10.993
> $5.0	7.5	0.3684	– 1.4	1.96	0.722
> $10.0	15.0	0.1579	6.1	37.21	5.875
> $20.0	25.0	0.0526	16.1	259.21	13.634
> $30.0	35.5†	0.0526	26.6	707.56	37.218
Totals:		100.0000			72.153

M = 8.9 rounded from Exhibit 9-3.
† Arithmetic mean of losses in this open-ended class
S.D. = $\sqrt{72.153}$ = 8.494 (approx.), or $8,494

because that distribution uses the midpoint of each size class to represent all losses in that size class. (The arithmetic mean used in calculating this standard deviation in Exhibit 9-15 has been rounded in thousands to $8.9—computed directly from the individual losses as explained under the previous heading, "The Arithmetic Mean"—not the $9.3 computed in Exhibit 9-14 from the grouped loss data. A mean, or any other statistic, computed directly from individual data can be expected to be more accurate than a mean computed from grouped data.)

Standard Deviation of a Normal Distribution. As indicated, the variability of many real-world events can be accurately predicted through a symmetrical probability distribution, which statisticians call a "normal distribution." Exhibit 9-16 illustrates the typical "bell-shaped curve" of a normal distribution. This diagram looks much like the earlier diagram of a symmetrical probability distribution, but with one significant difference: the normal curve never touches the horizontal line at the base of the diagram. In theory, the normal distribution assigns some probability for every outcome regardless of its distance from the mean. The probability of a given outcome depends on the number of standard deviations that separate that outcome from the mean of the distribution. These relationships hold, symetrically both above and below the mean, for all normal distributions, regardless of the size of the mean or of the standard deviation.

Exhibit 9-16

The Normal Distribution—Percentages of Outcomes Within Specified
Standard Deviations of the Mean

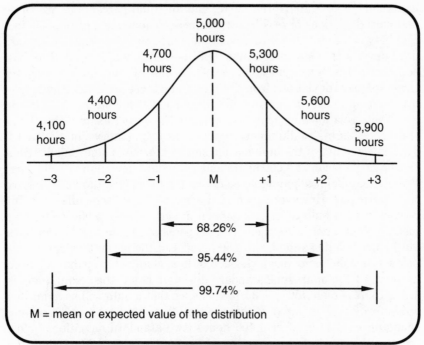

M = mean or expected value of the distribution

In all normal distributions, certain percentages of all outcomes fall
within a given number of standard deviations above or below the mean
of a distribution. For example, 34.13 percent of all outcomes are within
one standard deviation *above* the mean. Similarly, since every normal
distribution is symmetrical, another 34.13 percent of all outcomes fall
within one standard deviation *below* the mean. By addition, 68.26 percent
of all outcomes are within one standard deviation above or below the
mean. The portion of a normal distribution that is between one and
two standard deviations above the mean contains 13.59 percent of all
outcomes, as does the portion between one and two standard deviations
below the mean. Hence, the area between the mean and two standard
deviations above the mean contains 47.72 percent (34.13% + 13.59%) of
the outcomes, and another 47.72 percent are two standard deviations or
less below the mean. Consequently, 95.44 percent of all outcomes are
within two standard deviations above or below the mean.

Similarly, 2.15 percent of all outcomes are between two and three standard deviations above the mean and another 2.15 percent are between two and three standard deviations below the mean. Thus, 49.87 percent (34.13% + 13.59% + 2.15%) of all outcomes are three standard deviations or less above the mean, and an equal percentage are three standard deviations or less below the mean. The portion of the distribution between three standard deviations above the mean and three standard deviations below it contains 99.74 percent (49.87% × 2) of all outcomes. Only 0.26 percent (100% − 99.74%) of all outcomes lie *beyond* three standard deviations from the mean, and these are divided equally—0.13 percent above the mean and 0.13 percent below it.

These relationships may be applied to the earlier example involving the electric lights to illuminate signs along Promontory Point's tracks. The expected life of the bulb in each sign conforms to a normal distribution having a mean of 5,000 hours and a standard deviation of 300 hours. Promontory Point's maintenance crews try to replace the bulbs before they burn out. However, even if the maintenance schedule calls for replacing each bulb after it has been in service only 5,000 hours (the mean, or expected, life), there is a 50 percent chance that it will burn out before being changed, since 50 percent of the normal distribution is below this 5,000-hour mean. If each bulb is changed after having been used only 4,700 hours (one standard deviation below the mean), there is still a 15.87 percent (50% − 34.13%) chance that a bulb will have burned out before being changed. If this probability of burnout is still too high, changing each bulb after 4,400 hours (two standard deviations below the mean) reduces the probability of burnout to only 2.28 percent, the portion of a normal distribution that is more than two standard deviations below the mean. This probability can be calculated as 50% − (34.13% + 13.59%). A still more cautious practice would be to change bulbs routinely after only 4,100 hours (three standard deviations below the mean), so that the probability of a bulb burning out before replacement would be only 0.13 percent, slightly more than one chance in 1,000.

Using this same analysis, Promontory Point's management may select an acceptable probability that a bulb will burn out and can therefore schedule maintenance accordingly. Suppose, for example, that management would accept one chance in ten that a bulb would burn out before being replaced. That is, 90 percent of the bulbs should be replaced before they burn out. In terms of Exhibit 9-16, achieving this goal requires finding the point along the bottom of the diagram where 10 percent of the entire distribution (the portion of bulbs whose burnout could be tolerated) is below (to the left of) the time of replacement and the remaining 90 percent is above this point. This point will be somewhere between one and two standard deviations below the mean—that is, somewhere between 15.87 percent of the total distribution and 2.28

percent. Statisticians have shown that a value of 1.65 standard deviations below the mean cuts off the lowest 10 percent of any normal distribution. Thus, scheduling bulb replacement after 4,505 hours of use—computed as 5,000 − (1.65 × 300)—would ensure that only 10 percent of the bulbs burned out before replacement. For still greater assurance, say, 95 percent (instead of 90 percent), one must move 1.96 standard deviations below the mean or replace each bulb after 4,412 hours of use.

Coefficient of Variation. Given two distributions that have the same mean, the one with the larger standard deviation has the greater variability. However, when two distributions have different means, a new measure of variability—the coefficient of variation—should be used to compare their degree of variability.

The coefficient of variation of any probability distribution or other set of items is the quotient obtained by dividing that distribution's standard deviation by its arithmetic mean. For example, the coefficient of variation for the distribution of total points in rolling two dice equals 2.4 points divided by 7.0 points, or 0.34. For the light bulbs in the railroad's warning signs the coefficient of variation is 300 divided by 5,000, or 0.060. Notice the coefficient of variation is a ratio; like an index number, it does not measure any tangible quantity.

For the dollar amount of Promontory Point's derailment losses, a coefficient of variation may be computed from either the adjusted dollar amounts of individual losses as shown in Exhibit 9-4 or from the grouped data in Exhibit 9-15. Using individual loss data generates a mean derailment loss of $8,911 and a standard deviation of $8,231. Therefore, from this individual loss data, the coefficient of variation is $8,231 divided by $8,911, or 0.924. From the grouped data, the coefficient of variation is 0.915, computed as $8,494 divided by $9,287. The difference between these two computations of the coefficient of variation may or may not be significant. It is therefore important to know whether such a coefficient is computed from grouped data or from the generally more reliable individual loss data. Individual loss figures may, however, be too difficult or too expensive to obtain.

The coefficient is useful in comparing the variability of dissimilar distributions that have different shapes, means, or standard deviations. The distribution with the largest coefficient of variation has the greatest relative variability. The higher the variability within a distribution, the more difficult it is to make an accurate forecast of an individual outcome.

If—with respect to the forces that occasionally combine to cause "accidental losses"—the world can be assumed to be stable, then all past losses are only a sample of all possible losses, and that sample may or may not be representative. However, the greater the number of past losses, the larger the sample, the more reliable are the forecasts of future losses that both common sense (intuition) and statistical techniques can draw from that sample. The preceding discussion of probability analysis has assumed such a stable world. The following explanation of how to forecast losses by trending assumes a more dynamic world.

TREND ANALYSIS

Like probability analysis, trend analysis looks for patterns in past losses and then projects these patterns into the future. Unlike probability analysis, however, trend analysis looks for patterns of movement— that is, changes in loss frequency or severity that may coincide with changes in some other variable (such as production) that is easier to forecast accurately.

Estimates of the likelihood or the potential severity of losses derived from probability concepts discussed earlier assume a static, unchanging world. They assume, for example, that the frequency or severity of a particular type of loss has remained constant during both the period over which loss data has been gathered and the future period for which it is being forecast.

This assumption is true only in a limited sense. The assumptions that the future will repeat the past, and that data on all past losses has been drawn from a wholly static world, often are not justified. Past or future changes in an organization's operations, in technology, or in underlying economic or social factors (such as inflation, population growth, or crime rates) are likely to invalidate a projection based solely on historical data.

To improve projections of future losses, many risk management professionals use trend analysis to adjust loss data for anticipated changes in factors presumed to affect the frequency or severity of accidental losses. Although this trending must rest on informed judgment, trended projections may be more realistic than are the results of probability analysis alone. A simple example is an adjustment of forecasted future dollar amounts of losses for the anticipated rate of inflation.

Judgment often must temper projections of trend lines when extending far beyond the range of any past experience. "Automatic" use of any mathematic technique can produce unrealistic results. Used with discretion, however, these techniques permit some useful analysis.

For example, in estimating the property losses an organization will need to finance through retention if it adopts a particular deductible, an alert risk management professional will recognize that projected inflationary trends will increase the monetary value of a given amount of future physical damage. Installing a sprinkler system in a particular building is likely to produce increasingly significant savings in expected fire losses as the physical volume or financial value of the property in that building increases. Hence, inflation and growing concentrations of property values may increase the deductibles and investments in property loss prevention an organization decides to make. Reaching sound decisions on such matter requires trend analysis.

Intuitive Trending

Some trends in losses, or in other variables such as price levels, can be discerned by intuitive judgment. As an example of intuitive trending, consider Exhibit 9-17, which shows the number of disabling injuries Promontory Point's personnel have suffered per million employee hours worked (graphed vertically) over a period of seven years (graphed horizontally). Each dot (data point) in the chart indicates the rate, or frequency, of injuries in a given year. The downward trend of these data points clearly indicates that the organization's work injury record is improving.

A common-sense way of representing this trend uses a ruler to draw a line passing as nearly as possible through the data points. Extending the dotted portion of the trend line into the future gives some intuitive basis for forecasting a continued decline in work injuries, although it would not be reasonable to expect a zero injury rate. This trend line is the eye's "best estimate," drawn to minimize the total distances of all data points from the trend line. Arithmetic trending techniques only define more precisely the location of this distance-minimizing straight line.

The straightness of this trend line implies that the work injury record has been improving steadily. That is, the injury rate has been falling by a constant number each year. This constancy accounts for the straight, or linear, shape of the trend line. However, in many situations, a totally linear trend is unrealistic because it would suggest, for example, that injuries would eventually cease to occur. In this and other situations, a curved trend line might reflect past loss data and reasonably expected future losses more accurately. When a trend line is curved, it is known as a *curvilinear trend line*.

Exhibit 9-18 shows how to estimate a curvilinear trend line, again solely on intuition, that closely approximates past losses. Again, the curvilinear trend line is located to minimize the total of the distances of each of the plotted dots from the trend line. Risk management professionals can plot past losses in this way and then judge whether a linear or a curvilinear trend line most accurately projects past losses into the future.

Exhibit 9-17
Generalized Form of Hand-Drawn Linear Trend Line

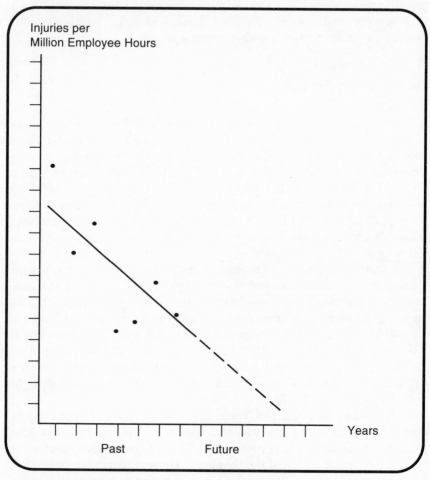

Arithmetic Trending Techniques

Because computing a curvilinear trend line is complex, most risk management professionals will turn to a trained statistician when the need arises. However, linear trending, which is more straightforward and has many uses, is a procedure that should be within the analytic repertoire of every risk management professional.

Exhibit 9-19 presents data suitable for linear trending. Arithmetic techniques can develop an equation that precisely locates a linear trend

Exhibit 9-18
Generalized Form of Hand-Drawn Curvilinear Trend Line

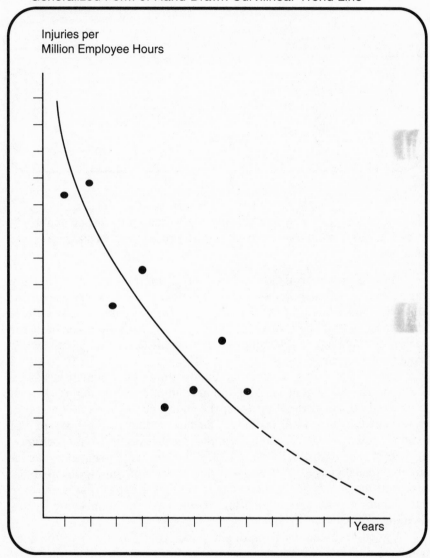

line like that in Exhibit 9-17. Exhibit 9-19 shows the number of derailment losses Promontory Point suffered and the number of ton-miles of cargo (in hundreds of thousands) in each year from 19X1 to 19X4. This information can be used to project trends that relate the number of derailment

Exhibit 9-19

Relationships of Losses to Exposure (Ton-Miles of Freight)

Year	Annual Number of Losses	Ton-Miles (x 100,000)
19X1	4	35
19X2	4	60
19X3	5	72
19X4	6	95
	19	262

losses to (1) time (through a process known as "time series analysis") and (2) annual ton-miles carried (through a process known as "regression analysis").

Time Series Analysis.   Time series analysis assumes that the variable to be forecast (known as the *dependent variable*) varies predictably with time (the *independent variable*). *Linear time series analysis* also assumes that the change in the dependent variable is constant for each unit of change in the independent variable (the change is the same from year to year).

Exhibit 9-20 plots Promontory Point's annual derailment losses on a graph. The dependent variable (annual number of derailment losses) is charted on the vertical (y) axis; the independent variable (years) is shown on the horizontal (x) axis. The heavy dots in the body of the exhibit show that 4, 4, 5, and 6 derailment losses occurred, respectively, in each of the years 19X1 through 19X4 (which, for convenience, can be simply labeled years 1, 2, 3, and 4). The objective of time series analysis is to find the equation for the linear trend line that best fits these four data points and to project this line to forecast the number of future derailment losses.

A good first step in calculating a linear trend line is to plot the data points and sketch an approximate trend line. Such a sketch helps to intuitively estimate the two determinants of any linear trend line. The first determinant is the point where the line crosses the vertical y axis, labeled "a" in the diagram and technically known as the "y-intercept," or the value of y when x equals zero. The second determinant is the "slope" of the line, the amount by which y increases or decreases with a one-unit increase in x. The length of the dashed line labeled "b" signifies the slope. The values of a and b depend on the values of the depen-

Exhibit 9-20
Diagram of Linear Time Series Analysis Trend Line

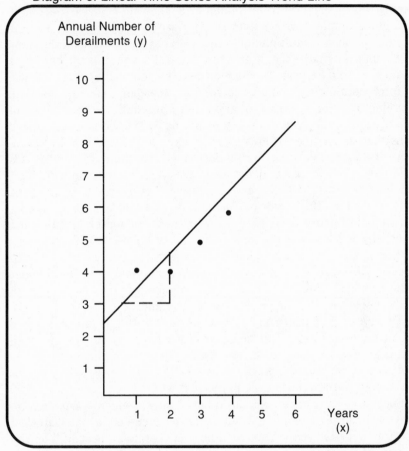

dent and independent variables represented by the four plotted data points. The general equations for a and b follow:

$$a = \frac{(\text{Sum y})(\text{Sum } x^2) - (\text{Sum x})(\text{Sum xy})}{n(\text{Sum } x^2) - (\text{Sum x})^2}$$

$$b = \frac{n(\text{Sum xy}) - (\text{Sum x})(\text{Sum y})}{n(\text{Sum } x^2) - (\text{Sum x})^2}$$

In these equations, n indicates the number of data points, or the number of paired x and y values, which is four in this case. For clarity, these formulas also use the symbol "Sum" to mean the sum of the variable following the symbol. For example, "Sum y" means the sum of the annual numbers of losses, 19 in all.

Exhibit 9-21 shows the calculation of a trend line of the annual number of derailment losses, using the above formulas. Columns 1 and 2 simply repeat the data from Exhibit 9-19, showing the years as single digits (for example, 1 rather than 19X1). Each figure in Column 3 represents the product of multiplying each x value by the y value on the same line. Column 4 squares the figures in Column 1. The totals of these four columns—10, 19, 51, and 30—enable one to solve for a and b, as shown.

Interpreting these results is, for the most part, straightforward. The value of 3 for a in the equation indicates that, at the y-intercept when x equals zero (year 19X0), y would be 3. The value of 0.70 for b means that the number of losses can be expected to increase by seventenths of a loss each year. (Had b been negative, the number of losses would have been forecast to decrease each year, as they do in Exhibit 9-17). Furthermore, if this trend or pattern continues, the number of losses in year 5 (19X5) can be forecast as $3 + 5(0.7) = 6.5$, making it reasonable to forecast either 6 or 7 derailment losses in 19X5 and 7—actually, 7.2 losses, computed as $3 + (6 \times 0.7)$—in 19X6.

The equation for such a linear time series trend is $y = a + bx$. In this case, the dependent variable, y, is the forecast number of derailment losses; the independent variable, x, is the number of years beyond 19X0; a is the y-intercept; and b is the slope of the line.

Two potentially confusing aspects of interpreting linear trend lines need to be recognized. First, a linear trend line may not be accurate when it approaches the horizontal x axis. Despite the linearity of the equation and the line, the dependent variable that is graphed vertically usually does not approach zero in the real world.

Second, for any past year, the value of the dependent variable computed by the linear trend line is not likely to exactly equal the historical value for that past year. Any trend line represents a "best fit," on the average, of a straight or smoothly curved line to actual historical data for all past years. For any given year, the projected trend value will probably differ somewhat from the actual outcome, both in the past and in the future. The size of this difference between actual and projected values will also vary somewhat. For example, in Exhibit 9-20, the historical outcome for Year 1 is farther from the projected trend line than is the outcome for Year 2.

Regression Analysis. Regression analysis is—in most respects, and especially in the computational steps—just like time series analysis. From the standpoint of risk management, the only important difference between them lies in the assumptions that characterize each.

Time series analysis assumes that the dependent variable (such as the annual number of losses) varies only with the passage of time. Given

Exhibit 9-21
Computation of Linear Time Series Trend Line

(1) Years x	(2) Losses y	(3) xy	(4) x^2
1	4	4	1
2	4	8	4
3	5	15	9
4	6	24	16
10	19	51	30

$$a = \frac{(\text{Sum } y)(\text{Sum } x^2) - (\text{Sum } x)(\text{Sum } xy)}{n(\text{Sum } x^2) - (\text{Sum } x)^2} \qquad b = \frac{n(\text{Sum } xy) - (\text{Sum } x)(\text{Sum } y)}{n(\text{Sum } x^2) - (\text{Sum } x)^2}$$

$$a = \frac{(19)(30) - (10)(51)}{4(30) - (10)^2} \qquad b = \frac{4(51) - (10)(19)}{4(30) - (10)^2}$$

$$= \frac{570 - 510}{120 - 100} \qquad = \frac{204 - 190}{120 - 100}$$

$$= \frac{60}{20} \qquad = \frac{14}{20}$$

$$= 3 \qquad = 0.70$$

any future year, the trend line can be extended to forecast the expected number of losses in that year.

In contrast, regression analysis assumes that there may be many other independent variables that may be useful predictors of the dependent variable. For example, the annual number of derailment losses may be affected by such factors as the volume of freight transported, the number of inches of snow (or some other measure of adverse weather conditions), or the speed at which trains traverse particularly hazardous stretches of rail.

Regression analysis substitutes one of these other variables (freight volume, snowfall, or speed) for time as the independent variable that predicts the number of future derailments. In fact, time series analysis is nothing more than a special case of regression analysis in which time is the independent variable.

Therefore, any reasonable causative factor that can be measured and predicted with more accuracy than accidental losses can be an independent variable. Regardless of the variables used, the procedures for computing the a and b determinants of the linear trend line remain the same. (By turning to an expert statistician, a risk management professional can develop either curvilinear or linear trend lines, which take account of many variables simultaneously. An example is an equation that would forecast the number or dollar amounts of losses in a future year based on combined effects of forecast freight volumes, weather conditions, price levels, and perhaps other independent variables more easily predictable than the losses themselves.)

If, for example, Promontory Point's risk management professional wished to use annual ton-miles (in 100,000-ton-mile units) as a predictor of the annual number of derailment losses, a diagram might be developed. Exhibit 9-22 graphs annual ton-mileage horizontally on the x axis as the independent variable and annual number of derailment losses vertically on the y axis as the dependent variable. The four data points in the exhibit correspond to the pairs of losses and ton-miles shown in Exhibit 9-19, and the solid portion of the linear regression line approximates the trend of the historical data. The dashed extension of the regression line projects annual numbers of derailment losses for ton-mileages (in units of 100,000) beyond the range of this particular historical data. Developing such a diagram and approximating a regression line help one visualize and confirm the results obtained by computing the values of a and b for the actual linear regression line.

The procedure for calculating values for a (y-intercept) and b (slope) determinants of the regression line relating derailment losses to ton-miles, as seen in Exhibit 9-23, is the same procedure for computing a time series analysis trend line. As computed at the bottom of Exhibit 9-23, the indicated value for a is 2.46 derailments, and the value for b is 0.035. If the number of derailment losses is linearly related to ton-miles for all possible volumes of freight, the 2.46 value for a means that, even if annual ton-mileage were zero (that is, the railroad was not operating), it would still suffer 2.46 (actually 2 or 3) derailment losses each year. The 0.035 value for b implies that, with each 100,000 increase in ton-miles, 0.035 additional derailments can be expected. One could also say that one additional derailment can be expected with approximately each additional 2,857,000 ton-miles (computed as 100,000 ton-miles × 1/0.035).

While arithmetically correct, these values may not be valid for very low or very high freight volumes, again indicating the need to temper mathematics with reason. One should not extend a regression line too far beyond the bounds of past experience.

Exhibit 9-22
Diagram of Linear Regression Line

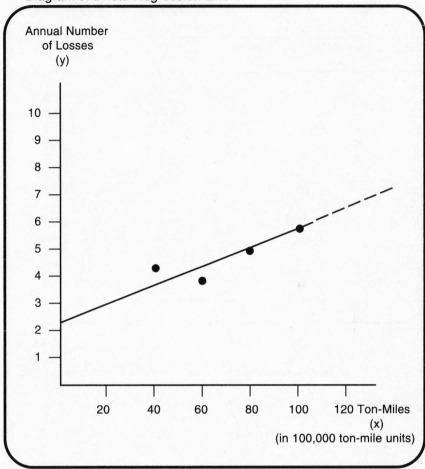

To forecast losses from these regression results, assume the railroad expects to carry 10 million (or 100 hundred thousand) ton-miles of cargo in 19X5. The expected number of derailments can be computed as follows:

$$y = 2.46 + 100(0.035)$$
$$= 2.46 + 3.50$$
$$= 5.96 \text{ losses}$$

Fractional derailments being impossible—there may be five or six, but

Exhibit 9-23
Computation of Linear Regression Line

(1) Ton-Miles (x)	(2) Losses (y)	(3) (xy)	(4) (x)²
35	4	140	1,225
60	4	240	3,600
72	5	360	5,184
95	6	570	9,025
262	19	1,310	19,034

$$a = \frac{(19)(19,034) - (262)(1,310)}{4(19,034) - (262)^2} \qquad b = \frac{4(1,310) - (262)(19)}{4(19,034) - (262)^2}$$

$$= \frac{361,646 - 343,220}{76,136 - 68,644} \qquad = \frac{5,240 - 4,978}{76,136 - 68,644}$$

$$= \frac{18,426}{7,492} \qquad = \frac{262}{7,492}$$

$$= 2.46 \qquad = 0.035$$

nothing in between—a reasonable forecast would be for six derailments in a year when the railroad carries 10 million ton-miles of cargo.

This forecast, like the others described in this chapter, should be accepted only if the underlying assumptions are valid. Therefore, it is important to know these assumptions and recognize the potential limitations in these forecasting techniques.

While probability and trend analyses can be very powerful tools for forecasting future losses, they must be used with care. Their results must be interpreted with reason and not with blind acceptance just because they may seem to possess some mathematical mystique. Furthermore, perhaps more for risk management than for some other uses of these forecasting techniques, the seeming scarcity of loss data, when compared with the apparent wealth of data in other management specialties, makes forecasts of accidental losses more difficult.

SUMMARY

Probability analysis and trend analysis can be used effectively in projecting future losses and in making rational decisions for dealing with their consequences. Valid forecasts require the following:

1. Gathering historical data not only on the frequency and severity of losses but also on the circumstances (physical conditions, levels of output, or state of the economy, for example) that logically may be related to the frequency or severity of these losses. This data should be complete, expressed on consistent bases, relevant to risk management (especially with respect to valuation of losses), and organized to facilitate the analysis.

2. Experimenting with this data enables one to detect patterns, either patterns of stability or patterns of change, which themselves can be reasonably predicted and then used as a basis for forecasting losses. Where patterns of stability exist, where it seems reasonable to view past losses as samples from a fixed set of all possible losses, one should concentrate on probability analysis. Where loss frequency or severity seems related to other variables, one can compare loss frequency or severity with these other variables through time series or regression analysis.

3. Remaining wary of drawing *fixed* conclusions from inadequate data, realizing that new discoveries of data (either from new losses or from better records of old losses) may provide new information for making better forecasts. On the one hand, one should be willing to draw tentative conclusions on the basis of the available data, but on the other hand, one should also be ready to modify these conclusions when additional data become available.

It is often said that the more the world changes, the more it stays the same. The basic truth underlying this saying may well be that some aspects of the world (and of the accidents the world generates) are constant, while others are changing. Probability analysis can help a risk management professional identify what is unchanging despite the apparent randomness of accidents. Trend analysis can help the risk management professional project what changes the future is likely to bring.

Chapter Notes

---

1. The Commissioners 1980 Standard Ordinary Male Mortality Table, 1970-1975, available in many standard insurance references.
2. Federal Bureau of Investigation and Federal Highway Administration data reported in *MVMA Motor Vehicle Facts and Figures* (Detroit: Motor Vehicle Manufacturers Association, 1990), p. 93.

CHAPTER 10

Risk Management Applications of Forecasts

Applying probability and trend analyses to loss forecasting involves making realistic forecasts in situations somewhat more complex than the elementary cases described in Chapter 9. This chapter describes how to recognize these more complex situations and how to break them down for closer scrutiny and, therefore, more precise forecasts. These concepts and procedures enable a risk management professional to do the following:

- Apply probability analysis to compute (1) the joint probability that any number of losses, or any given dollar total amount of losses, may occur in a given period and (2) the probability that any one of a variety of losses may occur at any given time.
- Use trend analysis to combine the effects of several independent trends, each of which may affect the frequency or severity of future losses.
- Use the fundamental notation and logic of probability and trend analyses to draw on the expertise of statisticians or other quantitative experts in developing further forecasting models, which, while more complex than those described in this chapter, rest on the same fundamental principles described here.

This chapter describes elementary models and examples of forecasting techniques to illustrate their significance and their mechanics. It is important to understand the computational procedures that these forecasting techniques employ. With this understanding, the risk management professional can, when working with larger quantities of real-world data, rely on much more rapid and sophisticated computers and data processing equipment that may be available to develop these and other forecasts. First, however, must come the basic understanding.

SOME FURTHER CALCULATIONS INVOLVING PROBABILITIES

Chapter 9 introduced two basic types of forecasting tools: (1) probability analysis for situations where the world is presumed to be stable and the future is expected to repeat the past without change and (2) trend analysis for situations involving change, where a number of variables move together and some can be used as predictors of others. Somewhat more advanced aspects of each of these two types of analysis are helpful in dealing with more complex situations. For example, probability analysis can be extended to multiple combinations of events, and trend analysis can be extended to situations where combining the effects of several independent variables permits more accurate forecasting of dependent variables.

Chapter 9 defined the concept of probability and explained how to develop probability distributions to estimate the probabilities of specific individual events. The probability calculations that follow carry this analysis further to determine the probabilities of various combinations of events.

Basic Notation

Probability calculations usually are expressed in some generally useful symbols. The symbol p( ) means "probability of" the item in parentheses, so that p(A) means "the probability of A" occurring in a given period, where A represents any specified event. Similarly, p(A and B) is a shorthand expression for "the probability of A and B," both occurring in a given period. The symbol p(A or B) stands for "the probability that either A or B, or possibly both," will occur within a specified period. This notation is flexible because any event or combination of events can be designated in the parentheses.

The symbol "n" also appears frequently in probability calculations to designate the number of separate units from which a probability is developed or to which it is applied. To illustrate, if Promontory Point Railroad made 20,000 trips, or "runs," during 19X1-19X4, when the railroad suffered 19 derailments, then the probability of a derailment on any particular run could be computed as 19/20,000, which equals 0.000950. More generally, the symbol "n" typically designates the number of trials or exposures (here, runs) from which an empirical probability is derived. The symbol "m" designates the number of occurrences of the event whose probability is sought, 19 in this case. Thus, the general equation for the probability of a derailment is expressed as follows:

$$p(\text{derailment}) = m/n = 19/20{,}000 = 0.000950$$

and, by algebraic manipulation,

$$m = np = (20{,}000)(0.000950) = 19$$

In a slightly different, predictive context, "n" can represent the number of train runs Promontory Point plans for 19X5. Since p is the best estimate (based on the available data) of the probability of derailment on any one run, then n times p, (np), is the number of derailments the railroad can expect in 19X5. Given that p equals 0.000950, if Promontory Point forecasts making 7,000 runs in 19X5, the railroad can expect 7 derailments that year (6.65 to be precise, but fractional derailments are impossible). Symbolically, expected derailments equal the number of runs times the probability of derailment on one run, expressed as follows:

$$\text{expected derailments} = (np) = 0.000950 \times 7{,}000 = 6.65$$

"Expected derailments per year" can be interpreted as the average (arithmetic mean) number of derailments *expected* to occur annually in the long run, not necessarily the number that *will* occur in the next twelve months.

The concept of long-run, expected value is so common in working with probabilities that a symbol, E( ), is used as shorthand for "the expected number or value" of the event specified in the parentheses. If D stands for the annual number of derailments in the year in which Promontory Point makes n runs, then

$$E(D) = np$$

which can be read as "the expected annual number of derailments equals the number of runs times the probability of derailment on any one run." The following probability calculation would be used for the first derailment example:

$$E(D) = np = (20{,}000)(0.000950) = 19$$

Most probability calculations rest upon two assumptions, which, while usually obvious, should be made explicit in order to avoid mistakes where these assumptions are not true. The first assumption is that the probability, p, remains constant and is valid for the future events whose probability is being calculated. This is true whether the value for p is derived from experience (as for derailments) or wholly from logic (like the *a priori* probabilities involved in rolling dice). In other words, the world that has generated any particular value for p is assumed to remain unchanged so that p also applies to the future.

The second assumption is that an event either occurs or does not occur—there are no other possibilities. The occur/not occur alternatives are mutually exclusive and together they exhaust all possibilities. Therefore, the probability of any event occurring, p(A), and the probability of it not occurring, p(not A), add up to one. For example, since the probability of a derailment on any one run is 0.000950, then the probability that there will be no derailment on that run is 0.999050. In general, the following is true:

$$p(A) + p(\text{not } A) = 1$$

and, by algebraic manipulation,

$$p(A) = 1 - p(\text{not } A)$$

$$p(\text{not } A) = 1 - p(A)$$

In these equations, A may represent a single event or a set of events. These equations are useful when the probability of A is unknown and may be difficult to compute directly. In these situations, it is often easier to find the probability of A by computing p(not A) and subtracting the result from one.

This basic notation applies to all probability analyses. Two applications most useful in risk management are computations of joint probabilities (the probability that two or more events will occur together in a given time period) and of alternative probabilities (the probability that any one of two or more events will occur in a given time period).

Joint Probabilities

A joint probability, also often called a *compound probability*, is the probability that two or more events will all happen within a given period. Examples are the probability that two train derailments will occur in a particular month, that eight men will all die within one year, or that Sheltering Arms Hospital will suffer both a fire loss and a theft loss within one month.

Before computing the joint probability of two or more events, it is necessary to determine whether these events are independent. Two events, A and B, are independent if the occurrence or nonoccurrence of one does not affect the probability that the other will or will not occur. If A and B are independent, the probability of A is unchanged by the occurrence or nonoccurrence of B. Similarly, the probability of B is unchanged by the occurrence or nonoccurrence of A. For example, the probabilities that two railcars, widely distant from one another, will burn are independent of each other, since a fire at one will not endanger the other. However, if the two railcars are close enough that fire can spread from one to the other, their probabilities of fire loss are not independent. Specifically, each railcar alone may have a 2 percent chance of fire in a given year, but if the railcars are close together, a fire in one of them will raise the probability of fire in the other.

For Independent Events. If two or more events are independent, the joint probability that all the events will occur is the product of their separate probabilities. That is, if the two railcars mentioned above are widely distant, the probability they will both burn in one year, $p(2\text{ fires})$, is equal to the probability of fire in one, $p(F1)$, times the probability of fire in the other, $p(F2)$, expressed as follows:

$$p(2\text{ fires}) = p(F1)p(F2)$$

$$p(2\text{ fires}) = (0.02)(0.02) = 0.0004$$

For Dependent Events. If the two railcars are close enough to be affected by one fire, the joint probability that both will burn is determined by multiplying the probability of fire in one times the probability of fire in the second, given that there already is a fire in the first. The probability of fire in the second railcar is known as *conditional probability* because this probability is conditioned by the existence of fire in the first. Generally, if the probability of event B is conditional upon event A, the notation for "the probability of B given A" is $p(B|A)$.

Assume, for example, that the two railcars mentioned above are sufficiently close that fire can spread from one to the other, or that a fire from an outside source may strike both railcars. Assume further that it has been observed over the years (creating an empirical probability) that on 40 percent of the occasions when one railcar catches fire, the other railcar also catches fire. Then, even though the probability of fire in one or the other remains at 2 percent, leaving $p(F1) = 0.02$, the conditional probability of fire in the second railcar, given fire in the first, increases to 40 percent (in notation, $p(F2|F1) = 0.40$).

With conditional probabilities—when the probability of one event changes depending upon whether another event has already occurred—it is especially important to specify not only the nature but also the sequence of the events whose joint probability is being computed. Assume, for example, that Railcar One is much older than Railcar Two and therefore more likely to catch fire. Assume also that the probability of fire in Railcar One, denoted as $p(F1)$ is 0.05, while the corresponding probability for Railcar Two is 0.01. Furthermore, perhaps because Railcar One contains a more flammable cargo than does Railcar Two or because Railcar One is upwind from Railcar Two, let the probability of a fire spreading from Railcar One to Railcar Two be 0.60, while the probability of fire spreading in the other direction is 0.10. That is, $p(F2|F1)$

$= 0.60$, while $p(F1|F2) = 0.10$. Then, the probability that Railcar Two will catch fire after and as a result of a fire in Railcar One is equal to the probability that Railcar One will catch fire times the probability that this fire will spread to Railcar Two, expressed as follows:

$$p(\text{F1 followed by F2}) = p(F1)p(F2|F1) = (0.05)(0.60) = 0.03$$

Conversely, the probability that a fire will begin in Railcar Two and spread to Railcar One is computed by the following:

$$p(\text{F2 followed by F1}) = p(F2)p(F1|F2) = (0.01)(0.10) = 0.001$$

Notice that each of these calculations derives the probability of a particular sequence of events and does not include any allowance for any other sequence (such as both cars simultaneously being ignited by a fire whose origin is outside either car).

The General Case. When dealing with events whose probabilities are dependent upon one another, it is important to specify the sequence in which they occur. When dealing with events whose probabilities are independent, the sequence is unimportant because the occurrence or nonoccurrence of one event does not affect the probability of the other. Therefore, the formula for the joint probability of two events that are not independent is also the general formula for all joint probabilities regardless of independence. This formula follows:

$$p(\text{A followed by B}) = p(A)p(B|A)$$

This formula is applicable to independent events because if A and B are independent, $p(B|A) = p(B)$.

This general formula for the joint probability of two events can be extended to find the joint probability of any number of events. However, the formula rapidly becomes very lengthy as the number of separate events increases. The key point is that joint probabilities are computed by multiplication of either unconditional or conditional probabilities depending on whether the events are independent or dependent.

To illustrate this general formula further, the probability of rolling 8 fours in 8 rolls of one die (independent events) is 1/6 (the probability of a four on each roll) multiplied by itself as follows:

$$p(\text{8 fours}) = (1/6)(1/6)(1/6)(1/6)(1/6)(1/6)(1/6)(1/6)$$

$$= (1/6)^8$$

$$= 1/1,679,616$$

Other Joint Probability Calculations. As another illustration, if the probability that a train depot will suffer a fire, $p(F)$, is 0.005 and the probability that it will be looted if fire occurs, $p(L|F)$, or "the probability of looting given a fire," is 0.60, then the probability that the building will burn and then be looted in the wake of the fire is as follows:

$$p(F \text{ followed by } L) = p(F)p(L|F) = (0.005)(0.60) = 0.003$$

Notice that this is the probability of fire followed by looting, which is not the same as the probability of looting followed by fire or as the probability of looting and fire occurring in two unrelated events. The figures above do not allow calculating these latter two probabilities. In general, great care should be taken in defining the events whose probability is being computed.

Joint probabilities can also be used to compute the likelihood that an organization will *not* suffer a loss. To illustrate, suppose that the probability that one of Sheltering Arms Hospital's ambulance drivers will be injured in a job-related traffic accident during the next year is 0.03. Because $p(\text{not } A) = 1 - p(A)$, the probability of no injury to the driver is 0.97. For two drivers whose probabilities of injury are assumed to be independent (their vehicles will not collide with one another), the probability that neither will be injured is $(0.97)(0.97)$, or $(0.97)^2$, which is 0.9409, or roughly 94 percent.

As the number of drivers increases, the probability that none will suffer injury decreases until, with 76 drivers, the probability of *no* injuries among these drivers falls to less than 10 percent (because 0.97^{76} is less than 0.10). To generalize, it follows that any organization with even a moderate number of employees is likely to experience at least one workers compensation claim in a given year, even though the probability of injury to any one employee is relatively small.

With extremely small probabilities of loss (extremely large probabilities of no loss) the number of separate exposure units must become quite large before some loss is virtually certain. For Promontory Point, for example, the 0.999050 probability that any one train will reach its destination *without* derailment means that, for any two trains, there is a 0.998101 probability that both will reach their destinations without derailment, this probability being computed as $(0.999050)^2$. As the number of train runs increases, however, the probability of *no* derailments falls (though not as rapidly as in the above work injury example). It is not until Promontory Point has 2,423 separate train runs that the probability of no derailment falls to less than 10 percent because $(0.999050)^{2423}$ is less than 0.10.

These examples illustrate two basic points. First, as the number of exposure units (here, workers or train runs) increases, some eventual loss becomes a virtual certainty. Second, the smaller the probability of loss to any one exposure unit, the greater is the number of units required to reach a given probability (here, more than 90 percent) that *some* loss will occur.

What is true for the probability of loss within a given number of exposure units in one year is also true for a single exposure unit over a number of years: some loss is likely to occur. For example, assume that the probability is 1 in 8 (0.125 or 12.5 percent) that, during a given winter, Bigh Pass, a crucial stretch of mountain track along one of Promontory Point's routes, will be closed by heavy snow at least once. The equation to compute the probability that Bigh Pass will *not*, during four consecutive years, ever be closed by snow follows:

$$p(\text{no snow closure for 4 years}) = (1 - 0.125)^4$$
$$= (0.875)^4$$
$$= 0.586$$

or slightly less than 59 percent. The probability that Bigh Pass will not be closed by snow in a decade is $(0.875)^{10}$, which is approximately 26.3 percent. In other words, there is an almost 74 percent chance $(1 - 0.263 = 0.737)$ that, unless special measures are taken to keep Bigh Pass open, it will be closed by snow at least once every ten years. The higher this probability, the more consideration Promontory Point may wish to give to stationing adequate snowplows near Bigh Pass.

Alternative Probabilities

An alternative probability is the probability that any *one* of two or more events will occur within a given time. Examples are the probability that either a three or a five will come up in one roll of one die, the probability that a card drawn from a deck will be either a five or a club, and the probability that Sheltering Arms will suffer either a fire loss or a burglary loss within the next year.

For computing alternative probabilities, the first step is to determine whether the events involved are mutually exclusive. Two or more events are *mutually exclusive* only if the occurrence of one makes the other *impossible*. For example, rolling a three on a die makes it impossible to roll a five on the same roll, so three and five on one roll of one die are mutually exclusive events. An ambulance driver involved in an accident can be uninjured, injured, or killed immediately. Since his or her physical condition cannot fall into two of these categories, the three are mutually exclusive.

Similarly, the probabilities that Promontory Point will suffer no derailment loss in a particular year, that it will suffer one derailment, that it will suffer two derailments, and that it will suffer more than two derailments are probabilities of four mutually exclusive events because in no one year can the number of derailment losses fall into any two of these categories.

Events that are not mutually exclusive include drawing a five or a club from a deck on one draw (because the five of clubs may be drawn) and, for Promontory Point, suffering both derailment and snow closure losses in a particular year.

For Mutually Exclusive Events. For mutually exclusive events, the probability that any one of them will occur is the sum of their separate probabilities. Thus, the probability of rolling either a 3 or a 5 on one roll of one die is p(3 or 5) = 1/6 + 1/6 = 2/6 = 1/3.

Another set of mutually exclusive events concerns the dollar amounts of individual losses. Since a given loss measured by a specified valuation standard can be only one particular dollar amount, no individual loss can fall into two categories of loss size. A loss is, for example, either (1) less than $5,000 or (2) equal to or more than $5,000. In a probability distribution of losses by size, the probability of a loss equal to or less than a given figure is the sum of the probabilities of losses up to this figure (see Column 3 of Exhibit 9-7). In general, the *sum* of the probabilities of all possible mutually exclusive events—events that are both mutually exclusive and collectively exhaustive—is always one.

Probabilities of mutually exclusive events are also germane to those risk management situations where loss can be caused by one of two perils, but not by more than one. For example, Promontory Point might lose a particular railcar by fire or by flood, but not by both perils. Suppose the probability that a given railcar will be destroyed by fire in a given year is 0.04 and the probability of this railcar being lost to flood in that year is 0.06. Thus, the probability of the railcar being lost to either fire or flood during that year is expressed as follows:

$$p(\text{flood or fire}) = 0.04 + 0.06 = 0.10$$

This computation assumes that the probabilities of flood and of fire are independent—that the occurrence of flood does not affect the probability that fire will occur, and vice versa.

For Events That Are Not Mutually Exclusive. When two or more events can occur within a specified time, they are not mutually exclusive. For such events, the probability that at least one, and possibly both or all, of them will occur is their separate probabilities minus the joint probability that they will both or all occur. (With more than two events that are not mutually exclusive, the computations become quite complex. This discussion of alternative probabilities for non-mutually exclusive events is therefore restricted to cases involving only two events.)

For example, the probability of drawing a five from a deck of cards without jokers is 1/13, the probability of drawing a club is 1/4, and the probability of drawing the five of clubs is 1/52. Therefore, the probability of drawing a five or a club is computed as follows:

$$p(5 \text{ or club}) = 1/13 + 1/4 - 1/52$$
$$= 4/52 + 13/52 - 1/52$$
$$= 16/52$$
$$= 4/13$$

Subtracting the joint probability of events that are not mutually exclusive is necessary to avoid overstating the probability of the alternative events by double-counting the five of clubs as both a five and a club.

The problem of double-counting becomes more serious with events having larger probabilities. Suppose that the climate in a particular area is such that the probability of rain at noon on any given day is 50 percent and the probability that the noon temperature will exceed 70 degrees is 80 percent. On some days, it is both raining and over 70 degrees at noon, so rain and heat (above 70 degrees) are not mutually exclusive. If the joint probability of rain and heat is not subtracted, the probability of either rain or heat, or both, is mistakenly calculated as p(rain or heat) = 0.50 + 0.80 = 1.30. This is an impossible result because, by definition, no probability can exceed 1.0. The following is the proper calculation:

$$p(\text{rain or heat or both}) = 0.50 + 0.80 - (0.50)(0.80)$$
$$= 0.50 + 0.80 - 0.40$$
$$= 0.90$$

Thus, there is a 90 percent probability that at noon it will be raining or the temperature will exceed 70 degrees, *or both*.

Calculating the alternative probability of two events, but *not* both, involves (1) identifying each of the mutually exclusive ways the events may occur, (2) computing the probability of each of these ways, and (3) adding the resulting probabilities. For example, the probability of heat or rain but not both at noon on a particular day is equal to the probability of heat and no rain plus the probability of rain and no heat. These two combinations of circumstances are the only two ways of having rain or heat but not both. Since the probability of rain is 0.50 and the probability of heat is 0.80, the alternative probability of the two events is calculated as follows:

$$p(\text{rain and no heat}) = (0.50)(1 - 0.80)$$
$$= (0.50)(0.20)$$
$$= 0.10$$
$$p(\text{no rain and heat}) = (1 - 0.50)(0.80)$$

$$= (0.50)(0.80)$$

$$= 0.40$$

p(rain or heat but not both) $= 0.10 + 0.40 = 0.50$

In risk management, alternative probabilities of events that are not mutually exclusive arise when dealing with two or more perils that can each cause loss—either operating independently or occurring simultaneously. For example, the cargo inside one of Promontory Point's railcars could be struck by both water damage (by less than total flooding) and pilferage (theft of less than an entire railcar). A given shipper's property, a given railcar, or even the contents of all railcars of an entire train could suffer both water damage and pilferage losses on a single run, and the occurrence of one peril is not likely to change the probability of the occurrence of the other (thus making water damage and pilferage independent events). Here, the railroad's risk management professional might well want to know the probability that a given shipment will suffer either water damage or pilferage loss, or perhaps both.

To illustrate, assume that the probability of pilferage loss to a shipment is 0.09 and the probability of flood loss is 0.06. The probability of loss by pilferage or water damage *or both* is therefore computed as follows:

p(pilferage or water damage or both) $= 0.09 + 0.06 - (0.09)(0.06)$

$$= 0.15 - 0.0054$$

$$= 0.1446$$

Computing the probability of pilferage or water damage *but not both* requires summing the probabilities of the two mutually exclusive ways that this result can occur. These are the probabilities of (1) pilferage but no water damage and (2) water damage but no pilferage. Computing these two probabilities and finding their sum yields the following:

p(pilferage but no water damage) $= (0.09)(1 - 0.06)$

$$= (0.09)(0.94)$$

$$= 0.0846$$

p(water damage but no pilferage) $= (0.06)(1 - 0.09)$

$$= (0.06)(0.91)$$

$$= 0.0546$$

p(pilferage or water damage but not both) $= 0.0846 + 0.0546 = 0.1392$

The probability of either kind of damage but not both is smaller than the probability of either kind of damage and possibly both because the first probability excludes the chance of their both happening.

SOME FURTHER TREND ANALYSIS

As noted in Chapter 9, probability analysis assumes the world is stable. Trend analysis assumes that it is dynamic—that whatever stability exists lies in the constancy of the patterns of movement, the trends of change. In such a presumably dynamic world, the losses that a risk management professional seeks to forecast frequently are analyzed as the joint result of several trends, all acting simultaneously. Therefore, a risk management professional may often wish to use trend analysis to forecast levels of exposures, numbers or sizes of losses, or the costs of insurance or retention—any of which may be the joint result of several trends operating independently. Forecasting any such variable requires combining these trends to find the net result.

For example, the risk management professional for an organization that retains its automobile physical damage losses may, for forecasting purposes, envision each year's losses as the joint result of three trends in (1) the number of vehicles the organization operates, (2) the frequency of losses per 100 vehicles, and (3) the costs of repairing a given amount of physical damage. Forecasting each of these trends separately and combining the result is likely to generate a more accurate forecast of annual vehicle losses than would trying to predict annual losses directly.

Similarly, an organization wishing to budget its annual aggregate workers compensation premiums for each of the next four years may find little predictable pattern in these annual aggregate costs. Without some clear pattern, a reliable forecast may not be feasible. Meaningful patterns may emerge when the organization's risk management professional analyzes annual aggregate workers compensation costs as the combined result of separate, more predictable trends in (1) the size of the organization's work force, (2) the changes in the wage and salary rates the organization pays its employees, and (3) the levels of workers compensation benefits mandated by the states in which this organization's employees work. Relatively simple procedures can be used to determine, or at least estimate, the combined effects of such trends.

The procedure involved is essentially addition: two or more trends are combined by applying them in sequence. In the railroad example, annual dollars of loss of net income and loss from derailments on a particular rail route are presumed to be the joint result of two trends. The first trend relates annual amounts of Promontory Point's net income losses from derailment losses (in constant dollars) to output (in ton-miles of freight). The second is the trend of rail-freight rates per ton-mile of a given cargo shipped along this route (which converts constant dollars to current dollars of net income loss).

In this example, constant dollar losses are forecast through regression analysis against output (with dollars of loss being the dependent variable and forecast ton-miles the independent variable). As a second step, these trended constant dollar losses are inflated by a forecast of freight rates on this route.

This approach to forecasting the combined effects of two or more trends rests on an important assumption: the two trends are independent. In this case, ton-mileages and the general level of freight rates are not related to one another in any defined pattern. If this were not the case, then this additive, sequential combining of trends would not be valid.

Combining Trends—Defining the Model

Business forecasters often develop *models*—systems of graphs, equations, or other relationships that describe, in a simplified way, how the real world appears to work. When used for forecasting, a model identifies and describes the effects of all relevant causes of the dependent variable being forecast.

The elementary model presented here assumes that there are two independent variables, ton-miles of freight carried and changes in freight charges, that are useful predictors of annual dollar totals of Promontory Point's net income losses from derailments on a particular route. These losses are the dependent variable. Because this is a most elementary model, it does not take into account important factors such as weather (where, arguably, low temperatures and high levels of precipitation increase derailment losses), expenditures on track maintenance (where higher expenditures presumably mean fewer derailments), years of experience of the engineer and crew (more years usually meaning lower derailment losses), the time interval since the last major derailment (where, the shorter this interval, perhaps the more likely a crew is to be particularly careful, thus reducing derailments), and even the mere passage of time (which may change the conditions that generate each trend). These are just some of the factors that might reasonably be used as predictors of annual dollar amounts of net income losses from derailments, assuming these predictors could themselves be reasonably forecast. But, for understanding the procedure and for practicing how to apply it, two independent variables (ton-miles and rail cargo rates) are sufficient.

The First Predictor: Ton-Miles. It is reasonable to assume that the frequency and annual totals of derailment losses a railroad suffers each year will increase or decrease as the volume of its freight hauling increases or decreases. To test this assumption, Exhibit 10-1 computes the regression equation that relates Promontory Point's annual derailment losses to its annual ton-miles of cargo carried during the years 19X1 through 19X4. In this exhibit and in the equation it derives, ton-miles is the independent variable (X, expressed in hundreds of thousands of miles) and the annual dollar amount of derailment losses is the dependent variable (Y, expressed in thousands of constant 19X4 dollars).

The ton-mileages in Column 1 of Exhibit 10-1 are taken directly from Exhibit 9-23. The dollar losses in Column 2 are from Exhibit 9-3. The remaining columns and computations in Exhibit 10-1 parallel those in Exhibit 9-23. The resulting equation for the regression line indicates that the annual dollar total of losses (Y) can be expected to increase by $1,192 for each 100,000 ton-mile increase in cargo carried.

The negative $35,610 value for "a" in the equation erroneously suggests that derailment losses would be less than zero if the railroad ceased to operate and ton-mileages were zero. Because a linear regression line often results in distortions at its extremes, this result can be ignored for practical purposes. This regression equation should not be used for making predictions beyond the range of ton-mileages (3,500,000 through 9,500,000) from which it was computed.

It is important not to ascribe false accuracy to the results shown in any exhibits in the remainder of this chapter. The forecast that expected, annual dollar totals of loss will rise or fall by $1,192 each time annual ton-mileages rise or fall by 100,000 is only a best estimate, based on available data and the assumptions underlying the model. To the extent that these assumptions are not true, and to the extent that other causal factors are ignored in the model, the accuracy of this forecast is limited. At best, actual results can only be expected to fall within a range of this single-value forecast. The width of this range depends on many factors, analysis of which requires statistical expertise beyond the scope of this text.

The Second Predictor: Cargo Rates. Changes in the general level of prices are usually forecast through time series analysis. Exhibit 10-2 computes a linear trend line of changes in historic rail cargo rates from 19X1 through 19X4. The actual index figures in Column 2 are taken from Exhibit 9-2, and the computation follows the procedure portrayed in Exhibit 9-21. The resulting equations suggest that if the economic conditions of 19X1 through 19X4 do not change and price levels move linearly, then the price index can be projected to increase by 11.45 index points each year.

Many forecasting models assume that price levels change by a constant, curvilinear *rate* (or percentage) from year to year rather than by a constant *number* of index points. The assumption of a constant percentage rate of change yields a curvilinear, rather than a linear, trend line. As years pass, any positive or upward rate of change means larger

Exhibit 10-1
Regression fo Annual Derailment Losses Against Annual Ton-Miles

	(1) Ton-Miles (x 100,000) (X)	(2) Losses (x $1,000) (Y)	(3) XY	(4) X²
	35	9.8	343.0	1,225
	60	32.9	1,974.0	3,600
	72	45.1	3,247.2	5,184
	95	82.0	7,790.0	9,025
Totals:	262	169.8	13,354.2	19,034

$$a = \frac{(\text{sum } Y)(\text{sum } X^2) - (\text{sum } X)(\text{sum } XY)}{n\,(\text{sum } X^2) - (\text{sum } X)^2}$$

$$= \frac{(169.8)(19,034) - (262)(13,354.2)}{4(19,034) - (262)^2}$$

$$= \frac{3,231,973.2 - 2,498,800.4}{76,136 - 68,644}$$

$$= \frac{266,827.2}{7,492}$$

$$= \underline{\underline{-35.61}}$$

$$b = \frac{n(\text{sum } XY) - (\text{sum } X)(\text{sum } Y)}{n\,(\text{sum } X^2) - (\text{sum } X)^2}$$

$$= \frac{4(13,354.2) - (262)(169.8)}{4(19,034) - (262)^2}$$

$$= \frac{53,416.8 - 44,487.6}{76,136 - 68,644}$$

$$= \frac{8,929.2}{7,492}$$

$$= \underline{\underline{1.192}}$$

$$Y = -35.61 + 1.192X$$

Losses (x $1,000) $= -35.61 + 1.192$ Ton-Miles (x 100,000)

Exhibit 10-2

LinearTrend of Cargo Rates

	(1) Years (X)	(2) Index (Y)	(3) XY	(4) X^2
	1	115.2	115.2	1
	2	125.9	251.8	4
	3	140.2	420.6	9
	4	148.6	594.4	16
Totals:	10	529.9	1,382.0	30

$$a = \frac{(\text{sum Y})(\text{sum } X^2) - (\text{sum X})(\text{sum XY})}{n\,(\text{sum } X^2) - (\text{sum X})^2}$$

$$= \frac{(529.9)(30) - (10)(1,382.0)}{4(30) - (10)^2}$$

$$= \frac{15,897.0 - 13,820.0}{120 - 100}$$

$$= \frac{2,077}{20}$$

$$= \underline{\underline{103.85}}$$

$$b = \frac{n(\text{sum XY}) - (\text{sum X})(\text{sum Y})}{n\,(\text{sum } X^2) - (\text{sum X})^2}$$

$$= \frac{4(1,382.0) - (10)(529.9)}{4(30) - (10)^2}$$

$$= \frac{5,528 - 5,299}{120 - 100}$$

$$= \frac{229}{20}$$

$$= \underline{\underline{11.45}}$$

$$\text{Index} = Y = a + bX$$

$$= 103.85 + 11.45 \,(\text{Year})$$

Exhibit 10-3
Comparison of Linear and Constant Percentage-Change
Projection of Cargo Rates

Year	Linear Projection (11.45 points/yr.)	Percentage Projection[†] (8.86%/yr.)
19X4	148.60	148.60
19X5	160.05	161.76
19X6	171.50	176.10
19X7	182.95	181.70
19X8	194.40	208.69
19X9	205.85	227.17
19Y0	217.30	247.30
19Y1	228.75	269.21
19Y2	240.20	293.07
19Y3	251.65	319.03

†Rounded to two decimal places.

and larger annual increases, while a persistent negative or downward rate of change implies an increasingly rapid fall. Since rates of change can vary, projecting a constant-rate curvilinear trend over many years can lead to unrealistic results.

Exhibit 10-3 demonstrates that linear and curvilinear trends can forecast strikingly different results, especially in more distant years. In the linear projection, each succeeding year's forecast is 11.45 ton-mile units greater than the last; in the percentage projection, each year's forecast is 8.86% greater than the last. As more years pass, the 8.86% growth is much more rapid than the 11.45 ton-mile growth. Because these two types of trending techniques produce such markedly different results, long-range forecasts can prove quite inaccurate. To improve accuracy, both in the long and the short run, it is important to do the following:

1. Obtain as much relevant data as possible for computing trends, especially current data that can be particularly valuable in making short-term forecasts.
2. Experiment with both linear and curvilinear trending techniques to see which approach better fits actual historical data and presumably will better project the future. (A simple way to experi-

ment is to graph both the historical data and the linear or curvilinear trend lines, as shown in Chapter 9, to make an intuitive judgment as to the better "fit." Alternatively, a statistician may be consulted, especially for crucial forecasts whose importance justifies the cost of such special expertise.)

3. Redraw or recalculate trend lines to incorporate new data, either adding to the total volume of data upon which the trends are based or, if conditions are changing so that the earliest data no longer reflects existing conditions, deleting any inapplicable early loss data.

These steps help refine the forecasting model by adding to the historical data on which the model is founded and clarifying the patterns of change on which it relies. This discussion purposely focuses on a most elementary model in order to illustrate the principles involved. The model here involves only four years' data and two variables. A large organization with many years' experience may wish to use a model with five or six trended variables and perhaps two decades' accumulated data. For the risk management professionals in many smaller organizations, however, even such a simple model as the one explained here can sharpen forecasts of future losses.

An Illustrative Forecast

Exhibit 10-4 demonstrates one technique for forecasting Promontory Point's annual derailment losses in both constant 19X4 and current dollars based on the following:

1. The regression equation in Exhibit 10-1 that relates derailment losses to ton-miles.
2. A forecast from Promontory Point's senior management that because of an expected general economic decline in the region Promontory Point serves, ton-mileages will be 8 million in 19X5, 5.5 million in 19X6, and 4.3 million in 19X7.
3. A forecast from the railroad's finance department that the 8.86 percent increase in the rail cargo rates will continue for 19X5, but the price level will increase only 7.00 percent in 19X6 and, in 19X7, the general level of prices will fall 5.00 percent from their 19X6 level.

The forecasts in (2) and (3) above should enhance the accuracy of the forecasts that the risk management professional could make. Without this information from other departments, these risk management forecasts might have to rely on linear or curvilinear projections of both future ton-mileages and future cargo rates.

Exhibit 10-4
Forecasts of Annual Derailment Losses for 19X5, 19X6, and 19X7

Assumptions

For 19X5
1. Ton-Miles = 8,000,000 (or 80 x 100,000)
2. Cargo rates continue to rise at 8.86% over 19X4 level

For 19X6
1. Ton-Miles = 5,500,000 (or 55 x 100,000)
2. Rates rise at 7.00% over 19X5 level

For 19X7
1. Ton-Miles = 4,300,000 (or 43 x 100,000)
2. Rates fall 5.00% from 19X6 level

Computations

For 19X5
1. Losses (in thousands of constant 19X4 dollars)

$$L = -\$35.61 + 1.192(80)$$
$$= -\$35.61 + \$95.360$$
$$= \$59.75$$

2. Adjusted for cargo rate change (8.86% increase for 19X4)

$$\text{Losses} = (\$59.75)(1 + 0.0886)$$
$$= \$65.04$$

For 19X6
1. Losses (in thousands of contstant 19X4 dollars)

$$L = -\$35.61 + \$1.192(55)$$
$$= -\$35.61 + \$65.56$$
$$= \$29.95$$

2. Adjusted for cargo rate change (7.00% increase over 19X5)

$$\text{Losses} = (\$29.95)(1 + 0.0886)(1 + 0.0700)$$
$$= \$34.89$$

For 19X7
1. Losses (in thousands of constant 19X4 dollars)

$$L = -\$35.61 + 1.192(43)$$
$$= -\$35.61 + \$51.256$$
$$= \$15.65$$

2. Adjusted for cargo rate change (5.00% decrease from 19X6)

$$\text{Losses} = (\$15.65)(1 + 0.0886)(1 + 0.07)(1 - 0.05)$$
$$= \$17.32$$

Exhibit 10-4 recaps these assumptions and performs the computations that apply the regression equation for 19X5, 19X6, and 19X7. These computations involve two separate steps. The first is to compute losses in constant dollars based on projected ton-mileages. These computations are similar for all three years, involving only substitution of different ton-mileage figures for each of the three years. The resulting loss projections—$59,750 in 19X5, $29,950 in 19X6, and $15,650 in 19X7—are in constant 19X4 dollars.

The second step in the computations for each of these three years converts these constant dollar losses to current dollars, reflecting 19X5, 19X6, and 19X7 projected rate levels. These rate-adjusting computations differ among the three years because of different projected percentages in price level changes and because of the differing number of years for which the constant 19X4 dollar losses need to be adjusted.

Thus, for 19X5, the price level change merely involves multiplying $59.75 by (1 + 0.0886), reflecting an 8.86 percent increase in cargo rates from 19X4 to 19X5. Consequently, 19X5 losses are forecast to be $65,040 in 19X5 dollars. For 19X6, the rate level adjustment involves multiplying the amount of losses in constant dollars by two factors: (1 + 0.0886) to bring these losses to 19X5 levels and (1 + 0.0700) to reflect the 7.00 percent rate level increase from 19X5 to 19X6. By this procedure, expressed in 19X6 dollars, losses are projected to be $34,890 in 19X6. For 19X7, when cargo rates are projected to fall by 5.00 percent, three factors are needed to adjust to the 19X7 rate level: (1 + 0.0886) to reach the 19X5 rate level, (1 + 0.0700) to reach the 19X6 rate level, and (1 − 0.0500) to reflect the 19X7 projected price level decrease. Weighted by these three factors, 19X7 losses in then-current dollars can be forecast as $17,320. (These price-adjustment factors are equivalent to 1.0886, 1.0700, and 0.9500, respectively. Had the projected changes in cargo rate levels been a constant 8.86 percent for each of the three years, the respective rate level adjustment factors could have been expressed as 1.0886, 1.0886^2, and 1.0886^3.)

SUMMARY

Accidental losses pose demands on an organization's resources—demands to finance recovery from losses that actually do occur and, perhaps more importantly, to prevent or reduce the size of potential losses before they occur. Forecasts of accidental losses should therefore be viewed as forecasts of the demands on an organization's risk management capacities—demands that are met by selecting and implementing appropriate risk management techniques. In this context, therefore, making risk management decisions becomes a matter of choosing those risk management techniques that will most effectively and efficiently meet the demands posed by actual and potential accidental losses.

Chapter 9 and this chapter have described elementary procedures for forecasting these demands. Drawing upon the common-sense descriptions of probability and trend analyses in Chapter 9, this chapter has developed more precise notation and procedures for computing the joint probability of two or more events, alternative probabilities of any one of several possible events, and equations for trend lines that bring together the combined effects of the several factors that may influence the frequency or severity of an organization's losses. Against these forecast demands, Chapters 11 and 12 develop and apply decision rules for selecting those risk management techniques that will best meet these needs.

CHAPTER 11

Cash Flow Analysis as a Decision Criterion

This chapter develops a criterion for selecting risk management techniques or combinations of techniques. Applied to the forecasts of losses developed in Chapters 9 and 10, this criterion allocates an organization's risk management resources to meet most cost-effectively the demands that potential and actual accidental losses place upon that organization.

This criterion calls for maximizing the present value of an organization's long-term, after-tax net cash flows. Most organizations use this same rule for making sound business decisions. For both profit-seeking and nonprofit organizations, maximizing the present value of net cash flows is the decision guideline that best enhances the organization's ability to apply resources to fulfill its basic objectives.

Using cash flow analysis to select risk management techniques puts risk management decisions on the same basis, made by the same logic, as most other decisions in well-managed organizations. Cash flow logic unifies risk management with other management specialties by enabling the risk management professional to make and defend choices of risk management techniques in the same way other managers make their decisions. Specifically, cash flow analysis enables the risk management professional to do the following:

- Explain how any proposal, including a proposed risk management technique, would affect the flows of cash into and out of an organization.
- Compute the present value of the net cash flows of proposals that call for the commitment of an organization's resources to an asset or activity.

111

- Express and evaluate proposals, including alternative risk management techniques, in terms of their net cash flows and rates of return.

THE IMPORTANCE OF CASH FLOWS

An organization's net cash flow during any period is its cash receipts minus its cash disbursements during that period. If receipts exceed disbursements, net cash flow is positive. If disbursements exceed receipts, it is negative. It is through its net cash flow—plus any credit the organization can use as a substitute for cash—that the organization can command resources to pursue its objectives. Projecting net cash flows likely to be generated by alternative assets or activities gives management a valid criterion for choosing those assets or activities that promise the most benefit to the organization.

Command Over Resources

Cash, in hand or in the bank, enables an organization to obtain things to fulfill its objectives. Cash—more precisely, purchasing power, including credit—is a means to other ends, indeed usually a *necessary* means to *all* other ends. The greater an organization's positive net cash flow, the more it can do. In contrast, negative cash flow reduces an organization's ability to pursue its goals. Thus, net cash flow serves as a barometer of an organization's strength, a measure of its short-range capabilities and of its long-range value to its owners and to those whom it serves.

Net cash flow measures an organization's ability to function effectively better than its accounting profits or surpluses measured in accrued revenues and expenses. Unlike profits or budget surpluses, which may be affected by changes in accounting receivables, payables, or other accruals that are not means of paying for things, net cash flow measures an organization's ability to buy or otherwise command needed resources.

Using present values of net cash flows as a decision criterion also promotes other organizational objectives (such as profits, public service, or humanitarian or political objectives) that guide an organization's decisions. Seeking cash is not a final objective in itself. It is only a means to the organization's more meaningful goals, virtually all of which require cash. Because cash flow is a means to so many other (usually higher) ends, a decision rule based on maximizing the present value of an organization's net cash flows is, in a sense, "objective-neutral." The greater the present value of the purchasing power an organization can command in the long run, the more fully it can realize its organizational objectives. The risk management professional should coordinate the cash needs of risk management techniques with the organization's other needs for cash.

Evaluating Alternative Uses of Resources

In selecting assets or activities to which to commit an organization's resources, senior management should give priority to those alternatives that promise the net cash flows having the greatest present value. The simplicity of this decision rule is often complicated by situations where an asset or an activity requires immediate cash expenditures (as well as perhaps further expenditures in the future), especially on assets or activities that can be expected to generate cash receipts only in future periods. Such situations, where cash expenditures or cash receipts are spread over several accounting periods, can best be dealt with by a procedure known as *capital budgeting*, which formalizes decisions based on net cash flows.

Capital budgeting distinguishes between operating expenditures and capital expenditures. *Operating expenditures* involve the acquisition of resources that will be consumed in a relatively short period, usually one year or less. *Capital expenditures* involve assets or activities that are relatively long-lived and promise to generate cash receipts or to require cash disbursements in future accounting periods. For example, when Promontory Point Railroad acquires a new locomotive, the cash receipts attributable to that locomotive will be received over the entire useful life of the equipment—perhaps twenty or even fifty years depending upon technology, maintenance, and whether the expected life of the locomotive is cut short by an unexpected major accident. If Promontory Point were to build a new railway station, the benefits it would generate might be received over a period of forty, fifty, or more years.

A capital budget is a plan for making long-term capital investments in order to achieve an organization's objectives. Capital budgeting is the decision-making process involving the evaluation of various alternative capital investment proposals in terms of the cash outlays they require and the present values of the cash inflows they are likely to generate. Because most organizations have more worthwhile investment opportunities than they have available cash to invest, priority should be given to those uses of cash that promise to be most productive, that is, the uses for which the organization projects the greatest present value of future net cash flows.

THE TIME VALUE OF MONEY

Capital budgeting techniques recognize that money has a time value. This time value of money arises because investing money over time in a project or in a financial investment generates ("earns") more money. The additional amount of money earned by a given dollar over a given time period is the *time value* of that dollar over that period. Computing the present value of a sum of money to be received in the future incorporates its time value.

The Present Value Concept

A dollar presently available, "in hand," has a greater time value than does a dollar to be received in the future because the dollar in hand can be invested to start earning money now. In contrast, a dollar to be received in the future cannot be invested to generate earnings until that future date. The greater the rate of return a dollar in hand can earn, the greater is its value relative to a future dollar. Conversely, the longer the time period until a future dollar is to be received, the lesser is its present value when compared with the value of a dollar in hand. The two factors that determine the present value of a particular sum are the appropriate interest rate and the length of time before that sum becomes available for use.

Interest Rate. The appropriate interest rate is the cost associated with the use of money, normally expressed as a percentage rate for each year the money is being used. Except in those cases where money has been borrowed from an outside lender, this time value cost does not usually entail any explicit outlay for the use of money. Instead, this time value cost is an implied cost, an "opportunity cost," of using money for one purpose rather than for another. Selecting one use for money necessarily commits funds that could otherwise have been invested in an alternative project. Expressed as an interest rate, the cost of money used for one purpose is the rate of return that money could have earned had it been put to the best alternative use.

An organization typically earns an after-tax rate of return on funds put to use in its normal operations. For illustrative purposes, assume an organization can generate internally 18 percent after taxes from its normal operations. Putting money to a use other than normal operations involves a sacrifice, an opportunity cost, of this 18 percent. This 18 percent is this organization's time value of this money.

In contrast, when an organization borrows funds at, say, an after-tax cost of 10 percent per year, its cost of using these particular funds for one year is the after-tax 10 percent charged by the lender. Notice that here interest cost is not the same as opportunity cost. The organization's time value of money for evaluating proposed uses of cash remains 18 percent, not the 10 percent charged by the lender. Because the organization can earn 18 percent on money from any source, the "opportunity cost" of putting this money to any use remains 18 percent.

When funds are used over several years—as is often the case in risk management, particularly for loss prevention devices—this implicit opportunity cost rate applies to each year the funds are used. Therefore, on the basis of the organization's opportunity cost, its financial officer usually specifies a minimum rate of return, a "hurdle rate," which all acceptable proposals must meet or exceed.

Length of Time. The second determinant of the time value of money is the length of time (the number of years or units of time) for which that money could be invested at a specified interest rate. To illustrate, if money can earn a rate of 10 percent per year, the use of $100 has a time value of $10 for that one-year period—$100 earns $10 in one year at a 10 percent interest rate. With a 10 percent interest rate, an initial sum of $100 increases to $110 at the end of one year. Expressed differently, $110 in hand one year from now has a present value of $100 if the interest rate is 10 percent per year.

Computations of Present Values

Computations of present value may involve (1) a present payment, (2) a single future payment, (3) a series of equal future payments, or (4) a series of unequal future payments.

A Present Payment. The present value of a present payment (either a receipt or a disbursement) is the face amount of that payment. No discounting is required to take account of the use value of that current payment before it is received or disbursed because there is no period of time prior to receipt or disbursement. For example, $100 received or disbursed now—in a present accounting period—has both a face value and a present value of $100. The present payment most frequently encountered in capital budgeting situations is the initial outlay required by a proposed asset or activity, such as purchasing fire extinguishers and training employees in their use.

A Single Future Payment. Appendix A at the end of this chapter, "Present Value of $1 Received at the End of Period," gives present values of $1 received at the end of various periods of time at various rates of interest. This table shows present value factors for each pair of determinants of the time value of money—the rate of interest and the length of time. The present value factors indicate the amount that must be invested today at a given interest rate for a given number of years to receive $1 as a single payment at the end of that number of years.

For example, using a 10 percent annual interest rate, the present value of $1 received at the end of one year is $0.909, or about 91 cents. This result is obtained by multiplying $1 by the present value factor, 0.909, in the one-year row of the 10 percent column of Appendix A. This factor is equal to dividing $1 by $1.10, which is the present value of $1 now divided by the present value of $1 one year from now at 10 percent. Conversely, if approximately 91 cents is invested today for one year, earning 10 percent interest per year, the interest is 9 cents and the amount resulting at the end of that year is $1.

If interest is compounded annually for two years, a little more than 82 cents must be invested initially to produce an ending amount of $1. The present value factor in Appendix A is 0.826, indicating that 82.6 cents is needed initially if the ending amount is to be $1 after two years at 10 percent annual interest. At the end of one year, 82 cents grows to 91 cents, and at the end of the second year, the 91 cents grows to $1. Viewed prospectively, the present value of $1 to be received two years hence at interest compounded annually at the rate of 10 percent per year is 82.6 cents.

Notice the inverse relationship between the present value of $1 and the number of years during which money initially invested earns interest. As one increases, the other decreases. For example, with interest compounded annually at the rate of 10 percent, $1 in hand today has a present value of $1. The $1 in hand one year from now has a present value of about 91 cents. An amount of $1 in hand 10 years from now has a present value of about 38 cents, and $1 in hand 50 years from now has a present value of about a penny. These present values can be confirmed by applying the appropriate present value factors from Appendix A to $1.

There is also an inverse relationship between the present value of $1 and the rate of interest. The higher the rate of interest for any given time period, the lower the present value, and vice versa. For example, at 10 percent interest, the present value of $1 received at the end of one year is about 91 cents because at 10 percent interest, 91 cents earns 9 cents. At 12 percent, the present value of $1 under the same conditions is only about 89 cents ($0.893) and at 20 percent about 83 cents ($0.833). As an extreme example, at a 50 percent annual interest rate, the present value of $1 to be received one year from now is about 67 cents ($0.667) because 67 cents will earn 33 cents in interest if the interest rate is 50 percent for one year.

A Series of Equal Future Payments. The present value of a series of future payments is equal to the sum of the present values of each of the separate payments. Exhibit 11-1 shows the present values for a series of three payments of $1 received at the end of one, two, and three years when the interest rate is 10 percent per year compounded annually. The present value of a single payment of $1 at the end of one year under these conditions is $0.909. Similarly, the present value of $1 received at the end of two years is $0.826, and the present value of $1 received at the end of three years is $0.751. These present values are computed from the present value factors in Appendix A, using the 10 percent column, lines 1, 2, and 3, respectively. If the three present values are added, the sum of $2.486 is the present value of $1 received at the end of *each* year for a period of three years at interest compounded annually at the rate of 10 percent. Stated differently, $2.486 is the amount that must be invested today at 10 percent interest per year compounded annually in order to receive $1 at the end of each of the next three years, after which the investment is exhausted.

Appendix B, also located at the end of this chapter and entitled "Present Value of $1 Received Annually at the End of Each Period for N Periods," provides the same result without requiring the summing of the separate present values from Appendix A. Appendix B presents these sums directly. For example, Appendix B can be used to determine the present value of $1 received annually for a period of three years at interest compounded annually at the rate of 10 percent. In the 10 percent column of Appendix B, where n, the number of years, equals 3, the present value factor is 2.487. This present value factor, applied to future payments of $1 each, yields a present value of $2.487 (or $1 × 2.487). Except for the slight difference due to rounding, this amount is the same as the $2.486 calculated by adding the three separate present value factors from Appendix A.

The present value factors in Appendix B are derived from those in Appendix A. The top line is the same in both tables because $1 is received at the end of only one year, and the present value factors in the first row of each table are the same for each rate of interest. The values on line 2 of Appendix B equal the sums of the present values shown on lines 1 and 2 in Appendix A. For example, at 10 percent interest in Appendix A, the figures for the first and second years are 0.909 and 0.826. The present value at 10 percent on line 2 in Appendix B is the sum of those two figures, 1.736. Because the present value factors are rounded to three decimal places, comparisons between the two tables may differ by one thousandth.

Exhibit 11-1 also shows another perspective for determining the present value of a stream of equal annual payments. The present value of a three-year stream of $1 annual payments at 10 percent interest is $2.487. Starting with a fund of $2.486852, add 10 percent interest for the first year and subtract $1 at the end of the first year. At the beginning

Exhibit 11-1

Present Value of a Stream of Equal Payments at 10% Interest

Equal to the Sum of Present Values of the Future Payments

	Future Values – at the end of		
Present Value	1 year	2 years	3 years
$0.909 ←	$1		
0.826 ←		$1	
0.751 ←			$1
$2.486			

Equal to the Sum of the Future Payments plus Interest on the Balance Remaining After Each Payment[†]:

	First	Second	Third
Beginning Balance	$2.486852	$1.735537	$0.909091
Plus Interest (10%)	0.248685	0.173554	0.090909
	2.735537	1.909091	1.000000
Less Payment	1.000000	1.000000	1.000000
Ending Balance	$1.735537	$0.909091	$0.

[†] To demonstrate that payments exhaust the beginning balance, values in this portion of the exhibit have been computed to be accurate to six places to the right of the decimal. Rounded to three decimal places, the beginning balance computed in the lower portion of the exhibit would be 2.487, shown in the upper portion. (This differs from the 2.486 total of the Appendix A values because Appendix A presents rounded values.)

of the second year, start with $1.735537. Repeat the process of adding interest and subtracting $1 at the end of each year for the second and third years. When the third dollar is subtracted, the amount remaining in the fund is $0. This computation demonstrates that investing approximately $2.49 at 10 percent interest enables one to pay $1 at the end of each year over a three-year period.

The difference represents the interest earned by the investment, a total of approximately 51 cents ($3.00 − $2.49 = $0.51). Exhibit 11-1 shows that 91 cents invested for a one-year period at 10 percent earns about 9 cents interest. Similarly, 82.6 cents invested for a two-year period earns about 17 cents, and 75 cents invested for a three-year period earns about 25 cents. These earnings add to 51 cents.

Notice that the present values are for future payments of $1. If the future payments differ from $1, their present value is calculated by multiplying each future payment by the present value factor for the specified interest rate and time period. For example, to calculate the present value of a single payment of $100 to be received at the end of three years at interest compounded annually at the rate of 10 percent, determine the present value factor for $1 to be received under these conditions. The proper factor from Appendix A is 0.751. Multiplying this factor by $100 shows that $75.10 is the present value of $100 to be received at the end of three years at interest compounded annually at the rate of 10 percent. Similarly, if the interest rate remains 10 percent, but the single payment to be received at the end of three years is $7,800, the present value of that future payment is $7,800 times the present value factor, 0.751, or $5,857.80.

To calculate the present value of $100 received annually at the end of each year for three years at interest compounded annually at the rate of 10 percent, use Appendix B to find the present value factor for a stream of $1 payments for three years at 10 percent interest. The factor is 2.487. Multiplying this factor by $100 indicates that the present value of the stream of equal $100 annual payments is $248.70. If the payment were $7,800 each instead of $100, the present value of this stream of payments would be 2.487 times $7,800, or $19,398.60.

A Series of Unequal Future Payments. When different dollar amounts are to be received at the end of different periods, each period's cash inflow must be separately valued, using the present values for single payments in Appendix A. The present value of the entire stream of unequal payments is the sum of the present values of the individual payments.

Exhibit 11-2 shows the present values of a stream of unequal payments ($2, $3, and $4) at 10 percent interest. The present value of the $2 to be received at the end of the first year is 2 times $0.909, or $1.818. Similarly, the value of $3 to be received at the end of the second year is three times the value of $1 to be received at the end of that period, or $2.478. The present value of $4 at the end of three years is $3.004, making the present value of the three years' payments $7.300.

METHODS FOR EVALUATING CASH FLOWS

Capital budgeting decisions apply cash flow criteria in either of two ways. One involves determining whether a particular investment

Exhibit 11-2

Present Value of a Stream of Unequal Payments at 10% Interest

Equal to the Sum of Present Values of the Future Payments

Present Value	1 year	Future Values – at the end of 2 years	3 years	Present Value Factor
$1.818 ⟵	$2			0.909
2.478 ⟵		$3		0.826
3.004 ⟵			$4	0.751
$7.300				

proposal is expected to meet some predetermined minimum acceptable level of performance. For example, Promontory Point's financial policy may specify that any proposed capital investment (such as a locomotive or a newly-built railway station) must be expected to earn a minimum rate of return of 20 percent annually during its expected useful life before that project can be given further consideration. The rate of return an organization considers minimally acceptable often represents the interest rates it must pay to borrow funds or the interest rates it can earn by investing its funds in a financial instrument rather than its own activities.

The second way of applying cash flow criteria to capital budgeting decisions involves selecting the most promising proposal by computing the rate of return each proposal promises to earn on the investment it requires. For example, assume that three capital investment proposals exceed Promontory Point's predetermined minimum acceptable 20 percent rate of return. Suppose one is expected to earn 25 percent, the second 30 percent, and the third 35 percent. The selection process involves allocating cash to the proposal expected to earn the highest rate of return, 35 percent. Other things being equal, the proposal that yields the highest return is the best.

Corresponding to these two ways of applying net cash flow criteria are two different evaluation methods. One, the net present value method, takes the first approach of computing whether, at a specified rate of interest, the present value of a proposal's net cash flows is positive or negative. The second evaluation method, the time-adjusted rate of return method (also often called the internal rate of return method) computes the interest rate at which the present value of a proposal's net cash flows is zero. Both these methods are explained below, as is the profitability index for ranking projects with positive net present values.

Two major conditions are necessary for the successful application of these evaluation methods to capital budgeting decisions. One is that the benefits and costs associated with a particular proposed investment project must be measurable in monetary terms. Nonmonetary considerations are beyond the scope of these evaluation methods.

The second condition relates to unpredictability. Capital budgeting decisions involve investments that are expected to extend well into the future. Such long-term investment projects are subject to both speculative and pure risks. In most cases, the longer the expected life of an investment project, the less predictable is its rate of return. The discussion in this chapter assumes that present and future cash flows are known with certainty. Chapter 12 examines problems associated with making decisions when the future is, in some degree, unpredictable.

To evaluate capital investment proposals one must know the following:

1. The amount of the initial investment
2. The acceptable annual rate of return, expressed as a percentage of the initial investment
3. The estimated useful life of the proposal, the number of years (or other periods) for which it will produce cash flows
4. The amount of differential annual after-tax net cash flows associated with the proposal

Exhibit 11-3 illustrates the evaluation of a capital investment proposal using, first, the net present value method and, then, the time-adjusted rate of return method. The proposal involves the acquisition of an asset for $30,000 cash. The estimated useful life of the asset is three years, and it is expected that the asset will generate additional annual after-tax net cash inflows of $12,000, or a total of $36,000 over three years, with no salvage value.

Net Present Value Method

The net present value method can be used only when there is a predetermined minimum acceptable rate of return. Typically, this minimum acceptable rate of return will be given to, not established by, a risk management professional. This given rate applies to the cash inflows and outflows from any proposal the organization may consider, including a proposed risk management technique.

Any proposal whose projected cash inflows have a present value greater than the present value of the required outflows is acceptable by this criterion. In Exhibit 11-3, for instance, the additional annual net cash inflows are a constant $12,000 each year, and the only required cash outflow is the $30,000 initial cost of the asset. The first step in using

Exhibit 11-3

Evaluating a Capital Investment Project

Factors:

    Initial investment – $30,000

    Useful life – 3 years

    Differential annual after-tax net cash flow – $12,000 net inflow

Evaluation by the Net Present Value Method:

Present value of differential inflows ($12,000 x 2.487)	$29,844
Less: Present value of initial investment	30,000
Net present value (negative)	($ 156)

Evaluation by the Time-Adjusted Rate of Return Method:

$$\frac{\text{Initial investment}}{\text{Differential cash inflow}} = \frac{\$30,000}{\$12,000} = 2.500 = \text{present value factor}$$

Interpolation to Find the Time-Adjusted Rate of Return (r):

	Rate of Return	Present Value Factor	Present Value Factor
	8%	2.577	2.577
	r		2.500
	10%	2.487	
Differences:	2%	0.090	0.077

  r =   8% +[(0.077/0.090) x 2%]

      =   8% + 1.71%

      =   9.71%

the net present value method is to calculate the present value of the additional annual after-tax net cash flows.

Appendix B indicates that the present value factor for $1 received annually at the end of each year for three years at 10 percent interest compounded annually is 2.487. Multiplying this present value factor by $12,000 yields the present value of the differential net cash inflows, $29,844. In other words, $29,844 is the amount that would have to be invested today at 10 percent interest compounded annually to receive $12,000 at the end of each year for a period of three years. The net present value of the proposal is the present value of the differential net cash inflows minus the present value of the investment. The net present value of this proposal is a negative $156, computed by subtracting the $30,000 initial investment the proposal requires from the $29,884 present value of the proposal's future cash inflows. This negative result shows that the proposal will not generate the minimum acceptable rate of return of 10 percent.

Time-Adjusted Rate of Return Method

Exhibit 11-3 also illustrates the same result, using the time-adjusted rate of return method. Since the price of the asset is $30,000 and acquiring that asset is expected to generate $12,000 a year for three years, $30,000 is the present value of $12,000 received annually for a period of three years at some unspecified time-adjusted rate of return. Dividing $30,000 by $12,000 gives a present value factor for the proposal of 2.500. Therefore, 2.500 is the present value of $1 received annually for a three-year period at the yet undetermined time-adjusted rate of return for this proposal. One can determine this rate by finding the present value factor that comes closest to 2.500 in the three-year row of Appendix B. The factor of 2.500 lies between 2.577 for an 8 percent return and 2.487 for a 10 percent return over a three-year period. Therefore, the time-adjusted rate of return for this proposal is between 8 and 10 percent, compounded annually.

Finding a more precise time-adjusted rate of return for this proposal requires an interpolation process, such as that illustrated in the lower portion of Exhibit 11-3. The total difference between the present value factors for 8 percent and 10 percent returns is 0.090 (computed as 2.577 − 2.487). The difference between the present value factor for an 8 percent return and the present value factor for this proposal is 0.077 (2.577 − 2.500). Since lower present value factors are associated with higher rates of return for any given number of years, the asset has a time-adjusted rate of return that is higher than 8 percent. It is higher by an amount equal to 0.077/0.090 of 2 percent. (The two percentage points are the difference between the two columns in Appendix B used for this interpolation.) Because 0.077/0.090 of 2 percent is approximately 1.71 percent, the time-adjusted rate of return on this project is approximately 9.71 percent (8 percent + 1.71 percent), which is less than the minimum acceptable rate of return of 10 percent.

Exhibit 11-4 illustrates an alternative process for interpolating, using the same figures shown in the lower portion of Exhibit 11-3. This alternative procedure is based on the fact that the exact rate of return, r, lies at the same relative point in the interval between any two known rates of return as the relative point that the present value factor for r occupies in the interval between the present value factors for these known rates of return. For example, if the present value factor for the rate of return being sought lies two-thirds of the way between the present value factors for two known rates of return, then the rate of return being sought also is approximately two-thirds of the way between

Exhibit 11-4
Alternative "Cross-Products" Procedure for Interpolation

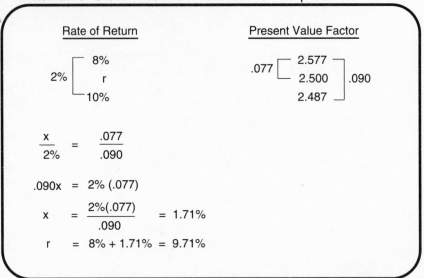

the two known rates of return. In Exhibit 11-4, let x represent the rate-of-return interval between 8 percent and r; it follows that the interval between 8 percent and 10 percent is 2 percent and that the intervals between the respective present value factors for these rates of return are 0.077 and 0.090. The ratio x/2% equals the ratio 0.077/0.090. When two ratios are equal, the cross products of their respective numerators and denominators are also equal. Consequently, as shown in Exhibit 11-4, 0.090x equals 2 percent (0.077). By further algebraic manipulations, x equals 1.71 percent, making r equal to 9.71 percent (8 percent + 1.71 percent). The interpolations shown throughout the remainder of this text, while presented in the format of Exhibit 11-3, can also be performed by the procedure in Exhibit 11-4.

Had the cost of the asset been $27,000 instead of $30,000, and the other three factors remained unchanged, the net present value of the proposal would have been positive, as shown in Exhibit 11-5. The present value of the differential net cash flows would exceed the present value of the initial investment: $29,844 exceeds $27,000 by $2,844.

To use the time-adjusted rate of return method here, divide $27,000 by $12,000. The result is a present value factor of 2.250. Appendix B shows that 2.250 lies between the present value factors for 15 percent and 16 percent. Knowing that the rate of return is between 15 percent and 16 percent may be adequate for many purposes, certainly

Exhibit 11-5

Evaluating an Alternative Project

Factors:
   Initial investment – $27,000
   Useful life – 3 years
   Differential annual after-tax net cash flow – $12,000 net inflow
   Minimum acceptable rate of return – 10% annually

Evaluation by the Net Present Value Method:

   Present value of differential inflows ($12,000 x 2.487) $29,844

   Less: Present value of initial investment   27,000

   Net present value $ 2,844

Evaluation by the Time-Adjusted Rate of Return Method:

$$\frac{\text{Initial investment}}{\text{Differential cash inflow}} = \frac{\$27,000}{\$12,000} = 2.250 = \text{Present value factor}$$

Interpolation to Find the Time-Adjusted Rate of Return (r):

	Rate of Return	Present Value Factor	Present Value Factor
	15%	2.283	2.283
	r		2.250
	16%	2.246	
Differences:	1%	0.037	0.033

r = 15% + [(0.033/0.037) x 1%]
   = 15% + 0.89%
   = 15.89%

for showing that the rate exceeds the 10 percent minimum. In many cases, it is not necessary to calculate the more precise rate of return by hand, since many calculators and computer programs can perform this calculation. Risk managers should know the procedure, however, including the interpolation technique, so that they can spot-check the reasonableness of the results obtained by other means.

Exhibit 11-6 illustrates the application of capital budgeting evaluation techniques to a proposal for which the estimated differential annual net after-tax cash flows are *not* uniform. The initial investment is $10,000; the estimated useful life is six years; and the differential annual after-tax next cash flows are as shown in Exhibit 11-6. The minimum acceptable rate of return is 16 percent. Since the annual net cash flows are not uniform, the present value of each year's differential net cash flows must be calculated separately using the factors from Appendix A.

As shown in Exhibit 11-6, this present value equals $9,881, which is less than the $10,000 present value of the initial investment. The net present value of the proposal is therefore negative $119.

Using the time-adjusted rate of return method for evaluating this proposal requires calculating two present values—one each for two different rates of return (16 percent and 15 percent). The present value of the differential net cash flows at a 16 percent rate of return was calculated when evaluating the proposal by the net present value method. As also shown in Exhibit 11-6, at 15 percent, the present value of the net cash inflows is $10,220. By interpolation, the time-adjusted rate of return is 15.65 percent compounded annually, less than the specified minimum acceptable rate of 16 percent. The proposal should therefore be rejected.

Profitability Index

The discussion to this point has shown how both the net present value method and the time-adjusted rate of return method can be used to distinguish acceptable from unacceptable proposals. In addition, both methods can rank the order of preference of several acceptable proposals. Under the time-adjusted rate of return method, the best proposal is the one with the highest rate of return, the second best has the second highest rate, and so on. With the net present value method, any proposal that has a positive net present value is acceptable.

Ranking acceptable proposals by the net present value method requires computing a profitability index. This index is the ratio of the present value of the differential annual after-tax cash inflows expected from a proposal divided by the present value of the cash outflows the proposal requires. For most proposals, the present value of the required investment will equal the initial required cash outlay, undiscounted by any present value factors. The best proposal has the highest profitability index, and lower ranking proposals have progressively lower profitability indices.

Notice that the profitability index of a proposal that just meets the minimum acceptable rate of return is 1.0—the present value of the expected net cash flows equals the present value of the required investment when both are discounted by the present value factor for the minimum acceptable rate of return. All acceptable projects have a profitability index of at least 1.0; therefore, any proposal with a profitability index less than 1.0 is unacceptable when measured by specified minimum acceptable rates of return.

Exhibit 11-6

Evaluation of a Capital Investment Project—Unequal Cash Flows

Factors:

Initial investment – $10,000
Useful life – 6 years
Minimum acceptable rate of return – 16% annually
Differential annual after-tax net cash inflows at the end of each year:

Year	Inflows
1	$1,000
2	2,000
3	3,000
4	3,000
5	4,000
6	5,000

Evaluation by the Net Present Value Method:

Year	Cash Inflows	Present Value Factor (16%)	Present Value
1	$1,000	0.862	$ 862
2	2,000	0.743	1,486
3	3,000	0.641	1,923
4	3,000	0.552	1,656
5	4,000	0.476	1,904
6	5,000	0.410	2,050

Present value of net cash inflows:		$9,881
Present value of differential inflows	$ 9,881	
Less: Present value of initial investment	10,000	
Net present value (negative)	($ 119)	

Evaluation by the Time-Adjusted Rate of Return Method:

Year	Cash Inflows	Present Value Factor (15%)	Present Value
1	$1,000	0.870	$ 870
2	2,000	0.756	1,512
3	3,000	0.658	1,974
4	3,000	0.572	1,716
5	4,000	0.497	1,988
6	5,000	0.432	2,160

Present value of net cash inflows: $10,220

Interpolation to Find the Time-Adjusted Rate of Return (r):

Rate of Return	Present Values	Present Values
15%	$10,220	$10,220
r		10,000
16%	9,881	
1%	$ 339	$ 220

Differences:

$$r = 15\% + [(\$220/\$339) \times 1\%]$$
$$= 15\% + 0.65\%$$
$$= 15.65\%$$

COMPUTING DIFFERENTIAL ANNUAL AFTER-TAX
NET CASH FLOWS

After-tax net cash flows, positive or negative, determine the rate of return on a proposal that involves investment of a specified amount of cash. However, the examples presented thus far have not explained how these differential after-tax net cash flows are calculated—in each case, they have simply been stated as a "given." In practice, using capital budgeting techniques often requires computing net cash flows from more basic data on revenues and expenses. Some explanation of the computation of net cash flows is therefore in order.

The net cash flow from a proposal in any year (or sometimes shorter period) equals the cash inflows it produces minus the cash outflows it requires. If inflows exceed outflows in any year, the net cash flow from that proposal is positive for that year. If outflows exceed inflows, net cash flow is negative. Thus, subject to the possible effect of income taxes, the net cash flow from a proposal in a given period equals the cash revenues it generates minus the cash outlays it requires during that period.

For profit-seeking organizations, income taxes, like other cash outlays, must be deducted from cash revenues in computing net cash flows. Taxes are treated like any other cash outlay and do not alter the basic procedure for computing net cash flows. The complication from income taxes arises from the fact that these taxes are computed as a percentage of *taxable income*, not as a percentage of net cash inflows. Taxable income recognizes some noncash revenue and expense items. Therefore, in computing the cash outflow for income taxes, noncash revenue and expense items must be considered. For organizations not subject to income taxes, these noncash items can be ignored, thus simplifying cash flow calculations for public and other nonprofit entities.

In capital budgeting decisions, the main noncash item affecting income tax is depreciation of long-lived assets. *Depreciation* is the periodic accounting expensing of the initial cost or acquisition price of an asset over the useful life of that asset. Depreciation is not a cash outflow in the period in which the expense is recognized. That outflow usually occurs when the asset is purchased. This expense merely recognizes the outlay in a way that spreads the cost of the asset over the years it produces revenue, thus matching expenses with revenues period by period. (Many organizations also have other substantial noncash revenue and expense items that are properly recognized by their accrual accounting systems but have no cashflow effects until they generate actual receipts or outlays. All such noncash items are ignored in cashflow calculations until they result in an actual receipt or expenditure.)

The following illustrations compute depreciation expense by the straight-line method. Salvage value is assumed to be zero unless otherwise specified. Thus, for example, if the initial investment in an asset with a seven-year useful life is $35,000, the annual depreciation expense is $5,000. While not a cash outflow, depreciation should be added to other expenses when computing taxable income. For ease of calculation, income taxes, unless otherwise specified, are assumed to be 50 percent of taxable income.

Exhibit 11-7 illustrates the procedure for computing the differential annual after-tax net cash flow (NCF) from a proposal. It also evaluates this proposal by both the net present value and the time-adjusted rate of return methods. The proposal involves Promontory Point's purchase of an automated accounting system that costs $35,000 and has an expected useful life of seven years. Use of this system will add $500 annually to the railroad's maintenance expenses and $100 a year to its property insurance outlay, both of which are cash expenses. Notice that maintenance and insurance expenses are *differential* expenses—the railroad's *total* cash outlays for all maintenance and all insurance are far more than $500 and $100 a year, respectively. Under this proposal, the differential cash revenues to the railroad, attributable to more prompt and accurate billing of customers, are $12,000 a year. (Again, this is a differential amount because the railroad's total revenues from all operations are many times $12,000.)

The procedure for computing differential annual after-tax net cash flows from this system starts by subtracting annual differential cash expenditures, other than income taxes, from differential cash revenues. The result is annual differential before-tax net cash flows ("before-tax NCF").

While income taxes are like every other cash outflow in that they must be deducted from cash inflows to arrive at the net cash flow for any period, income taxes must be computed separately because they are a percentage of taxable income. Taxable income is equal to before-tax NCF minus depreciation, which is a noncash expense. Here, annual depreciation expense is $5,000 ($35,000/7 years), making taxable income $6,400 and differential income taxes $2,560. After the deduction of the cash outflow for taxes, this system's annual after-tax net cash flow ("after-tax NCF") becomes $8,840.

For organizations not subject to income taxes, after-tax net cash flows are equal to before-tax net cash flows. Actual receipts and disbursements of cash have the same effects on public and other nonprofit organizations as they do on profit-seeking ones, but income taxes are not an expense for nonprofit entities. Therefore, the noncash expense of depreciation (which must be accounted for in computing income taxes) also has no effect on net cash flows of nonprofit organizations. For

Exhibit 11-7

Calculation of Differential Annual After-Tax Net Cash Flow

Computation of Differential Accual NCF

Differential cash revenues		$12,000
Less: Differential cash expenses (except income taxes):		
Maintenance expense	$ 500	
Insurance expense	100	600
Before-tax NCF:		$11,400
Less: Differential income taxes:		
Before tax NCF	$11,400	
Less differential depreciation		
expense ($35,000/7 years)	5,000	
Taxable income	$ 6,400	
Income taxes (40%)		2,560
After-tax NCF:		$8,840

Evaluation of Differentiai Annual NCF

Factors:

    Initial Investment – $35,000
    Useful Life – 7 years
    Differential annual after-tax NCF – $8,840
    Minimum acceptable rate of return – 14% annually

Evaluation by the Net Present Value Method:

Present value of differential NCF ($8,840 x 4.288)	$37,905.92
Less: Present value of initial investment	35,000.00
Net present value	$ 2,905.92

Evaluation by the Time-Adjusted Rate of Return Method:

$$\frac{\text{Initial investment}}{\text{Differential NCF}} = \frac{\$35,000}{\$\ 8,840} = 3.959 = \text{Present value factor}$$

Interpolation to Find the Exact Time-Adjusted Rate of Return (r):

	Rate of Return	Present Value Factor	Present Value Factor
	16%	4.039	4.039
	n		3.959
	18%	3.812	
Differences:	2%	0.227	0.080

r =   16% +[(0.080/0.227) x 2%]
   =   16% + 0.70%
   =   16.70%

example, if the accounting system whose net cash flows are computed and evaluated in Exhibit 11-7 had been purchased by the Erewhon Municipal Water Authority instead of by Promontory Point, the annual net cash flows to EMWA from this system, either before or after taxes, would have been $11,400 (the result of the first subtraction at the top of Exhibit 11-7) rather than the $8,840 net cash flow to Promontory Point. Unlike Promontory Point, EMWA would not have had to pay $2,560 in income taxes each year. Thus, EMWA would have a higher time-adjusted rate of return on this accounting system than would Promontory Point.

This $8,840 after-tax NCF for a profit-seeking organization like Promontory Point is equivalent to "differential annual after-tax net cash flow" in previous exhibits in this chapter. Exhibit 11-7 shows how this $8,840 after-tax NCF can be evaluated by either the net present value method or the time-adjusted rate of return method. This evaluation reveals that this system surpasses the minimum acceptable rate of return of 14 percent compounded annually. Discounted at 14 percent, the net present value of the system is $2,905.92. The time-adjusted rate of return is 16.70 percent per year.

The present value to EMWA of its $11,400 NCF over seven years (assuming the utility also required a 14 percent minimum annual rate of return) would be $48,883.20 ($11,400 × 4.288). For EMWA, therefore, the net present value of this investment would be $13,883.20 ($48,883.20 − $35,000). With respect to the time-adjusted rate of return, the present value factor for this accounting system to EMWA would be approximately 3.070 ($35,000/$11,400), in contrast to the 3.959 present value factor for Promontory Point. Therefore, for EMWA, the time-adjusted rate of return for this accounting system, computed by the same procedure illustrated at the bottom of Exhibit 11-7, would be 26.18 percent.

Regardless of whether or not the organization must consider the effect of income taxes, this procedure for computing net cash flow and determining the net present value or the time-adjusted rate of return provides a basis for evaluating all risk management investments.

SUMMARY

Capital budgeting is a process for evaluating alternative investment proposals. This chapter has examined the techniques that evaluate net cash flows for the time value of money by the net present value method, the time-adjusted rate of return method, and the profitability index method. Investment proposals are expected to generate future positive net cash inflows. Differential net cash flows are calculated by measuring changes in cash inflows and changes in cash outflows that would result from the proposal.

The discussion in this chapter has assumed that cash flows are predictable with certainty when, in fact, they are somewhat unpredictable. A significant source of unpredictability is the possibility of accidental losses, which can affect projected cash flows from any investment proposal. The risk management techniques for dealing with these actual and potential losses also alter projected cash flows. Chapter 12 takes account of these accidental losses and of the risk management techniques for countering them, showing how to make risk management decisions that enhance an organization's net cash flows.

These elements of uncertainty are deferred to the next chapter. For the moment, it is sufficient to understand the essentials of capital budgeting as a decision-making technique.

Appendices to Chapter 11

Appendix A
Present Value of $1 Received at the End of Period

Years Hence	1%	2%	4%	6%	8%	10%	12%	14%	15%	16%
1	0.990	0.980	0.962	0.943	0.926	0.909	0.893	0.877	0.870	0.862
2	0.980	0.961	0.925	0.890	0.857	0.826	0.797	0.769	0.756	0.743
3	0.971	0.942	0.889	0.840	0.794	0.751	0.712	0.675	0.658	0.641
4	0.961	0.924	0.855	0.792	0.735	0.683	0.636	0.592	0.572	0.552
5	0.951	0.906	0.822	0.747	0.681	0.621	0.567	0.519	0.497	0.476
6	0.942	0.888	0.790	0.705	0.630	0.564	0.507	0.456	0.432	0.410
7	0.933	0.871	0.760	0.665	0.583	0.513	0.452	0.400	0.376	0.354
8	0.923	0.853	0.731	0.627	0.540	0.467	0.404	0.351	0.327	0.305
9	0.914	0.837	0.703	0.592	0.500	0.424	0.361	0.308	0.284	0.263
10	0.905	0.820	0.676	0.558	0.463	0.386	0.322	0.270	0.247	0.227
11	0.896	0.804	0.650	0.527	0.429	0.350	0.287	0.237	0.215	0.195
12	0.887	0.788	0.625	0.497	0.397	0.319	0.257	0.208	0.187	0.168
13	0.879	0.773	0.601	0.469	0.368	0.290	0.229	0.182	0.163	0.145
14	0.870	0.758	0.577	0.442	0.340	0.263	0.205	0.160	0.141	0.125
15	0.861	0.743	0.555	0.417	0.315	0.239	0.183	0.140	0.123	0.108
16	0.853	0.728	0.534	0.394	0.292	0.218	0.163	0.123	0.107	0.093
17	0.844	0.714	0.513	0.371	0.270	0.198	0.146	0.108	0.093	0.080
18	0.836	0.700	0.494	0.350	0.250	0.180	0.130	0.095	0.081	0.069
19	0.828	0.686	0.475	0.331	0.232	0.164	0.116	0.083	0.070	0.060
20	0.820	0.673	0.456	0.312	0.215	0.149	0.104	0.073	0.061	0.051
21	0.811	0.660	0.439	0.294	0.199	0.135	0.093	0.064	0.053	0.044
22	0.803	0.647	0.422	0.278	0.184	0.123	0.083	0.056	0.046	0.038
23	0.795	0.634	0.406	0.262	0.170	0.112	0.074	0.049	0.040	0.033
24	0.788	0.622	0.390	0.247	0.158	0.102	0.066	0.043	0.035	0.028
25	0.780	0.610	0.375	0.233	0.146	0.092	0.059	0.038	0.030	0.024
26	0.772	0.598	0.361	0.220	0.135	0.084	0.053	0.033	0.026	0.021
27	0.764	0.586	0.347	0.207	0.125	0.076	0.047	0.029	0.023	0.018
28	0.757	0.574	0.333	0.196	0.116	0.069	0.042	0.026	0.020	0.016
29	0.749	0.563	0.321	0.185	0.107	0.063	0.037	0.022	0.017	0.014
30	0.742	0.552	0.308	0.174	0.099	0.057	0.033	0.020	0.015	0.012
40	0.672	0.453	0.208	0.097	0.046	0.022	0.011	0.005	0.004	0.003
50	0.608	0.372	0.141	0.054	0.021	0.009	0.003	0.001	0.001	0.001

18%	20%	22%	24%	25%	26%	28%	30%	35%	40%	45%	50%
0.847	0.833	0.820	0.806	0.800	0.794	0.781	0.769	0.741	0.714	0.690	0.667
0.718	0.694	0.672	0.650	0.640	0.630	0.610	0.592	0.549	0.510	0.476	0.444
0.609	0.579	0.551	0.524	0.512	0.500	0.477	0.455	0.406	0.364	0.328	0.296
0.516	0.482	0.451	0.423	0.410	0.397	0.373	0.350	0.301	0.260	0.226	0.198
0.437	0.402	0.370	0.341	0.328	0.315	0.291	0.269	0.223	0.186	0.156	0.132
0.370	0.335	0.303	0.275	0.262	0.250	0.227	0.207	0.165	0.133	0.108	0.088
0.314	0.279	0.249	0.222	0.210	0.198	0.178	0.159	0.122	0.095	0.074	0.059
0.266	0.233	0.204	0.179	0.168	0.157	0.139	0.123	0.091	0.068	0.051	0.039
0.225	0.194	0.167	0.144	0.134	0.125	0.108	0.094	0.067	0.048	0.035	0.026
0.191	0.162	0.137	0.116	0.107	0.099	0.085	0.073	0.050	0.035	0.024	0.017
0.162	0.135	0.112	0.094	0.086	0.079	0.066	0.056	0.037	0.025	0.017	0.012
0.137	0.112	0.092	0.076	0.069	0.062	0.052	0.043	0.027	0.018	0.012	0.008
0.116	0.093	0.075	0.061	0.055	0.050	0.040	0.033	0.020	0.013	0.008	0.005
0.099	0.078	0.062	0.049	0.044	0.039	0.032	0.025	0.015	0.009	0.006	0.003
0.084	0.065	0.051	0.040	0.035	0.031	0.025	0.020	0.011	0.006	0.004	0.002
0.071	0.054	0.042	0.032	0.028	0.025	0.019	0.015	0.008	0.005	0.003	0.002
0.060	0.045	0.034	0.026	0.023	0.020	0.015	0.012	0.006	0.003	0.002	0.001
0.051	0.038	0.028	0.021	0.018	0.016	0.012	0.009	0.005	0.002	0.001	0.001
0.043	0.031	0.023	0.017	0.014	0.012	0.009	0.007	0.003	0.002	0.001	
0.037	0.026	0.019	0.014	0.012	0.010	0.007	0.005	0.002	0.001	0.001	
0.031	0.022	0.015	0.011	0.009	0.008	0.006	0.004	0.002	0.001		
0.026	0.018	0.013	0.009	0.007	0.006	0.004	0.003	0.001	0.001		
0.022	0.015	0.010	0.007	0.006	0.005	0.003	0.002	0.001			
0.019	0.013	0.008	0.006	0.005	0.004	0.003	0.002	0.001			
0.016	0.010	0.007	0.005	0.004	0.003	0.002	0.001	0.001			
0.014	0.009	0.006	0.004	0.003	0.002	0.002	0.001				
0.011	0.007	0.005	0.003	0.002	0.002	0.001	0.001				
0.010	0.006	0.004	0.002	0.002	0.002	0.001	0.001				
0.008	0.005	0.003	0.002	0.002	0.001	0.001	0.001				
0.007	0.004	0.003	0.002	0.001	0.001	0.001					
0.001	0.001										

Appendix B

Present Value of $1 Received Annually at the End of Each Period for N Periods

Years (N)	1%	2%	4%	6%	8%	10%	12%	14%	15%	16%
1	0.990	0.980	0.962	0.943	0.926	0.909	0.893	0.877	0.870	0.862
2	1.970	1.942	1.886	1.833	1.783	1.736	1.690	1.647	1.626	1.605
3	2.941	2.884	2.775	2.673	2.577	2.487	2.402	2.322	2.283	2.246
4	3.902	3.808	3.630	3.465	3.312	3.170	3.037	2.914	2.855	2.798
5	4.853	4.713	4.452	4.212	3.993	3.791	3.605	3.433	3.352	3.274
6	5.795	5.601	5.242	4.917	4.623	4.355	4.111	3.889	3.784	3.685
7	6.728	6.472	6.002	5.582	5.206	4.868	4.564	4.288	4.160	4.039
8	7.652	7.325	6.733	6.210	5.747	5.335	4.968	4.639	4.487	4.344
9	8.566	8.162	7.435	6.802	6.247	5.759	5.328	4.946	4.772	4.607
10	9.471	8.983	8.111	7.360	6.710	6.145	5.650	5.216	5.019	4.833
11	10.368	9.787	8.760	7.887	7.139	6.495	5.988	5.453	5.234	5.029
12	11.255	10.575	9.385	8.384	7.536	6.814	6.194	5.660	5.421	5.197
13	12.134	11.343	9.986	8.853	7.904	7.103	6.424	5.842	5.583	5.342
14	13.004	12.106	10.563	9.295	8.244	7.367	6.628	6.002	5.724	5.468
15	13.865	12.849	11.118	9.712	8.559	7.606	6.811	6.142	5.847	5.575
16	14.718	13.578	11.652	10.106	8.851	7.824	6.974	6.265	5.954	5.669
17	15.562	14.292	12.166	10.477	9.122	8.022	7.120	6.373	6.047	5.749
18	16.398	14.992	12.659	10.828	9.372	8.201	7.250	6.467	6.128	5.818
19	17.226	15.678	13.134	11.158	9.604	8.365	7.366	6.550	6.198	5.877
20	18.046	16.351	13.590	11.470	9.818	8.514	7.469	6.623	6.259	5.929
21	18.857	17.011	14.029	11.764	10.017	8.649	7.562	6.687	6.312	5.973
22	19.660	17.658	14.451	12.042	10.201	8.772	7.645	6.743	6.359	6.011
23	20.456	18.292	14.857	12.303	10.371	8.883	7.718	6.792	6.390	6.044
24	21.243	18.914	15.247	12.550	10.529	8.985	7.784	6.835	6.434	6.073
25	22.023	19.523	15.622	12.783	10.675	9.077	7.843	6.873	6.464	6.097
26	22.795	20.121	15.983	13.003	10.810	9.161	7.896	6.906	6.491	6.118
27	23.560	20.707	16.330	13.211	10.935	9.237	7.943	6.935	6.514	6.136
28	24.316	21.281	16.663	13.406	11.051	9.307	7.984	6.961	6.534	6.152
29	25.066	21.844	16.984	13.591	11.158	9.370	8.022	6.983	6.551	6.166
30	25.808	22.396	17.292	13.765	11.258	9.427	8.055	7.003	6.566	6.177
40	32.835	27.355	19.793	15.046	11.925	9.779	8.244	7.105	6.642	6.234
50	39.196	31.424	21.482	15.762	12.234	9.915	8.304	7.133	6.661	6.246

18%	20%	22%	24%	25%	26%	28%	30%	35%	40%	45%	50%
0.847	0.833	0.820	0.806	0.800	0.794	0.781	0.769	0.741	0.714	0.690	0.667
1.566	1.528	1.492	1.457	1.440	1.424	1.392	1.361	1.289	1.224	1.165	1.111
2.174	2.106	2.042	1.981	1.952	1.923	1.868	1.816	1.696	1.589	1.493	1.407
2.690	2.589	2.494	2.404	2.362	2.320	2.241	2.166	1.997	1.849	1.720	1.605
3.127	2.991	2.864	2.745	2.689	2.635	2.532	2.436	2.220	2.035	1.876	1.737
3.498	3.326	3.167	3.020	2.951	2.885	2.759	2.643	2.385	2.168	1.983	1.824
3.812	3.605	3.416	3.242	3.161	3.083	2.937	2.802	2.508	2.263	2.057	1.883
4.078	3.837	3.619	3.421	3.329	3.241	3.076	2.925	2.598	2.331	2.108	1.922
4.303	4.031	3.786	3.566	3.463	3.366	3.184	3.019	2.665	2.379	2.144	1.948
4.494	4.192	3.923	3.682	3.571	3.465	3.269	3.092	2.715	2.414	2.168	1.965
4.656	4.327	4.035	3.776	3.656	3.544	3.335	3.147	2.752	2.438	2.185	1.977
4.793	4.439	4.127	3.851	3.725	3.606	3.387	3.190	2.779	2.456	2.196	1.985
4.910	4.533	4.203	3.912	3.780	3.656	3.427	3.223	2.799	2.468	2.204	1.990
5.008	4.611	4.265	3.962	3.824	3.695	3.459	3.249	2.814	2.477	2.210	1.993
5.092	4.675	4.315	4.001	3.859	3.726	3.483	3.268	2.825	2.484	2.214	1.995
5.162	4.730	4.357	4.003	3.887	3.751	3.503	3.283	2.834	2.489	2.216	1.997
5.222	4.775	4.391	4.059	3.910	3.771	3.518	3.295	2.840	2.492	2.218	1.998
5.273	4.812	4.419	4.080	3.928	3.786	3.529	3.304	2.844	2.494	2.219	1.999
5.316	4.844	4.442	4.097	3.942	3.799	3.539	3.311	2.848	2.496	2.220	1.999
5.353	4.870	4.460	4.110	3.954	3.808	3.546	3.316	2.850	2.497	2.221	1.999
5.384	4.891	4.476	4.121	3.963	3.816	3.551	3.320	2.852	2.498	2.221	2.000
5.410	4.909	4.488	4.130	3.970	3.822	3.556	3.323	2.853	2.498	2.222	2.000
5.432	4.925	4.499	4.137	3.976	3.827	3.559	3.325	2.854	2.499	2.222	2.000
5.451	4.937	4.507	4.143	3.981	3.831	3.562	3.327	2.855	2.499	2.222	2.000
5.467	4.948	4.514	4.147	3.985	3.834	3.564	3.329	2.856	2.499	2.222	2.000
5.480	4.956	4.520	4.151	3.988	3.837	3.566	3.330	2.856	2.500	2.222	2.000
5.492	4.964	4.524	4.154	3.990	3.839	3.567	3.331	2.856	2.500	2.222	2.000
5.502	4.970	4.528	4.157	3.992	3.840	3.568	3.331	2.857	2.500	2.222	2.000
5.510	4.975	4.531	4.159	3.994	3.841	3.569	3.332	2.857	2.500	2.222	2.000
5.517	4.979	4.534	4.160	3.995	3.842	3.569	3.332	2.857	2.500	2.222	2.000
5.548	4.997	4.544	4.166	3.999	3.846	3.571	3.333	2.857	2.500	2.222	2.000
5.554	4.999	4.545	4.167	4.000	3.846	3.571	3.333	2.857	2.500	2.222	2.000

CHAPTER 12

Making Risk Management Decisions Through Cash Flow Analysis

This chapter shows how to select the best risk management technique by combining the forecasts developed in Chapters 9 and 10 with the cash flow analysis developed in Chapter 11 to formulate a risk management decision rule. This rule can guide an organization in making the most cost-effective allocations of its risk management resources to meet the demands that accidental losses may place on that organization. Given a loss exposure and alternative risk management techniques, the rule developed in this chapter answers the question: Which technique(s) should be used? For example, should the exposure be avoided or insured, or should both insurance and loss prevention be used?

This chapter elaborates the traditional cash flow decision framework to take account of risk management considerations, catalogs the effects that various risk management techniques are likely to have on an organization's cash flows and rates of return, and sets forth the logic of cash flow analysis for selecting risk management techniques. These techniques enable a risk management professional to accomplish the following:

- Explain to other operating managers and to senior management the effects that the loss exposures inherent in a proposed capital budgeting project are likely to have on the organization's cash flows.
- Accurately assess the proposals when deciding among them.
- Identify, measure, and evaluate the effects that each risk management technique can be expected to have on a particular loss exposure.
- Recognize when the assumptions that underlie cash flow analysis

139

might create potential difficulties in using the analysis for risk management.

This chapter illustrates how each risk control and risk financing technique could be applied to a specific exposure facing Sheltering Arms: fire damage to a building on the hospital's grounds. Analysis of this exposure highlights the differing effects that alternative risk management techniques are likely to have on the hospital's cash flows, uses of cash, and therefore profitability or operating efficiency. The particular illustrations presented here are specific, but the types of cash flows they illustrate tend to be universal. These illustrations and the risk management techniques on which they focus are as follows:

1. Ignoring risk management concerns
2. Recognizing expected losses
3. Preventing or reducing losses
4. Segregating exposure units
5. Using contractual transfer for risk control
6. Avoiding exposures
7. Retaining losses as current expenses
8. Retaining losses through a funded reserve
9. Retaining losses through borrowed funds
10. Financing losses through a captive insurer
11. Financing losses through a separate insurer
12. Using contractual transfer for risk financing

Illustration 2, recognizing (but "doing nothing" to manage) a loss exposure, is the most basic illustration, the one against which the cash flow and rate of return effects of each of the other risk control and risk financing techniques should be compared. Illustrations 3 through 12 should be examined separately and contrasted with "doing nothing," Illustration 1. These illustrations are not cumulative. This sequence allows each risk management technique to be analyzed on its own merits for its own contribution to an organization's net cash flows. However, the procedures shown here can also be used to analyze the combined cash flow effects of several risk management techniques, particularly combinations of risk financing and risk control techniques, in other real-world situations.

None of these illustrations includes retaining losses through an unfunded reserve. This option has been purposely omitted because the cash flow effects of an unfunded reserve are identical to the cash flow effects of retaining losses as current expenses. An unfunded reserve represents no formal commitment or source of funds. It is merely an accounting recognition of an anticipated expenditure designed to more nearly match the timing of expenses and revenues among accounting periods.

CASH FLOW ANALYSIS OF RISK MANAGEMENT TECHNIQUES

Traditional cash flow analysis omits any mention of risk management considerations. The annual differential after-tax NCFs that an asset or activity are projected to generate are typically presumed to be highly predictable. Except perhaps in the most hazardous of situations, little consideration is given to the possibility that, for example, an investment that is projected to have a ten-year useful life will be destroyed by fire three years after it has been installed.

Similarly, most cash flow analyses do not explicitly recognize that the *one-time* costs of implementing risk management techniques should often be *added* to the initial investment in a proposal, while other *continuing* risk management expenses should be *deducted* from its projected annual NCFs. Some more sophisticated analyses recognize that NCF may be predictable only as a probability distribution rather than as a fixed stream, but even these analyses may assume that variations in NCF from year to year arise from speculative risks (such as changes in market conditions) rather than from pure risks of accidental losses, liability claims, or other mishaps.

This chapter deals with risk management considerations within the traditional framework of cash flow analysis. Cash flow analysis offers one tool, although not a perfect one, for selecting the most appropriate risk management technique (or combination of techniques) to cope with exposures to accidental loss. This discussion considers how various risk management techniques may change the net present value or time-adjusted rate of return for a proposed asset or activity and then explores the extent to which the net present value or time-adjusted rate of return can be used to select the most cost-effective risk management technique(s).

While each of the following illustrations features the cash flow effects of only one risk control or risk financing technique, tracing the cash flows of the risk control techniques requires making an assumption about how any remaining risks are to be financed. Unless otherwise specified, these risk control illustrations assume that any losses are fully retained and paid as current expenses and that each risk financing technique is used without any other risk financing or risk control measure.

Cash Flows From Risk Management Decisions

Each of the following illustrations concerns the Ames Research Center (ARC), located in a three-story building owned by Sheltering Arms. The center was established four years ago when the hospital succeeded in attracting Dr. Ames, renowned for his research to develop innovative surgical procedures. Subject to the terms of a ten-year contract, Dr. Ames agreed to conduct his research under Sheltering Arms' auspices with the understanding that all revenue generated by this research would go to the hospital. The hospital projected that this revenue would average $60,000 annually. In exchange, Sheltering Arms provided Dr. Ames with a $200,000 grant to help establish the research facility and obtain necessary equipment. The hospital retained ownership of the building itself.

Over the past four years, fire losses to the building structure have averaged $16,000 annually in repair costs. The hospital is not responsible for fire damage to the building's contents, furnishings, and fixtures, all of which belong to Dr. Ames. The doctor had also agreed to hold the hospital harmless for any liability claims that might arise out of his use of the building, and Sheltering Arms' risk management professional is satisfied that Dr. Ames has purchased adequate insurance to meet his obligations under this agreement. In short, the hospital's only significant loss exposure attributable to the ARC is physical damage to the building itself, principally because of fire. This commitment, made four years ago, has six years to run.

Illustration One: Cash Flows Ignoring Risk Management. Because the fire hazard is extreme, Sheltering Arms' risk management professional has been exploring various risk management techniques for dealing with this fire exposure, hoping to find a technique (or combination of techniques) that will effectively manage this exposure. The risk management professional has begun his work by developing the figures presented in Exhibit 12-1.

Notice that the figures in this exhibit, and this chapter's subsequent exhibits, reflect the fact that Sheltering Arms is a private hospital and, as such, must pay income taxes. If Sheltering Arms were a public, tax-exempt entity, the computations for differential income taxes would have been unnecessary. The entry for income taxes would have been zero (instead of $20,000), and the after-tax NCF would have been the same as the before-tax NCF ($60,000). The evaluation of this tax-exempt NCF would have followed the process that is shown in the bottom portion of Exhibit 12-1, substituting $60,000 for $44,000. If Sheltering Arms were a tax-exempt hospital (or any other type of tax-exempt organization), comparable changes would be made in other exhibits throughout this chapter.

Exhibit 12-1

Differential Annual After-Tax Net Cash Flow—
Risk Management Considerations Ignored

Calculation of NCF

Differential cash revenues	$60,000
Less: Differential cash expenses (except income taxes)	none
Before-tax NCF:	$60,000

Less: Differential income taxes:

Before-tax NCF	$60,000	
Less: differential depreciation expense ($200,000/10 years)	20,000	
Taxable income	$40,000	
Income taxes (40%)		16,000
After-tax NCF:		$44,000

Evaluation of this NCF

Factors:

    Initial Investment – $200,000
    Life of project – 10 years
    Differential annual after-tax NCF – $44,000
    Minimum acceptable rate of return – 12% annually

Evaluation by the Net Present Value Method:

Present value of differential NCF ($44,000 x 5.650)	$248,600
Less: Present value of initial investment	200,000
Net present value	$ 48,600

Evaluation by the Time-Adjusted Rate of Return Method:

$$\frac{\text{Initial investment}}{\text{Differential NCF}} = \frac{\$200,000}{\$\ 44,000} = 4.545 = \text{Present value factor}$$

Interpolation to Find the Time-Adjusted Rate of Return (r):

	Rate of Return	Present Value Factor	Present Value Factor
	16%	4.833	4.833
	r		4.545
	18%	4.494	
Differences:	2%	0.339	0.288

r = 16% + [(0.288/0.339) x 2%]
   = 16% + 1.70%
   = 17.70%

Exhibit 12-3

Differential Annual After-Tax Net Cash Flow—
Loss Reduction/Prevention Device

Calculation of NCF

Differential cash revenues		$60,000
Less: Differential cash expenses (except income taxes)		
Expected value of fire losses	$ 4,200	
Sprinkler maintenance	400	4,600
Before-tax NCF:		$55,400
Less: Differential income taxes:		
Before-tax NCF	$55,400	
Less: differential depreciation		
expense ($210,000/10 years)	21,000	
Taxable income	$34,400	
Income taxes (40%)		13,760
After-tax NCF:		$41,640

Evaluation of this NCF

Factors:

    Initial Investment – $210,000
    Life of project – 10 years
    Differential annual after-tax NCF – $41,640
    Minimum acceptable rate of return – 12% annually

Evaluation by the Net Present Value Method:

Present value of differential NCF ($41,640 x 5.650)	$235,266
Less: Present value of initial investment	210,000
Net present value	$ 25,266

Evaluation by the Time-Adjusted Rate of Return Method:

$$\frac{\text{Initial investment}}{\text{Differential NCF}} = \frac{\$210,000}{\$\ 41,640} = 5.043 = \text{Present value factor}$$

Interpolation to Find the Time-Adjusted Rate of Return (r):

	Rate of Return	Present Value Factor	Present Value Factor
	14%	5.216	5.216
	r		5.043
	15%	5.019	
Differences:	1%	0.197	0.173

r	=	14% + [(0.173/0.197) x 1%]
	=	14% + 0.88%
	=	14.88%

are considered. As Exhibit 12-2 reveals, without a sprinkler system, the investment would not have generated the required 12 percent annual rate of return. The fact that loss reduction increased the time-adjusted rate of return is a result of the particular details of this case. Not all loss prevention or reduction techniques improve profitability.

Illustration Four: Segregating Exposure Units. Segregation *of* of exposure units can be achieved either through *separation* (dividing one unit into two or more independent units, each normally used in daily operations) or by *duplication* (creating stand-by units that are used only when a regular unit has been lost). For example, dividing an inventory equally between two warehouses is separation; having duplicate records or spare parts for key machines is duplication.

In either case, segregation involves increasing the number of exposure units. Segregation makes these losses more predictable by reducing the variation in the total amount of these losses to a percentage of their expected value. With inventory in two widely separated warehouses, for example, the maximum possible loss from any one occurrence is reduced to one half what it was in the single warehouse. This reduces the variation in the amount of individual losses and in the annual totals of loss.

By the law of large numbers, an organization that has a larger number of independent loss exposures can more accurately predict its aggregate losses. In terms of net investment and NCF, this greater predictability of losses reduces the size of any contingency fund (funded reserve) needed to pay retained accidental losses. As the number of exposed units increases, any contingency fund an organization establishes to absorb retained losses can be reduced. This savings allows more of an organization's assets to be devoted to its normal productive activities, which generally yield a higher rate of return than can funds earmarked to pay accidental losses. Having a greater portion of its funds more productively invested increases an organization's overall rate of return.

To see how separation can reduce the amount of funded reserve needed to absorb retained losses, compare Exhibits 12-4 and 12-5. Exhibit 12-4 shows the cash flow implications if Sheltering Arms established a funded fire loss reserve equal to the full value of its initial $200,000 investment. Sheltering Arms' administrators might have judged such a fund necessary to restore any of Dr. Ames' property that might be irreplaceably damaged in a fire. If this fund can earn an 8 percent annual rate of return, then the resulting cash flows are as shown in Exhibit 12-4. The fund generates $16,000 of revenue each year before taxes. Using such a fund means that this investment yields an annual after-tax NCF of $44,000. However, because establishing a funded reserve equal to the initial grant doubles that investment, the resulting annual after-tax NCF yields a highly negative net present value and does not approach the 12 percent after-tax return the hospital requires.

(Some may wish to analyze the cash flows in this funded reserve example as merely a substitution between two rates of return: an 8 percent return on the $200,000 reserve replaces the 12 percent return the hospital requires on its assets as a whole. By this analysis, such a substitution·imposes on the funded reserve an additional cash cost of 4 percent (12 percent minus 8 percent) of $200,000, or an $8,000 cash outflow for the funded reserve. While this analysis would be correct if a 12 percent after-tax return could be guaranteed to the hospital, there is no such guarantee—actual returns may be greater or smaller. Throughout these examples, 12 percent is used only as a discount rate for the minimum *acceptable* rate of return, not as the assumed *actual* rate. In contrast, the figures in Exhibit 12-4 deal only with forecast actual results.)

If, instead of a single grant to Dr. Ames, Sheltering Arms had invested its $200,000 in ten separate research areas disbursed throughout the hospital, the predictability of any resulting fire losses would have been increased and their maximum likely size reduced. Assume that such segregation reduced aggregate expected losses to $15,000. Assume further that the standard deviation of this aggregate is such that the hospital could have been 99 percent certain that annual losses to the ten separate areas would not have exceeded $25,000. If the funded reserve, earning 8 percent each year, had been only $25,000, the resulting after-tax NCF would have been as shown in Exhibit 12-5.

Although the amount of the annual after-tax NCF is smaller with segregation ($36,200 rather than the $44,000 in Exhibit 12-4), reducing the required investment from $400,000 to $225,000 means that the NCF resulting from segregation more nearly approaches the hospital's minimum requirement. Segregation raises the net present value of the research facilities to a negative $20,470 (in contrast to the negative $151,400 in Exhibit 12-4) and generates a 9.75 percent annual time-adjusted rate of return.

Three of the conditions in this illustration may appear to limit its validity, but they do not. First, actual losses are assumed to equal expected losses. This is a more reasonable assumption with ten separate areas than with one research facility. Notice, however, that if actual losses to the ARC building exceed their $16,000 expected value, these losses would decrease the time-adjusted rate of return in that illustration, making segregation even more attractive in terms of predictability and profitability.

Second, establishing ten separate areas instead of one may be an extreme example of segregation, but a large number of separate units is not essential to the improved NCF that comes from a reduction in a

Exhibit 12-4
Differential Annual After-Tax Cash Flow—
Investment and $200,000 Funded Reserve

Calculation of NCF

Differential cash revenues

	From ARC	$60,000
	From funded reserve ($200,000 x 8%)	16,000
		$76,000

Less: Differential cash expenses (except income taxes)
Expected value of fire damage   16,000

Before-tax NCF: $60,000

Less: Differential income taxes:

Before-tax NCF	$60,000	
Less: differential depreciation expense ($200,000/10 years)	20,000	
Taxable income	$40,000	
Income taxes (40%)		16,000

After-tax NCF: $44,000

Evaluation of this NCF

Factors:

     Initial Investment – $400,000
     Life of project – 10 years
     Differential annual after-tax NCF – $44,000
     Minimum acceptable rate of return – 12% annually

Evaluation by the Net Present Value Method:

Present value of differential NCF ($44,000 x 5.650)	$248,600
Less: Present value of initial investment	400,000
Net present value (negative)	($151,400)

Evaluation by the Time-Adjusted Rate of Return Method:

$$\frac{\text{Initial investment}}{\text{Differential NCF}} = \frac{\$400,000}{\$\ 44,000} = 9.091 = \text{Present value factor}$$

Interpolation to Find the Time-Adjusted Rate of Return (r):

Rate of Return	Present Value Factor	Present Value Factor
1%	9.471	9.471
r		9.091
2%	8.983	
Differences: 1%	0.488	0.380

r = 1% + [(0.380/0.488) x 1%]
  = 1% + 0.78%
  = 1.78%

Exhibit 12-5

Differential Annual After-Tax Cash Flow—
Segregation with $25,000 Funded Reserve

<u>Calculation of NCF</u>

Differential cash revenues

From ARC	$60,000
From funded reserve ($25,000 x 8%)	2,000
	$62,000

Less: Differential cash expenses (except income taxes)

Expected value of fire losses	15,000
Before-tax NCF:	$47,000

Less: Differential income taxes:

Before-tax NCF	$47,000	
Less: differential depreciation expense ($200,000/10 years)	20,000	
Taxable income	$27,000	
Income taxes (40%)		10,800
After-tax NCF:		$36,200

<u>Evaluation of this NCF</u>

Factors:

Initial Investment – $225,000
Life of project – 10 years
Differential annual after-tax NCF – $36,200
Minimum acceptable rate of return – 12% annually

Evaluation by the Net Present Value Method:

Present value of differential NCF ($36,200 x 5.650)	$204,530
Less: Present value of initial investment	225,000
Net present value (negative)	($ 20,470)

Evaluation by the Time-Adjusted Rate of Return Method:

$$\frac{\text{Initial investment}}{\text{Differential NCF}} = \frac{\$225,000}{\$\ 36,200} = 6.215 = \text{Present value factor}$$

Interpolation to Find the Time-Adjusted Rate of Return (r):

	Rate of Return	Present Value Factor	Present Value Factor
	8%	6.710	6.710
	r		6.215
	10%	6.145	
Differences:	2%	0.565	0.495

r = 8% + [(0.495/0.565) x 2%]
  = 8% + 1.75%
  = 9.75%

funded reserve as potential loss severity is reduced. Establishing as few as three research areas within the hospital instead of one might have reduced the funded reserve to $100,000. Under these conditions, $100,000 would be liberated to earn at least the 12 percent rate of return the hospital requires of funds invested in its own operations instead of 8 percent in the loss reserve, a difference of at least $4,000 in before-tax earnings. Thus, adjusting the number of exposure units can greatly narrow the range of predictable loss severity even though the predictability of loss frequency may not be greatly enhanced.

Third, at the end of the useful life of any investment, the amount of a funded reserve presumably would be released back into the stream of an organization's cash flows—in essence, a cash inflow attributable to the recouping of the funded reserve. In order for an entire funded reserve to be recouped, any such fund must have been periodically restored to its original amount whenever a loss has been paid out of it. Additional computations to account for final recovery of the funded reserve would not alter the basic thrust of this example: segregation of exposure units reduces the commitment of resources that must provide assurance that losses can be restored from available funds.

Illustration Five: Using Contractual Transfer for Risk Control. Two risk management techniques involve contractual transfer: *contractual transfer for risk control*, where an entire activity and all its related exposures are transferred to another, and *contractual transfer for risk financing*, where an organization enters into a contract under which another—not an insurance company—agrees to pay for specified losses to that organization. In both cases, the organization being protected is the transferor and the other, protecting entity is the transferee.

Contractual transfer for risk control involves the shifting of a loss exposure through a change in the control of property, the subcontracting of an activity, or the transfer of a legal responsibility to another party. For example, Sheltering Arms could have transferred the exposure of fire damage to the ARC building by leasing appropriate research space for Dr. Ames to use for ten years for a $100,000 lump sum lease payment when the lease began. Added to the $200,000 grant, this lease payment would have raised the hospital's total investment in Dr. Ames' research to $300,000 but would have shifted to the landlord the exposure of fire damage to the leased building. Income tax regulations would have allowed Sheltering Arms, a private hospital, to write off $30,000 as a deductible expense in each of the ten years, a write-off similar to straight-line depreciation. The differential annual after-tax NCF to Sheltering Arms is computed and evaluated by the net present value and the time-adjusted rate of return methods in Exhibit 12-6.

of losses—is to smooth over time the highly fluctuating demands that retaining unpredictable losses would otherwise place on an organization's cash flows. Without a formal reserve, an organization's management may be highly uncertain of whether the organization will have access to the cash needed to finance recovery from a loss at the time a particularly substantial loss happens to occur.

Establishing a funded reserve from which to pay losses increases the initial investment in the asset or activity whose losses are to be restored from the fund—the amount of the fund must be added to the cost of the asset or activity as part of the initial investment. Beyond this large initial investment, however, the use of a funded reserve does not change the cash *outflows* that would otherwise arise from paying losses as current expenses. A funded reserve does create one significant cash *inflow* not present with other forms of retention: earnings on the fund held in the reserve. The reserve funds will normally be invested in highly liquid securities, that is, securities that can be quickly sold at a predictable price.

To illustrate, the cash flows to Sheltering Arms from a funded reserve earning 8 percent and used to pay the $16,000 expected value of fire losses to the ARC building would be as computed and evaluated in Exhibit 12-4. (While one of the purposes of using a funded reserve is to cushion the impact of losses of varying size, the assumption that each year's losses equal their $16,000 expected value does not change the logic of this analysis.) Because establishing and maintaining a funded reserve requires a higher initial investment, retaining losses in this way reduces the rate of return (compared with other forms of retention) whenever the funds placed in the reserve earn less than the funds employed in the organization's normal productive activities.

✓ **Illustration Nine: Retaining Losses Through Borrowed Funds.** An organization may borrow funds as needed to pay its accidental losses in order to keep its own funds productively employed within its normal operations. If an organization can earn more by investing funds in its operations than it costs that organization to borrow these funds (whether to pay losses or for any other purpose), borrowing will improve cash flows. The precise nature of the cash flows associated with borrowing depends upon the conditions of the loan.

Because of the diversity of possible borrowing arrangements, the cash flows arising from a loan to finance recovery from accidental losses cannot be fully generalized, but must be specified in each particular instance. For this reason, an organization's risk management professional will want to work especially closely with its financial officers, analyzing the various forms of short-term and long-term borrowing and the various terms upon which borrowed funds may be available to pay for accidental losses. Despite this diversity, one generalization—important to borrowing and to insurance and other contractual transfers—is that funds an organization receives to pay losses should not be considered a cash inflow. Any funds received to pay for accidental losses are disbursed immediately (or at least within the same accounting period) to finance recovery from these losses. Cash received and promptly paid out is merely a "wash transaction," a simultaneous receipt and disbursement of cash, not a net addition to the organization's usable NCF.

The concept of wash transaction is central to analyzing how borrowing to pay accidental losses affects an organization's NCF. Financing losses in this way earns a higher rate of return on funds kept active in the organization than does the effective interest rate at which the organization must borrow to pay for its losses.

Assume that Sheltering Arms borrows $16,000 on January 1 from its bank for one year at an annual effective before-tax interest rate of 16.67 percent. On December 31 of this same year, Sheltering Arms will have to pay the bank $18,667 (the $16,000 return of principal and $2,667 interest). Meanwhile, the hospital plans to use these borrowed funds to pay for expected losses to the ARC building whenever they may occur throughout the year and, more importantly, to keep invested in its operations the $16,000 of its own funds that would otherwise have been expended during the year to restore these losses.

Remember that the hospital's own funds generate a 12 percent annual after-tax internal rate of return. Since Sheltering Arms pays income taxes at a 40 percent rate, this is equivalent to a 20 percent rate of return before taxes. (Until needed to pay losses, the additional $16,000 borrowed on January 1 can also be used to generate this 12 percent after-tax return.) When a loss occurs, some or all of the borrowed $16,000 must be used to pay for it—just as, had the hospital not borrowed this money, it would have had to use its own funds. Using its own funds, however, would have required sacrificing the 12 percent after-tax internal rate of return on these funds. Since Sheltering Arms pays income taxes at a 40 percent rate, using borrowed funds costs only 10 percent after taxes.

Here, the benefit of borrowing is that the hospital gets to keep $16,000 more invested in its operations (of its own or borrowed funds) than it would have been able to use without borrowing. At a 20 percent rate of return before taxes, Sheltering Arms can earn $3,200 from these funds. The 12 percent after-tax earnings on this $16,000 additional investment amount to $1,920 ($16,000 times 0.12). Yet these funds cost only 10 percent, or $1,600, after taxes. The after-tax NCF, 2 percent of $16,000, is $320 ($1,920 minus $1,600).

At the end of the year, the $16,000 principal can be repaid to the bank, using the same $16,000 of the hospital's own money that, at the beginning of the year, it would have had to earmark for retaining the annual expected value of fire losses to the ARC building. The $16,000 principal borrowed and repaid is a wash transaction. However, the difference between the internal rate of return on this principal and the interest cost of the loan has generated an NCF of $320, 2 percent of the borrowed principal. As shown in Exhibit 12-8, borrowing under these circumstances benefits the hospital because the $1,920 added after-tax earnings on funds invested in the hospital's operations exceeds the $1,600 after-tax cost of borrowing.

An organization whose internal operations do not generate such a high rate of return (or an organization that faces higher costs of borrowing) is not likely to plan on using borrowed funds to pay losses except under emergency conditions. Relatively few organizations will normally find themselves in the favorable hypothetical position that Exhibit 12-8 portrays for Sheltering Arms. Instead, most organizations will find their position reversed—the after-tax cost of borrowed funds is typically higher than the after-tax rate of earnings forgone by using internal funds to pay losses. However, the depletion of cash from a particularly severe single loss or a series of smaller losses that aggregates to a substantial total may make borrowing necessary.

The illustration portrayed in Exhibit 12-8, retaining losses through borrowed funds, makes several simplifying assumptions that lessen the complications that could arise from complex financing arrangements.

First among these is the assumption that Sheltering Arms repays the entire loan in one payment at the end of the year rather than through, say, monthly or quarterly payments. The example also assumes that the only fee levied by the bank for this loan is the interest charged. Ignoring these or other banking intricacies, as well as other accounting and finance considerations, makes clearer the cash flow analysis of borrowing as a risk management technique.

This analysis also suggests why borrowing should be considered retention rather than transfer. Transfer has been previously defined in this text as involving the use of outside funds to pay losses, while retention has been defined as using internal funds to pay losses. Why, then, is borrowing outside funds not considered transfer? There are at least two reasons. First, borrowing reduces an organization's resources because credit is an important asset. An organization that borrows to pay its losses draws upon its own resources because it cannot borrow these same funds for other purposes.

A second reason for considering borrowing to be retention is that, unlike transfer to an insurer or a noninsurer, borrowing involves no transfer of risk, no shifting of uncertainty to an insurer or other transferee, arising out of the loss exposure originally facing the transferor. For example, Sheltering Arms' borrowing funds to pay for fire losses to

Exhibit 12-8

Differential Annual After-Tax Net Cash Flow—Retention Through Borrowed Funds

<u>Calculation of NCF</u>

Differential cash revenues

From ARC	$60,000	
From $16,000 used in operations (0.20 x $16,000)	3,200	
Total revenues:		$63,200

Less: Differential cash expenses (except income taxes)

Repayment of loan (1.20 x $16,000)		19,200
Before-tax NCF:		$44,000

Less: Differential income taxes:

Before-tax NCF	$44,000	
Less: Differential depreciation expense ($200,000/10 years)	20,000	
Taxable income	$24,000	
Income taxes (40%)		9,600
After-tax NCF:		$34,400

<u>Evaluation of this NCF</u>

Factors:

Initial Investment – $200,000
Life of project – 10 years
Differential annual after-tax NCF – $34,400
Minimum acceptable rate of return – 12% annually

Evaluation by the Net Present Value Method:

Present value of differential NCF ($34,400 x 5.650)	$194,360
Less: Present value of initial investment	200,000
Net present value	($ 5,640)

Evaluation by the Time-Adjusted Rate of Return Method:

$$\frac{\text{Initial investment}}{\text{Differential NCF}} = \frac{\$200,000}{\$ 34,400} = 5.814 = \text{Present value factor}$$

Interpolation to Find the Time-Adjusted Rate of Return (r):

	Rate of Return	Present Value Factor	Present Value Factor
	10%	6.145	6.145
	r		5.814
	12%	5.650	
Differences:	2%	0.495	0.331

$$\begin{aligned} r &= 10\% + [(0.331/0.495) \times 2\%] \\ &= 10\% + 1.34\% \\ &= 11.34\% \end{aligned}$$

the ARC building transfers none of this fire exposure to the lender. When funds are borrowed to pay particular losses (reducing an organization's otherwise available credit), the amount and terms of the loan are known and—except possibly for uncertainty regarding the borrower's ability or willingness to repay—the lender takes on no additional exposures to loss. With borrowing, the exposure to accidental losses remains with the borrower.

Illustration Ten: Financing Losses Through a Captive Insurer. An organization may establish an insurance subsidiary, or "captive," through which it may insure some or all of its loss exposures. The captive may be owned solely by this one parent organization or by a number of parents whose exposures the captive insures. The captive also may insure some loss exposures of organizations that are not owners of the captive.

Principally because of tax and regulatory issues, there exists considerable controversy over whether the use of a captive insurer constitutes retention or transfer for the parent organization. The present discussion of the cash flow effects of premiums paid by the parent to a captive briefly examines both perspectives—retention and transfer.

If the captive arrangement is considered to be retention, the premiums paid to the captive are not tax deductible and the cash flows to the parent would be similar to those shown in Exhibit 12-1, which ignores risk management considerations. The resulting annual after-tax NCF would be $44,000 minus whatever annual premium was paid to the captive.

If the captive arrangement is considered to be a transfer, the cash flow of the premium paid to the captive would be identical to those in the following discussion of financing losses through a separate insurer.

Illustration Eleven: Financing Losses Through a Separate Insurer. Rather than using internal funds to finance losses through some form of retention, an organization can turn to transfer, using funds originating in an outside organization to pay for losses. The most frequent form of transfer is to an insurer that agrees, in exchange for a premium, to pay to or on behalf of the insured losses or claims that fall within the scope of the insurance contract. Under such an arrangement, the premium for the insurance replaces the expected value of retained losses as a cash expense to the insured in the year in which the insurance premium is actually paid. In other respects, the computation of net present value and time-adjusted rate of return for insurance parallels those in previous illustrations.

Much depends on the size of the insurance premium, which may be greater than the expected value of the losses the insurance covers because the premium is designed to provide for the insurer's overhead (including profit). To simplify the discussion here, assume that Sheltering Arms purchases $200,000 of fire insurance on the ARC building. Under the insurance market conditions existing at that time, Sheltering Arms' fire insurer designed its premiums so that 60 percent of the gross premium was allocated to paying insured losses, expected to average $16,000 with 40 percent devoted to the insurer's overhead. The total annual premium for fire insurance on the ARC building, P, can be computed as follows:

$$60\% \text{ of } P = \$16{,}000$$

$$P = \frac{\$16{,}000}{0.60}$$

$$P = \$26{,}667$$

The premium is a tax-deductible expense. Exhibit 12-9 computes and evaluates the differential annual after-tax NCF from insuring the ARC building for a $26,667 annual premium. At a 12 percent annual rate of return, fully insuring the ARC building for this premium gives it a net present value of negative $41,800. The time-adjusted rate of return is 6.67 percent per year. Contrast this return with that from retaining all losses, either with a sprinkler system (14.88 percent) or without one (11.34 percent).

As long as the expected value of accidental losses is taken as the only cost of retention, insurance will usually produce a lower net present value or time-adjusted rate of return than will retention. This is because an insurance premium typically is larger than the expected value of the insured losses. How much lower the rate of return with insurance will be depends on (1) the size of the insurer's premium "loading" for its expenses and any profit (40 percent in this case), (2) the additional costs of retention to an organization, such as the expenses of performing the safety, loss settlement, and other services that otherwise would be provided by the insurer, and (3) the intangible burden of the uncertainty of knowing that retained losses may fluctuate greatly from year to year around their long-run expected value. Many organizations purchase insurance mainly to remove this uncertainty despite the lower net present value and time-adjusted rate of return on insurance when compared with retention.

/ **Illustration Twelve: Using Contractual Transfer for Risk Financing.** Another possible risk management technique is contractual transfer for risk financing, often associated with a "hold-harmless" agreement.

Under such an agreement, the transferor's protection may be broad or limited, strong or insecure, depending upon (1) the scope (both amount

Exhibit 12-9

Differential Annual After-Tax Cash Flow—Full Insurance

<u>Calculation of NCF</u>

Differential cash revenues	$60,000
Less: Differential cash expenses (except income taxes):	
Insurance expense	26,667
Before-tax NCF:	$33,333

Less: Differential income taxes:

Before-tax NCF	$33,333	
Less: differential depreciation expense ($200,000/10 years)	20,000	
Taxable income	$13,333	
Income taxes (40%)		5,333
After-tax NCF:		$28,000

<u>Evaluation of this NCF</u>

Factors:

> Initial Investment – $200,000
> Life of project – 10 years
> Differential annual after-tax NCF – $28,000
> Minimum acceptable rate of return – 12% annually

Evaluation by the Net Present Value Method:

Present value of differential NCF ($28,000 x 5.650)	$158,200
Less: Present value of initial investment	200,000
Net present value (negative)	($ 41,800)

Evaluation by the Time-Adjusted Rate of Return Method:

$$\frac{\text{Initial investment}}{\text{Differential NCF}} = \frac{\$200,000}{\$\ 28,000} = 7.143 = \text{Present value factor}$$

Interpolation to Find the Time-Adjusted Rate of Return (r):

Rate of Return	Present Value Factor	Present Value Factor
6%	7.360	7.360
r		7.143
8%	6.710	
Differences: 2%	0.650	0.217

r = 6% + [(0.217/0.650) x 2%]
   = 6% + 0.67%
   = 6.67%

and types) of losses for which the transferee agrees to pay and (2) the financial responsibility (both ability and willingness) of the transferee to pay for those losses that fall within the contractual transfer. Thus, effective use of contractual transfer for risk financing requires that (1) the transfer agreement clearly specify the transferor's losses for which the transferee agrees to be financially responsible and (2) the transferee have adequate financial resources to meet its obligations under the contractual transfer.

From the standpoint of the transferor, contractual transfer for risk financing generally involves the following types of cash flows:

1. The losses paid by the transferee are no longer expenses of the transferor.
2. The transferor *may*, depending on the terms of the transfer agreement, pay some compensation to the transferee for entering into the agreement.
3. The transferor may incur some administrative expenses enforcing the transfer agreement, such as in collecting indemnity payments from the transferee.

While contractual transfers for risk financing are typified by "hold-harmless" agreements for shifting liability exposures, such transfers can also shift property loss exposures. For example, to give Dr. Ames an added incentive for fire safety, suppose Sheltering Arms required Dr. Ames to sign a contract whereby he agreed to reimburse the hospital for the first $100 of each fire loss to the ARC building. Since eight fires are expected to occur each year due to the hazards inherent in the research activity, the hospital has projected $800 annual reimbursement from Dr. Ames and $160 additional administrative costs to the hospital. The NCF and rate of return on the hospital's grant are shown in Exhibit 12-10. Here, the expected $800 indemnity payments from Dr. Ames are treated as a source of incremental revenues, and the $160 administrative costs are incremental expenses.

The net present value resulting from this use of contractual transfer for risk financing is $19,130, and the rate of return is 14.3 percent. The same net present value and rate of return could have been computed by treating the $800 as a reduction in the expected value of fire losses rather than as an additional source of revenues.

CASH FLOW ANALYSIS AS A SELECTOR OF RISK MANAGEMENT TECHNIQUES

Cash flow analysis offers two alternative methods, the net present value method and the time-adjusted rate of return method, for most

Exhibit 12-10
Differential Annual After-Tax Net Cash Flow—
Contractual Transfer Through Risk Financing

Calculation of NCF

Differential cash revenues

From ARC	$60,000	
From Dr. Ames for fire losses	800	
Total cash revenues:		$60,800

Less: Differential cash expenses (except income taxes)

Expected value of fire losses	$16,000	
Administrative expenses	160	
Total cash expenses (except income taxes):		$16,160
Before-tax NCF:		$44,640

Less: Differential income taxes:

Before-tax NCF	$44,640	
Less: Differential depreciation expense ($300,000/10 years)	30,000	
Taxable income	$14,640	
Income taxes (40%)		5,856
After-tax NCF:		$38,784

Evaluation of this NCF

Factors:

Initial Investment – $200,000
Life of project – 10 years
Differential annual after-tax NCF – $38,784
Minimum acceptable rate of return – 12% annually

Evaluation by the Net Present Value Method:

Present value of differential NCF ($38,784 x 5.650)	$219,130
Less: Present value of initial investment	200,000
Net present value	$ 19,130

Evaluation by the Time-Adjusted Rate of Return Method:

$$\frac{\text{Initial investment}}{\text{Differential NCF}} = \frac{\$200,000}{\$ 38,784} = 5.157 = \text{Present value factor}$$

Interpolation to Find the Time-Adjusted Rate of Return (r):

	Rate of Return	Present Value Factor	Present Value Factor
	14%	5.216	5.216
	r		5.157
	15%	5.019	
Differences:	1%	0.197	0.059

$$
\begin{aligned}
r &= 14\% + [(0.059/0.197) \times 1\%] \\
&= 14\% + 0.30\% \\
&= 14.30\%
\end{aligned}
$$

profitably allocating an organization's financial resources. The present value method applies the rule that an organization should accept only those proposals that have a positive net present value when both the differential after-tax NCF and the initial investment are discounted at a minimum acceptable rate of return. When choosing among acceptable proposals by the net present value method, an organization should give first preference to the proposal with the highest profitability index.

Alternatively, the time-adjusted rate of return method applies the equally valid decision rule that an organization should rank alternative proposals in terms of the time-adjusted rate of return each promises. Foregoing sections of this chapter have demonstrated how the net present value or the time-adjusted rate of return from a proposal are affected by the costs of possible accidental losses and by the costs of risk management techniques to cope with these losses.

These decision rules should also be used to select risk management techniques. For this purpose, the net present value rule can be restated as follows: An organization should give first preference to that risk management technique that promises the highest net present value for the proposal to which that technique is applied. Similarly, the time-adjusted rate of return decision rule becomes the following: An organization should select the risk management technique that promises the highest time-adjusted rate of return on the proposal to which that technique is applied.

In order to select the technique giving the highest net present value or time-adjusted rate of return, however, an exhaustive list of all possibilities must be considered. This can be done by evaluating each proposal (such as the ARC building in the previous examples) not as a proposal alone but as a proposal coupled with a risk management technique. To illustrate, such a list of possibilities might resemble the following:

ARC Building with

Risk Control	Risk Financing
Through prevention/reduction	Through retaining losses as
Through segregation of exposure	current expenses
units	Through a funded or
Through contractual transfer	unfunded reserve
Through exposure avoidance	Through borrowed funds
	Through a captive insurer
	Through a separate insurer
	Through contractual transfer

Ignoring here the possibility of using two or more risk management techniques simultaneously, the above listing with respect to the ARC building is complete because it (1) allows for "doing nothing" about risk management (a phrase that usually signifies planned or unplanned retention), (2) includes the major types of risk management techniques, and (3) allows for comparison of the ARC building with all other proposals. If another proposal yields a higher net present value or time-adjusted rate of return than this ARC building can generate with any risk management technique other than exposure avoidance, the exposures associated with the ARC building should be avoided by investing in that other proposal.

Thus, expanding the final item in the above list makes the list into a complete enumeration of all possible proposals, each coupled with all possible risk management techniques. The list of alternatives is then at least six times longer than a list of traditional alternative capital investment proposals, which usually ignore risk management considerations. The rule for maximizing profit remains essentially the same: invest first in the proposal-with-risk-management-technique with the highest net present value or time-adjusted rate of return and give progressively lower ranking to alternatives with lower net present values or time-adjusted rates of return.

Advantages and Disadvantages of Cash Flow Analysis For Risk Management Decisions

The major advantages of using the above adaptation of cash flow analysis for selecting risk management techniques is that this procedure puts risk management decisions on the same footing as any other profit-maximizing decisions. The net present value and time-adjusted rate of return tests theoretically are proper for the organization that seeks to increase profits. They also are best for the non-profit organization striving to increase its operating efficiency. By using cash flow analysis, the risk management professional is "speaking the language of management," justifying his or her actions and supporting his or her proposals on a basis all managers should use and understand.

The disadvantages of cash flow analysis are the weaknesses of the assumptions that must be made to employ this analysis conveniently. First, in the above examples, each risk management technique has been dealt with individually, ignoring all the combinations of techniques that could have been employed. In practice, at least one risk control technique and one risk financing technique should be applied to every significant loss exposure. Risk control needs to be backed by risk financing for those risks that cannot be eliminated completely; risk financing becomes much less expensive when supported by effective risk control.

Another assumption has been that there are no degrees to which a particular technique can be used: for example, the ARC building was either sprinklered or unsprinklered (without any comparison of different sizes or types of sprinklers). This assumption leads to oversimplified yes/ no decisions rather than a more thorough analysis. A third assumption has been that damage by fire is the only loss involved while, in fact, a great variety of property, net income, personnel, and liability losses may result from a single event.

Fourth, the expected value of losses has been taken as a measure of the losses that actually occur regardless of the unpredictability of the future. Fifth, and in some respects most important, cash flow analysis assumes that the only goal of the organization is to maximize profits— that humanitarian and social values are irrelevant. For example, this approach attaches no explicit value to human life saved through prevention of an industrial accident or a river kept clean through an organization's efforts to avoid pollution.

The flaws inherent in these assumptions can be at least partially overcome. More lengthy net present value or time-adjusted rate of return computations, incorporating combinations of risk management techniques used in varying degrees to cope with several types of losses, can be performed, especially if a computer is available. Values can be assigned to humanitarian and social factors in order to include them in the computations.

The problem of unpredictability can be handled in several ways, one of the most straightforward being the "worry factor" method described below.

Adapting Cash Flow Analysis for Uncertainty

The procedures discussed above for making risk management decisions on the basis of net present values and time-adjusted rates of return assume, unrealistically, that accidental losses equal their expected value each year. Since accidental losses are not this predictable, the use of a risk management technique that exposes the organization to massive unanticipated losses naturally creates uncertainty as to whether the implemented risk management technique is, indeed, the one that contributes most to the organization's profitability or operating efficiency. Some degree of uncertainty is unavoidable with every risk management technique; the cost of this uncertainty needs to be considered when evaluating risk management alternatives.

The worry factor method assigns a "price tag" to this uncertainty, an implicit after-tax cost that, once identified, can be treated like any other cost, or cash outflow, in a cash flow analysis of any risk management technique. To apply the worry factor method, the first step is to assign (somewhat arbitrarily) a cost of worry to each alternative risk management technique. This cost should reflect the uncertainty to be suffered by the person(s) who must endure the uncertainty associated with each risk management decision. These would include primarily senior management or the owners of the organization, since often top management or the owners stand to lose the most from an unwise or unlucky risk management decision. The attitudes of these top managers or owners are often communicated to the risk management professional who assumes these worries as his or her own. The worry factor generally increases with the size of potential losses to be absorbed. Therefore, full insurance often has little worry factor associated with it on the assumption that insurance will pay all losses.

Applying the worry factor to risk management decisions requires the following two-step process:

1. Determine the amount of the worry factor, i.e., the cost of worry for each risk management technique for a given loss exposure.
2. Deduct this cost from the net cash inflow (or add it to the net cash outflow) for each period in which that technique would be used for that exposure.

The first step can be accomplished by asking the appropriate manager how much he or she would be willing to pay each year (or other period) to know exactly what that year's accidental losses will be. Once these losses are known, risk management decisions become comparable to other management decisions.

To complete the second step, subtract the value of the worry factor from the annual *after-tax* net cash inflow (or add it to the annual *after-tax* net cash outflow) from each risk management technique. The worry factor is deducted from the after-tax NCF because the worry factor is only an implicit expense, not a tax-deductible expenditure. Once the "after-worry" after-tax annual net cash flow is determined, it can be inserted into the net present value and time-adjusted rate of return evaluation computations and be evaluated just like the "before-worry" after-tax NCF.

To illustrate, refer to Exhibit 12-3, which computes and evaluates the annual after-tax NCF of an ARC building on which Sheltering Arms retains fire losses but installs a sprinkler system as a loss reduction measure. The after-tax net cash flow (computed without reference to the cost of worry) is $41,640, which, given the other facts in that example, yields a net present value, discounted at 12 percent, of $25,266 and a time-adjusted rate of return of 14.88 percent.

In this case, assume the hospital's senior administrators are very disturbed by the uncertainties associated with retaining the losses on the ARC building and would be willing to pay another $5,000 per year to ensure that fire losses to the building would actually equal the projected $4,200 value. As shown in Exhibit 12-11, deducting this $5,000 worry factor from the previously calculated annual after-tax NCF of 41,640

Exhibit 12-11
Differential Annual After-Tax Cash
Recognition of Worry Factor

Calculation of NC

Differential cash revenues
Less: Differential cash expenses (except incom
      Expected value of fire losses $4,20
      Sprinkler maintenance   400

Before-tax NCF:

Less: Differential income taxes:
      Before-tax NCF $55,400
      Less: differential depreciation
        expense ($210,000/10 years)   21,000
      Taxable income $34,400
      Income taxes (40%)   13,760

After-tax NCF: $41,640

Less: Worry Factor   5,000

After-worry NCF $36,640

Evaluation of this NCF

Factors:
        Initial Investment – $210,000
        Life of project – 10 years
        Differential annual after-tax NCF – $36,640
        Minimum acceptable rate of return – 12% annually

Evaluation by the Net Present Value Method:
        Present value of differential NCF ($36,640 x 5.650) $207,016
        Less: Present value of initial investment   210,000
        Net present value (negative)   ($ 2,984)

Evaluation by the Time-Adjusted Rate of Return Method:

$$\frac{\text{Initial investment}}{\text{Differential NCF}} = \frac{\$210,000}{\$36,640} = 5.731 = \text{Present value factor}$$

Interpolation to Find the Time-Adjusted Rate of Return (r):

Rate of Return	Present Value Factor	Present Value Factor
10%	6.145	6.145
r		5.731
12%	5.650	
Differences: 2%	0.495	0.414

$$
\begin{aligned}
r &= 10\% + [(0.414/0.495) \times 2\%] \\
&= 10\% + 1.67\% \\
&= 11.67\%
\end{aligned}
$$

2

36,640. The present value of this adjusted NCF, dis-
percent, is $207,016, giving a net present value of a nega-
84.

In terms of the time-adjusted rate of return method, the ARC building's present value factor adjusted for the cost of worry is 5.731, which
is equivalent to an 11.67 percent annual time-adjusted rate of return.
Contrast this 11.67 percent return with the 6.67 time-adjusted rate of
return on the ARC building if fully insured (Exhibit 12-9). If no worry
factor is associated with a fully insured ARC building, the gap in present
value factors (and rates of return) between insurance and retention
narrows. However, the projected rate of return for retention still remains higher than for insurance. In fact, had the worry factor associated
with retention been, say, $9,000, the worry-adjusted after-tax NCF on
the sprinklered ARC building would have been so low that fully insuring
an unsprinklered ARC building would have been more profitable than
retaining losses on a sprinklered one.

The worry factor method provides a fairly easy and understandable
method for adapting cash flow analysis to the uncertain environment in
which many risk management decisions must be made. This method
makes the cost of uncertainty explicit and adjustable to the attitudes
of senior management. Although necessarily somewhat arbitrary, this
method is sufficiently straightforward to appeal to the senior management of many organizations. In an organization where other, more complex methods of adjusting for the lack of certainty are used, the risk
management professional should seriously consider adopting that organization's methods of analysis.

SUMMARY

The selection of risk management techniques (the third step in the
risk management decision process) uses the net present value and time-
adjusted rate of return decision criteria developed in Chapter 11 to select,
from among the risk management techniques cataloged in Chapter 8,
those techniques that promise to most cost-effectively counter the adverse effects of accidental losses forecast by the statistical techniques
discussed in Chapters 9 and 10. Cash flow analysis provides decision
criteria for meeting those demands in ways that enhance the present
value of an organization's NCF and internal rates of return.

These decision criteria call for, first, identifying the effects exposures to accidental losses can be expected to have on an organization's
NCF if these exposures are not managed; second, tracing the cash flow

effects of each of the separate risk control and risk financing techniques that could be applied to each exposure; and, third, selecting the technique that is most cost-effective in promising to generate the highest net present value or time-adjusted rate of return.

CHAPTER 13

Risk Management Information Systems

All managers, indeed probably all persons, possess a "management information system" in the broadest sense. Such a system (or MIS) is a set of procedures (physical or mental) for gathering isolated facts (data) about one's environment, generating information (useful statements about the present or expected future condition of that environment), and reaching and implementing decisions about how to deal with that environment. In this generic sense, perhaps every creature that is able to manipulate or respond to its environment has some sort of management information system for protecting its own well-being. It follows that every organization, even those without a designated risk manager or risk management department, also has some sort of a risk management information system (or RMIS) for protecting the organization against the adverse effects of accidental losses by recognizing and coping with actual or potential accidental losses.

This chapter examines how a proper risk management information system, whether manual or computerized, can best be designed, implemented, and protected from accidental losses in ways that enhance the effectiveness of an organization's overall risk management program. Any management information system is a tool for achieving a particular managerial and organizational goal; a risk management information system is a tool for better protecting an organization against the adverse effects of actual and potential accidental losses, thereby lowering the organization's overall cost of risk. As a tool tailored to each organization's loss exposures and organizational mission, a risk management information system can be useful in any or all steps of the risk management decision process for any or all of an organization's operations.

Many perfectly good risk management information systems can be entirely manual, operating on the basis of traditional paper records and communications. Others demand computer-based facilities because of (1) the volume of exposure and loss data involved; (2) the number and locations of persons (inside or outside the organization) who must have access to exposure, loss, or other risk management data; or (3) the complexity of the risk control or risk financing conditions to be made on the basis of information derived from this data. Although manual risk management information systems are valid in many settings, this chapter focuses on computerized systems by explaining the following:

- The fundamental concepts underlying all proper management information systems
- The conditions under which a computerized, rather than a manual, risk management information system is appropriate
- The steps in, and the decisions required for, designing a computerized risk management information system
- The implementation and the management of a risk management information system, including managing the loss exposures that the system generates
- The applications of a risk management information system throughout the risk management decision process
- The exposures to accidental loss that a risk management information system creates or intensifies, and how these exposures should be managed

INFORMATION SYSTEMS—FUNDAMENTAL CONCEPTS[1]

As television sets changed Americans' personal life-styles in the 1950s and 1960s, computers have changed business life-styles through the past decade of this century. Just as television brought its own acronyms and jargon (TV, UHF, VHF, and "rabbit ears") into our homes, computers have brought terms such as "MIS" (management information system), "RMIS" (risk management information system, a special kind of MIS for dealing with risk management data and decisions), "mainframe" (a large, fast, and powerful computer, which often occupies a specially protected room, "mini" (a less powerful computer with lower capacity than a mainframe), "micro" (a desktop or smaller computer, often called a PC—personal computer), and "terminal" (a cathode-ray tube (CRT) or video-display tube (VDT) about the size of a portable television and a typewriter-style keyboard for communicating with a computer).

As managers throughout an organization come to use these and other computer tools and terminology for dealing more effectively with the quantitative aspects of their work and for improving their own performance, risk management professionals will want, or will feel pressured, to do the same. Like many activities and decisions throughout an organization, risk management also lends itself to a management information system and, more specifically to a risk management information system. To understand the purposes and components of an RMIS, it is best to begin with some fundamental concepts underlying all management information systems: (1) the distinction between information management and management information, (2) the distinction between operating data and management information, and (3) the costs and values of information and its management.

Information Management and Management Information

Information management and management information, while related, have significantly distinct meanings. *Information management* is the process by which management information is extracted from all the available data and manipulated so that it is available in the proper form to the managers who need it. *Management information* is that portion of all the information available within an organization that its managers need to know in order to make sound decisions.

Information Management. Information management is the process of managing information within an organization. It refers to any manager's concern with the creation, flow, and use of information in carrying out his or her responsibilities. Indeed, some managers refer to their "responsibility to manage the organization's information system." Although a computer is not essential for information management—both information and its management existed long before computers existed—many managers consider the computer an essential tool of information management.

Management Information. Management information refers to a particular type of information—information used by managers for particular purposes. For example, an organization's general management information system may contain information on many kinds of expenses; some of these costs (such as for workers compensation claims) will be of direct risk management concern. Some of this workers compensation and other costs of risk information will be useful for the organization's general financial management.

Other items, such as the workers compensation benefits paid to a particular employee for a specific disability or information about the causes of a variety of work-related injuries and illnesses, will be of more specific use within the risk management department in, for example, monitoring a particular employee's recovery and return to work or in identifying frequent causes of work injuries toward which preventive efforts should be directed. Depending on the purpose—general financial management, claims monitoring, or loss prevention—all of this data is potential management information. Management information is an extract of those facts needed by managers to carry out specific responsibilities from the mass of information on an organization's operations.

Management Information System (MIS). A management information system (MIS) is a particular kind of system. As usually defined, a system is a set of components that interact with one another from some purpose. A management information system is a group of people, a set of procedures, and (usually) data processing equipment that select, store, process, and retrieve data to reduce the uncertainty in decision making by yielding information for managers.[2]

Thus, the ultimate purpose of any MIS is to reduce uncertainty—a most important goal given the unpredictability of accidental losses. Notice, however, that the uncertainty to be reduced for an RMIS is not that which arises from the unpredictability of losses but, rather, the uncertainty associated with making decisions. An MIS, and particularly an RMIS, should be designed to give a manager the maximum confidence that, given the information available, a particular decision is the best one that can be made at that time.

An MIS reduces uncertainty in decision making by providing as much management information, in the most understandable and most useful form, as the decision requires. To do this, an MIS takes raw data about an organization's operations and generates from it useful management information.

Operating Data and Management Information

When discussing an MIS or an RMIS, it is important to distinguish between data and information. *Data* are isolated facts not placed in any meaningful context that would permit inferences or conclusions to be drawn. For example, a chronological listing of work injuries (perhaps showing the names of injured employees, the nature of the injuries, and the estimated ultimate dollar values of the claims) would be data. Arranged simply by the dates of injury, this data would not easily yield meaningful conclusions about the causes, costs, or control of these work injury exposures.

In contrast, *information* is data organized in ways that identify certain variables or conditions helpful in making decisions, that is, data put into a context for decision making. Within an organization, information about its operations guides its management.[3]

The distinction between data and information suggests a potential defect in many MIS and RMIS: they may be filled with data that does not provide adequate management information. For example, historical "loss runs" giving the date, the location, the perils, the coded category of cause, and the amount for individual losses provide an organization's risk management professional with much data, but they often go unread because the unorganized, isolated facts yield little information. However, once this data is organized and perhaps summarized by location, cause, date, time of day, or dollar size category, the risk management professional can begin to glean information useful in cost-effectively preventing or paying for these individual losses. A well-designed RMIS can structure this data properly, yielding true information and improving risk management performance.

Information: Costs and Values

Gathering raw data can be costly; deciding how to organize it into useful information and then producing the information itself can be still more expensive. In general, any organization should seek to gather only those data and generate only that information whose values are greater than their costs. This principle underlies much of the cost-benefit analysis for deciding among types of RMIS. Even before considering specific types of systems, however, it is useful to have in mind the types of costs and the values of information inherent in a computerized RMIS.

Costs of Information. The cost of obtaining, or capturing, information can be divided into the following five general categories:

1. Cost of Hardware. Since the cost of the hardware is the price actually paid for the purchase or lease of equipment, it probably is the easiest figure to determine.
2. Cost of Systems Analysis, Design, and Implementation. This includes all program development costs—from the design phase through the implementation phase.
3. Cost for Space and Environment Control Factors. This includes floor space, preparation, special temperature and humidity controls, and power control units. With large-scale computers, these costs can be significant.
4. Cost of Conversion. This includes both the one-time cost associated with conversion from a manual procedure to a computerized procedure and the cost of upgrading or converting from one computer system to another. The conversion cost is often considerably higher than the total costs of hardware, installation, and program development.
5. Cost of Operation. This includes the personnel, supplies, space,

utilities, and other costs associated with the maintenance and operation of the information management function.

Value of Information. Unlike the costs of information, the value of the information is extremely difficult to quantify and must be approached almost exclusively from a conceptual point of view. The value of information is based on the following ten considerations:

1. Accessibility. How easily and quickly can the information be accessed? It may be a matter of seconds through a cathode-ray tube (CRT) or a matter of hours through some batch method.
2. Comprehensiveness. Not how voluminous, but how comprehensive is the information in question? Does it convey meaning in its own right or only in relation to some other information?
3. Accuracy. To what degree is the information free from error? (Since no human information is infallible, an error rate—however small—is inevitable.)
4. Appropriateness. Is the information suited to the user's request or need?
5. Timeliness. How much time elapses from the transaction or event until the output is available to the user? Is information available when needed for activities and decisions?
6. Clarity. How ambiguous is the information? Can the inexperienced or occasional user understand it without aid?
7. Flexibility. How flexible is the information in its use? Can it be used for more than one decision or by more than one decision maker?
8. Verifiability. Can the information be easily verified?
9. Freedom From Bias. Has the information been free from any attempt to alter or modify it in order to support a preconceived conclusion? (If the information has been "screened," its objectivity—and hence value—has been reduced.)
10. Quantifiability. To what extent is the raw data numerical and susceptible to the kinds of mathematical manipulation for which computers are designed? (The more quantifiable the data, the more information a computer can generate from it and the greater the merit of investing in computer equipment and programs.)

RISK MANAGEMENT INFORMATION SYSTEMS[4]

A risk management information system, whether simple or complex, is a process for gathering, analyzing, and reporting data and information relevant to an organization's risk management program. That data, and the meaningful information derived from it for making risk control or risk financing decisions, may (1) encompass the entire scope of an organization's risk management program (including all loss exposures that the organization's senior management perceives as falling within the scope of "risk management" and all the risk control and risk financing tools for dealing with these exposures) or (2) focus more on a particular type of loss exposure (products liability, for example, for a firm facing many such claims) or on a particular risk management technique (such as prevention of employee injuries). The scope of any RMIS is unessential to the definition of the system. Also unessential to the definition is the particular use of any RMIS, which may range from transaction processing and standard risk management reporting to affording random access to a database and providing quantitative analysis to support risk management decisions. The essence of the definition is the gathering, analysis, and reporting of data and information in carefully specified ways that ensure the greatest accuracy and cost-effectiveness of the information generated and the decisions reached.

This discussion considers the historical development of risk management information systems, the components of an RMIS, and some potential benefits and limitations of such a system.

Evolution of Risk Management Information Systems

In the late 1950s and early 1960s, the only risk management information systems were manual procedures followed by the participants in insurance transactions—insurance buyers, insurers, brokers, and some outside claims administrators and consultants. During the mid-1960s, computers began to perform more of the repetitive tasks involved in insurance buying and selling. As computer technology advanced, continuing cycles of innovation gave rise to four recognizable states in the development of an RMIS: (1) transaction processing, (2) standard risk management reporting, (3) random data access, and (4) risk management decision support.

Not every RMIS in use today has progressed through these four stages. Some systems have bypassed the earlier phases to focus on risk management decision support, while others have been developed specifically for, and continue to perform most appropriately and cost-effectively, transaction processing, preparation of standard reports, or random access to data.

Stage 1: Transaction Processing. The earliest risk management applications of computerized insured loss and premium record keeping, beginning in the late 1960s, were developed by a few insurers to help selected insureds keep records on their insured losses and target risk control efforts on specific causes of frequent accidents. Shortly thereafter, comparable computer programs were marketed by independent vendors to all organizations wishing them.

These early transaction-processing systems were perceived as suffering from two significant defects. First, centered on insurance transactions, these Stage 1 systems were seen as not giving enough attention to an organization's overall cost of risk (insurance premiums + retained losses + risk control costs + risk management administrative expenses) and thus were not fully effective in communicating risk management concerns and achievements to senior management. Second, these early systems suffered from the apparent inability to capture credible data on a timely basis. Inaccurate, out-of-date information was not fully usable in making current risk management decisions and did not project to senior management a favorable impression of the risk management department.

Stage 2: Standard Risk Management Reporting. Stage 2 of RMIS development began in the late 1960s and early 1970s when the cost of risk concept became widely recognized and risk management professionals increasingly turned to independent vendors for computerized assistance in calculating and controlling their organizations' overall costs of risk. In addition, Stage 2 systems made significant steps toward building a stronger basis of communication on risk management matters not only with senior executives but also with managers throughout an organization.

By providing risk management professionals with a consistent basis for gathering, analyzing, and displaying cost of risk data from each of an organization's major departments, Stage 2 systems replaced the time-consuming practice of manually compiling tables of losses and premiums as well as other elements of the cost of risk in formats suitable for monthly, quarterly, or annual reports to an organization's board of directors, auditors, and owners.

While Stage 2 systems enabled risk management professionals to gather more data more quickly, much of the basic data continued to come from insurers rather than from within the organization. Moreover, vendors' ability to prepare a great variety of reports sometimes generated the criticism that their risk management clients were "buried in reams of computer paper"—much data, but little management information.

Stage 3: Random Data Access. In response to these criticisms, a number of independent vendors, brokerage organizations, and insurers began in the mid-1970s to offer their risk management clients more flexible risk management information systems through which they could not only design their own reports but also have "random access" to their own risk management data. Random, or direct, access to computerized data gives the computer user the ability to refer to a particular data item in a file or in a portion of a report without having to read the entire file or reproduce the entire report. In contrast, sequential access would require reading the entire file or reproducing the entire report from the beginning until the desired portion is reached.

To illustrate, when re-reading a familiar novel, a reader can have "random access" to particular passages by quickly finding the appropriate page; in contrast, when the novel is made into a movie, the viewer has only "sequential access" to a favorite portion by waiting for it to appear on the movie screen.

Random access to a database—to an organized collection of related computerized files that contain data relevant to a particular operation such as risk management—gave risk management professionals the ability to tailor their own reports and to respond quickly to requests for information from senior executives and other managers. This ability to extract data in any format on demand made at least three important contributions to effective risk management.

First, awareness of the risk management function increased through interaction with the risk management database, particularly among line management. After witnessing a successful application of the system, managers' interest in analysis was stimulated, enabling them to become sophisticated users of the RMIS.

Second, support of the risk management function typically improved as a direct result of satisfying line and staff management's information needs. Not recognizing the assistance that can be provided from the risk management department is often a major reason for limited support of the risk management function within organizations.

Third, communications dealing with risk management within an organization were improved with the risk management professional's ability to monitor and control costs, thereby increasing his or her ability to respond quickly to other managers' questions and problems.

Stage 4: Risk Management Decision Support. The focus of Stage 1 through Stage 3 was to store and display efficiently and accurately data useful in reviewing losses, insurance premiums, and other internal indicators of risk management performance. As more data was added to system databases, and as random access gave the risk management professional more opportunity to interact with the RMIS, the possibility of computers actually making risk management decisions became more realistic.

The key to interactive risk management decision support is the ability of the computer to respond to "what if" inquiries by using the data in its database to project the likely consequences of various alternative actions the risk management professional might recommend. Such forecasting has required the development of various analytical modules for loss forecasting, allocation of the costs of risk, and macroeconomic (economy wide) projections. Once having verified the assumptions underlying these forecasting and decision support capabilities, a risk management professional with a Stage 4 RMIS can use it in a variety of risks, including the following:

- Projecting the costs and benefits of the specific risk management measures being considered
- Forecasting changes in the organization's overall cost of risk and in each of the components of that cost
- Selecting cost-effective per-loss and annual aggregate retention levels
- Correlating actual safety practices (such as machine guards or safety training programs) with records of changes in accident frequency and severity rates
- Testing the adequacy of reserves for retained workers compensation or other losses

Access to broader databases, particularly through telephone (modem) interconnections of an organization's internal computers with external sources of data on financial markets, levels of economic activity, and regulatory developments can enhance the value of an RMIS as decision support both by increasing the reliability of the data on which these decisions are based and by broadening the types of decisions with which the computer can be helpful. (A modem—MOdulator + DEModulator—is a device that converts data to a form that can be transmitted, as by telephone, to data processing equipment, where a similar device reconverts it.)

It seems likely that future RMIS developments will bring the following, perhaps in additional stages:

- Much wider availability of mini and microcomputers that will be as accessible, familiar, and open to as wide a range of information as is the telephone today
- Use of RMIS communication capabilities among organizations—especially insurers and other providers of risk control and risk financing services—to negotiate the terms of purchase for insurance or other risk financing or risk controls
- Integration of an organization's risk management decision process with its other financial decision processes, all rooted in an MIS that coordinates all the organization's most crucial managerial decisions

Exhibit 13-1
Data and Information Flows With a Stage 4 RMIS

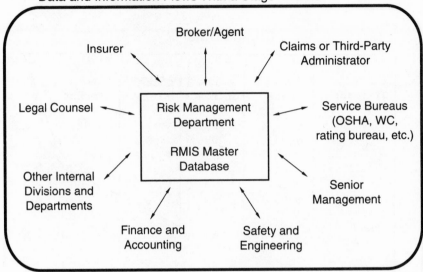

Such integration and coordination through a Stage 4 RMIS facilitates two-way exchanges between an organization's risk management department and others within and outside the organization, as shown in Exhibit 13-1.

Components of RMIS

An RMIS has the same four basic components as all management information systems: (1) relevant data, (2) procedures for gathering and manipulating the data to produce information, (3) computer equipment, and (4) personnel to operate the RMIS. In computer terminology, the data are often labeled the "database"; the computer programs, the procedures for managing the data, are known as "software"; and the computer equipment itself is known as "hardware."

Database. The database is the core of any RMIS, the "memory" in which is stored the basic information upon which the analytical software components of the RMIS operate. The following are the critical activities in database construction:

1. Selecting the types of data to be included and the quantity of each kind of data that the organization considers adequate to support reliable decisions

Exhibit 13-2
Example of RMIS File Display

Claims Data

Claimant	Acc Date	Cause of Loss	Loca-tion	Loss Amount
Smith, S.	900116	007	B1234	10027.20
Jones, M.	900315	208	AA007	75.00
Borwn, R.	890212	201	B 12	2830.00
Schultz, D.	900720	999	C0200	250.0
Abbot, B.	851017	100	SAA01	
Baker, D.	880511	033	J0500	
Cartha, E.	810908	999		
Zubrak, L.	891223	501		

2. Determining the format, types of summarizing, and random access capabilities required to perform the functions expected of the RMIS

3. Updating and periodically verifying the factual data that is the raw material for this system

Any RMIS based on a mainframe possesses a nearly inexhaustible limit of data storage; systems based on a micro or minicomputer, while less expensive than mainframes, necessarily have more limited storage capacity and require more thought as to the types and volumes of information to be stored in them.

In a computerized RMIS, data is stored (usually as magnetic charges) in files. As displayed on a computer screen, a file often appears as in Exhibit 13-2, which contains data records like the rows shown across the exhibit and data items like the vertical columns in the exhibit. The file segment in the exhibit, containing data on liability claims against an organization, consists of any number of records (like the first for claimant Smith, and the second for claimant Jones), with each record consisting of five data items (also known as attributes or data fields) within a given record.

Every proper RMIS must be built on data that is complete, accurate,

Exhibit 13-3
Frequent Database Components

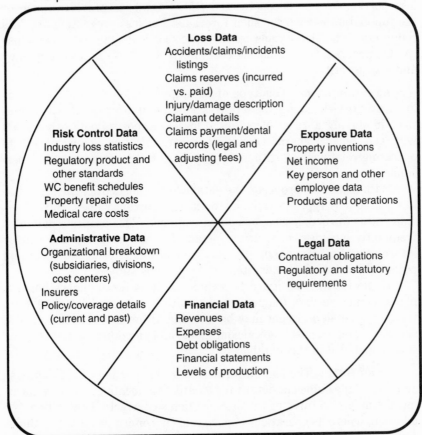

consistent, relevant, and timely. Otherwise, the inevitable results are described by the tested computer maxim: "Garbage In, Garbage Out," or GIGO. The types of data commonly recorded in an RMIS database can be classified as loss data, exposure data, legal data, financial data, administrative data, risk control data, and risk financing data. Some of these types of data are shown in Exhibit 13-3.

Loss Data. Details of an organization's past losses usually occupy the largest segment of its risk management database. From this loss data, risk management professionals, brokers and agents, and insurers can develop information on the frequency, severity, causes, and final settlement of past losses and can project reasonable reserves for current and future losses. Most risk management decisions require forecasts, such as forecasts of future losses and of the effects various risk control and risk financing techniques can have on the costs of those losses. The loss portion of a well constructed RMIS database provides much of the foundation needed for such forecasts. For loss prevention and loss reduction, extensive details on the precise circumstances of each loss can be most helpful in tailoring cost-effective controls of loss frequency and loss severity.

Exposure Data. This type of data, quite extensive and diverse, is important to risk management professionals and to insurers' representatives in staying abreast of potential losses. Exposure data often deals with the general characteristics of an organization, its property, its operating relationships with major suppliers and customers, and its personnel.

With respect to property, the database should identify the organization's assets by type, location, historical and current values, and ownership status (owned, leased, or held in bailment). This property data also frequently includes construction details for real property and vendor information for personal property as well as estimates of the maximum potential loss to which each item of property is subject.

If the RMIS is designed to include analysis for employee benefits plans, employee data (name, sex, age, occupation, and the like) from the personnel department may be in order. Other items, such as social security number, past medical conditions, and any other pertinent items can be included in this database.

Legal Data. The legal information in this portion of the database should include sufficient details for identifying, locating, and summarizing the major features of the organization's contractual obligations. In addition, where its operations expose it to civil or criminal liability under federal or state statutes, the database should provide references and perhaps brief summaries of the pertinent legislation. Finally, where an organization's alleged breaches of its common-law or statutory duties have led to specific legal claims against it, the database should provide information for identifying and tracking the status of these claims.

Financial Data. The financial section of many RMIS provides current data on and forecasts for revenues and expenses, cashflows, debt obligations and borrowing plans, levels of production, and other sources and uses for funds.

Administrative Data. If a firm's organizational structure is diverse, perhaps involving multiple departments, several subsidiaries, or widespread locations constituting different cost centers, the database should be constructed to reflect this hierarchy and to segregate risk management data to reflect this diversity. So structured, the database can greatly simplify risk management cost allocation, even if the organization is restructured.

To use the RMIS to analyze the losses the organization will retain, those covered by insurance, and the cost of that insurance coverage, the database needs to include information in coverage limits, deductibles, expiration dates, annual premiums, rating information, insurers, underwriters, and brokers/agents for each insurance policy protecting the organization. Comparable data on previous policies also should be retained within the RMIS because the data on them is likely to provide valuable trending information as well as perhaps valuable insurance coverage for claims arising out of the organization's past conduct.

Risk Control Data. To supplement the data in the other segments of the RMIS database, the risk control segment should include other facts that can help assess the quality of the organization's loss prevention efforts and to estimate the financial savings they generate. For such assessment, the database is likely to include industry-wide statistics on the frequency and severity of various types of accidents and claims and the standards applicable to work safety, product safety, and environmental protection that have been promulgated by federal and state regulatory agencies as well as by the relevant industry and trade groups. To estimate the financial benefits of risk control, the database should include relevant workers compensation benefit schedules, costs of real property and automobile repair, and indexes of medical care costs. These costs can be used in demonstrating the value of preventing accidents and claims.

Software. Software comprises the instructions that direct the computer to perform a given set of tasks. Without software a computer does virtually nothing except hum softly and perhaps flash a few lights to indicate that it has been turned on. This software, or programs, may be permanently stored in the mainframe, mini, or micro or may be loaded into the computer from magnetic tapes, disks, or punchcards when needed for a particular project. In addition, programs stored in a mainframe or other computer may be transferred, or "downloaded," into a smaller computer (or "uploaded" into a larger one). The kinds of software required for most RMIS applications include the following:

- Database management programs for adding to, updating, or restructuring data in the database
- Analysis software that performs statistical and financial procedures (for example, to forecast future losses based on actual or adjusted past loss data, to compute regression equations that relate the organization's loss experience to operational changes—such as new levels of production or the use of new safety equipment—and to compute cashflows and rates of return

based on projected loss experience as affected by different risk management techniques)

- Communications programs for transmitting database information or software programs among computers within or outside the organization

The most common types of software in current use include word processing programs, accounting and other reporting spreadsheets, database management systems, graphics packages, and special purpose programs, such as for payroll administration or RMIS, which may make use of several of these more generalized software programs. Software is becoming faster, more powerful, and more expensive (both in actual cost and in space).

An RMIS having somewhat limited built-in data storage capacity, or "memory," will typically rely on "batch" programs. "Batching" refers to the way in which changes are made to the database. In a batch system, all the data—or updating changes in the data—are entered into the computer at one session. Various processing programs then can be applied to that data, but the data cannot be changed while the processing program is operating.

In contrast, an RMIS with larger memory capacity often has what is known as "interactive" or "on-line" capabilities through which particular items in the database can be changed while a processing program is in operation. Such a system is described as interactive because the risk management professional or other computer user can direct specific "what if. . ." questions to the computer by changing the data or other assumptions with which the program is operating. The user is on-line with the computer, able to conduct a "conversation" with it rather than having to wait for the entire program to be completed under a batch system. In time, with sufficient recyclings of the programs, a batch system can deal with all the same questions as an interactive system. However, if the amount of data is great or the program is complex, a batch system operates at a much slower speed and consumes a great deal more costly computer time.

In selecting ready-made software programs for an RMIS—or in calling upon others within the organization or outside vendors or consultants to develop customized software programs—a risk management professional should bear in mind a number of questions regarding some desirable features of such software. Some of these features and some corresponding questions follow:

- *Reliability*—How dependable is the RMIS and what is the potential downtime associated with this product? Are there any discernible "bugs" within the software? What kind of guarantees does the vendor provide if problems develop?

- *User Friendly*—How easy to use is this system? Does it require extensive operator training? Are there "help" screens or English language prompts?
- *Flexibility*—What types of analyses or functions can it perform? Is the software adaptable enough to analyze a wide variety of risk control and risk financing options under differing scenarios? Does the software have the capability to tap into different databases within different hardware environments? Is there flexible reporting capability? Can reports be instantaneously generated on-site or do they need to be prepared elsewhere?
- *Degree of Integration*—Closely related to the system's flexibility, can the RMIS tie in with other existing company database files (such as the finance department) or with external organizations (such as insurers, brokers, or governmental agencies)?
- *Accuracy*—Are there enough proven editing capabilities and constraints to prevent inadvertent errors or intentional tampering? (Could February 32, 1985 be added as an acceptable date?)
- *Expandability*—Can the system grow along with the user's needs without requiring a complete overhaul every two or three years as needs grow or the organization changes?
- *Analytical Power*—What types of analytical capabilities are provided by the system? Is it simply a word processing/tracking system or can it provide cashflow analyses, modeling of different funding options, cost of risk allocation, or loss forecasting?
- *Security*—What types of security features are built into the software to prevent tampering or unauthorized access to different levels of sensitive data?

Hardware. Hardware is the physical equipment to which most people point when they speak of "the computer." It is the machinery that runs the software. The essential hardware components of any computer system are its central processing unit (CPU), an input device (such as a keyboard, "mouse," or touch-sensitive screen), an output or display device (such as a visual monitor in the form of a cathode ray tube or CRT), and a storage medium (such as computer tapes or disk drives). Most hardware systems also include an output device such as a printer, and many are also equipped with a communications device like a modem for linking computers and exchanging data and programs through telephone wires.

Computer hardware has chronologically evolved from mainframes (frequently room-sized assemblages of components) through minicomputers (now considered mid-sized, perhaps filling the space of a desk) to personal computers (or PCs, the size of a portable television or microwave oven) to the current "laptops" (which often fit into a normal briefcase.) Any of these devices can be interconnected to exchange information or to draw upon the data or software residing in a mainframe or minicomputer.

Hardware and software are the tools that risk management professionals can use to turn good data into good information that supports better decisions. Decision support is not the same as decision making; intelligent and informed humans are still essential for knowing what kinds of information to gather and analyze and for the actual choices that are the heart of risk management and other decision making. Data analysis and decision support often are highly repetitive tasks involving the management of large amounts of data—tasks for which the appropriate hardware and software are of great assistance to an actual human decision-maker. Because computers can do many tasks with much data very rapidly, they provide excellent decision support.

The type of computer equipment depends on the user's needs. Size is a major factor. The larger the database required, the more powerful should be the computer. To illustrate, for historical claims databases including five years' records of frequent losses and related information, a mainframe computer would provide the required storage capacity and speed. A 50,000 claim database would take seconds for a mainframe to sort, analyze, and generate a report; the same task could take much longer on a smaller computer. The number of work stations also governs the choice of computer equipment. Although sharing a computer terminal once was common, it is now quite likely that each user has an individual terminal.

Two important characteristics of any good hardware are reliability and expandability. It is important that any system be dependable and supported by readily available service facilities—that the hardware itself not create significant business interruption or downtime exposures. Back-up computers—extra minis or micros, or access to others' mainframes that can operate compatibly with the organization's own computers and have adequate available processing time—are essential. If the organization already has a general management information system, careful consideration should be given to using this system's hardware for the RMIS so that the RMIS and the MIS can be readily integrated.

Personnel. Of all the components of any management information system, and especially RMIS, people are the most important. It is people who supply and interpret the data; who design, build, install, and service the hardware; who conceive and write the software; who train and support those internal staff members who work with the RMIS; and people who use RMIS information for refining and supporting their decisions. It is also the people component of an effective RMIS whose cost—mainly consisting of salaries and fringe benefits—probably is rising the fastest.

The number of people required to operate an RMIS depends on the size and the requirements of the system. Some RMIS require a team of experts including computer programmers, analysts, and hardware/ software professionals. Other systems—particularly those relying on ready-made programs and one or two terminals attached to the general MIS—may require only one or two support personnel.

The needs and levels of expertise of the end users of the system— the organization's risk management professional, broker or agent, insurance underwriter, and claims administrator, for example—also affect personnel needs. If these individuals are computer literate, the need for additional personnel is reduced.

The personnel to operate an RMIS need not all come from within the organization. Persons with information systems expertise are often available on a part-time, consulting, or "loan" basis from insurers, brokerage organizations, hardware/software vendors, outside claims administration organizations, and a variety of consulting firms.

Potential Benefits and Limitations of RMIS

Although a risk management information system can be useful in a variety of ways, it also has limitations. Thus, the decision to establish such a system should consider both the benefits and the limitations at the outset.

Potential Benefits. A well-designed RMIS can perform many clerical, computational, communication, and decision activities more quickly and with greater accuracy than can people. As a result, an RMIS can increase the efficiency of a risk management program, reduce costs, improve communication, improve credibility for risk management, and enhance the quality of information for decisions.

Increased Efficiency. Eliminating or reducing paper work increases the risk management professional's time for analytical decision making. A well designed database management system within an RMIS can store, categorize, analyze, and extract needed data within seconds and reduce the chances of error, thus increasing the efficiency and the quality of decisions. For example, calls from varied sources to produce a loss forecast, a cost of risk allocation, or a summary of all claims over $50,000 at Location 5 could be produced in minutes instead of days.

Faster data compilation and analysis through RMIS generate more time for developing risk management recommendations. In addition, increased RMIS analytical capabilities (such as for loss forecasting, cost of risk allocation, cost/benefit analysis, and financial modeling) heighten the ability to perform sophisticated analyses and recognize opportunities for strengthening the risk management program. For example, a risk management professional deciding among several fire detection/suppression systems could use computerized simulations and financial models to determine which fire protection alternative would provide the most effective fire loss reduction for a given cost or, alternatively, which system would provide a given level of fire protection at the least cost. A somewhat more sophisticated RMIS could also portray the tradeoffs between the cost and fire protection each of these alternatives offers.

Reduced Costs. Senior management often finds attractive the savings that can be achieved through investing in an RMIS. These savings stem from fewer errors as manual operations are reduced, personnel expenses (to perform now-computerized tasks) are decreased, and responses to risk management needs are made more promptly.

For example, through random inquiry of an RMIS database, the risk management professional for a hospital determined that 30 percent of all workers compensation claims originated on one particular nursing shift. Further investigation revealed that there had not been enough nurses for the work this shift required; consequently, the overworked nurses suffered more back injuries. When the personnel department learned of this understaffing and subsequently increased the number of nurses on this shift, the incident rate of back injuries decreased markedly.

Improved Communication. Through computer networking and shared databases, properly computerized information is readily accessible simultaneously to many people both within and outside an organization. Moreover, computers can sort, manipulate, merge, summarize, and disseminate data with amazing speed. Therefore, an RMIS can be invaluable in presenting to departmental and senior management recommendations based on sound information and thorough analysis. The system can help present these recommendations concisely with graphic visuals and with clear calculations on how the recommendations would affect the organization's cost of risk.

An RMIS can be, on the one hand, as detailed as necessary for the risk management department's use in discussing, for example, renewals with underwriters or comparing various retention options, while, on the other hand, producing reports that present "the big picture" to senior and other managers. The timeliness of presenting this information is extremely important. A chief financial officer, for example, may ask the risk management professional for an historical trend for workers compensation losses over the past five years. Without an RMIS, this chore would require perhaps days of manually searching through old files. Many RMIS could present this material within perhaps minutes, depending on the system. Since less time is consumed in gathering and processing data, more staff and managerial time is available for interpreting the information and pondering its implications.

Particularly when integrated with an overall MIS, an RMIS can increase the risk management professional's contributions to the organization's day-to-day and strategic decisions. Through the MIS, the departments within the organization can communicate quickly with, and receive prompt advice from, the risk management department regarding routine activities. On a more strategic level, decisions such as whether to merge with another organization involve weighing risk management concerns—such as how the merger would change the new organization's loss exposures—as well as the purely business risks that traditionally dominate merger negotiations. With the use of an RMIS and with proper information, a risk management professional can measure the impact such a merger would have on the surviving organization's new cost of risk and can highlight for senior management the significance of such a change in the organization's overall costs.

Improved Credibility for Risk Management. Partly for psychological reasons, computer-generated material often gains more credibility than handwritten, or even typewritten, material. People tend to have more trust in computerized output because, unlike humans, computers cannot deviate from the programmed instructions and are thus unable to generate errors stemming from fatigue, ignorance, or emotion.

Computer-generated results can be wrong, however, because of human errors in programming or in providing the computer with incomplete or inaccurate data. For example, if a risk management department staff member has neglected to enter information about ten property losses, no computerized summary of total property losses to date will be meaningful. Similarly, if a clerical employee in a branch location has miscoded four back injuries as leg injuries in a quarterly report to an organization's headquarters, the resulting computerized summary will under-report back injuries and over-report leg injuries.

Nonetheless, computers can greatly improve the credibility of risk management information by "flagging" logical errors in the underlying data. For example, an RMIS liability claim tracking program can select for further human attention a claim report where the report date is prior to the occurrence date, where there is a reserve shown for a claim that is already closed, where a new claim is reported from a divested operation, or where the total of "claims paid-to-date" is less than the total "claims paid last quarter." By being programmed to highlight specified types of "things that should not be," a computer can greatly enhance the integrity of an organization's underlying risk management data.

Higher Quality Information for Decisions. Because of their strength in organizing data and developing decision models from it, computers can derive great quantities of information from a given body of data, thus providing more and higher quality information for humans to use in making decisions. Well-organized data typically yield the high quality of information statistical models need to support many risk management decisions.

Organized Data. The process of entering data into a computer requires much structuring of input into files, spreadsheets, and other formats from which a risk management professional can quickly access and manipulate this data, relying on the RMIS for both one-time queries and periodic reports. This structuring of data also facilitates analysis of all or some portion of the assembled data to reveal patterns in an organization's loss experience, claims management, risk financing costs, or other subjects of managerial concern. For example, computerized treatment of loss data permits calculations and comparisons of employee disability frequency and severity rates at different locations, under different operating conditions, or during different time periods—comparisons that would hardly be made cost-effectively without a computer.

Models. With a computer that has decision-support capabilities, a risk management professional can use various "What if. . .?" techniques to test the validity, or build simplified models, of the real world based on certain assumptions. These models permit "trying out" some decision alternatives. For example, a computer can answer such questions as: "What if we had agreed to a $50,000 per-loss deductible for the last three years instead of a $25,000 one—how would our insurance premiums and our retained losses have been different (assuming we had the same actual loss experience over the past three years)?" Although computers cannot make decisions, they can facilitate analysis of specific decision alternatives.

Potential Limitations. Because computers can do no more than they have been programmed to do and have access to only the data they have been given, no computerized RMIS can "perform miracles." Specifically, every RMIS is limited because (1) it can only perform analysis, not make decisions; (2) it cannot guarantee any reduction in an organization's accidental losses or cost of risk; (3) its quality of outputs is limited by the quality of the information it receives and the software it employs; (4) it entails additional expenses; and (5) it is ultimately dependent on people and subject to their weaknesses.

Only Analysis, Not Decisions. A computerized RMIS does not make decisions. It has no imagination or analytical insight and can only answer questions humans ask it on the basis of the data humans provide. Most fundamentally, it cannot initiate an inquiry or any thought process leading to a decision—it cannot even recognize the need for a decision to be made. In short, computers are wonderful at giving answers to precise questions, but only humans can create those questions and the data available to be processed for generating the answers.

No Necessary Loss/Cost Reduction. A computerized RMIS can reduce an organization's overall cost and risk in many ways such as cutting administrative costs and speeding the organization's response to changes in hazards and the resulting losses. However, an RMIS is a mere management information tool. It does not itself prevent accidental losses or make them less severe. In fact, as noted below, an RMIS creates or intensifies a number of exposures to accidental losses. Therefore, computerizing an already deficient risk management program does not significantly improve an organization's overall risk management effort.

Limited Quality of Inputs and Programs. When the data going into a computer is inaccurate, incomplete, or obsolete, no amount of computerized manipulation can generate reliable information or decision guidelines. Preventing "garbage in, garbage out" requires gathering accurate data on a timely basis, maintaining the integrity of the data as it is entered into and manipulated by the computer, and avoiding any attempts to infer from the data conclusions it cannot logically support.

RMIS Expenses. Although an RMIS improves the efficiency of an organization's overall risk management program and reduces its cost of risk, computerizing an existing manual RMIS does entail some additional costs. These include expenses associated with purchasing or leasing the hardware or software, along with expenditures for various computer supplies such as paper and printer ribbons. Personnel need training to understand the hardware and to operate the software—training that requires both direct educational expenses and loss of employees' normal productive time during their training sessions. In the aggregate, all these costs can be quite significant, ranging well into several thousand dollars annually for each regular RMIS user. Therefore, the decision to invest in a computerized RMIS can be examined through the same types of net cash flow analysis as any other major investment of the organization's financial, personnel, or other resources.

Human Error. The weakest link in most computerized RMIS systems is the people who design and operate them. Most of the problems with these systems are not fundamentally technical, but result from weaknesses in training operators and a failure to give operators access to expert technical support. Even problems that at first seem principally technical, such as software that is not "user friendly" or inappropriate system "defaults," are ultimately "people problems" in that they reflect poor decisions made by the people who designed or installed the RMIS.

DESIGNING RMIS

Securing the potential benefits and avoiding the potential disadvantages of an RMIS require that such a system be designed properly and tailored specifically to the needs of the organization. This designing and tailoring entails four phases: (1) analyzing the organization's particular RMIS requirements; (2) identifying the flows of information required to meet these needs; (3) determining the technological and financial feasibility of an RMIS to meet these needs; and (4) deciding whether to build, buy, or lease the hardware and software components of such a system.

Requirements Analysis

The purpose of a requirements analysis is to identify all intended users of the RMIS, their respective information needs, and the organization's present resources that might meet these needs. The four steps in performing a requirements analysis are to (1) identify all intended users, (2) conduct structured interviews of these users, (3) analyze the findings from these interviews, and (4) assemble this analysis into a report or recommendations.

Identifying Users. Potential intended "RMIS users" should include not only the people who will rely on the RMIS to manage information or to reach decisions but also people who will supply the data that the RMIS needs. While most users of an RMIS will be personnel within the risk management department, there will be a significant number of users who work in other departments within the organization as well as a few who work outside the organization. Of those outside the risk management department, some will supply data *to* the department, while others will receive information *from* the department. Within this context, likely users to be interviewed might include representatives of the following departments or functions:

- Internal to the Organization
  - Employee Health and Safety
  - Compensation and Benefits
  - Management Information Systems (or Electronic Data Processing, EDP)
  - Risk Management
  - Legal
  - Accounting
  - Purchasing
  - Senior Management

- Regional Management (or Department Heads)
- Local Management (such as Plant Managers)
- External to the Organization
  - Insurance Brokers/Agents
  - Insurers
  - Risk Management Consultants
  - External Legal Counsel
  - External Claims Administrators/Adjusters
  - Trade Associations
  - Personnel of Captives, Pools
  - Officials of State and Local Government

Conducting Interviews.   Questionnaires, tailored to each interviewee's function(s), should be structured to guide each interview but not to exclude valuable insights an interviewee may offer. The objective is to enable both the interviewer and the interviewee to understand, in a risk management context, one another's perceptions regarding the following:

- Data that currently is being collected and the procedures and reasons for its collection
- Additional data, or information from new or existing data, that is needed or desired
- Present data, or information derived from that data, that is not worth the cost and difficulty of gathering or analyzing it
- Gaps and bottlenecks in recurrent procedures for gathering data, analyzing it, or disseminating the resulting information.

Each interview should repeatedly emphasize the goal of designing the RMIS to enhance each interviewee's job performance and fulfillment of individual objectives. In addition to being among the interviewees, representatives of the organization's MIS department should be directly involved in, or available for consultation on, the entire interviewing process. MIS personnel have special expertise on the standards and constraints with which the new RMIS will need to comply and the capabilities of the organization's current and (potentially new) hardware and software.

It is good practice to send each interviewee a written summary of the key points of his or her interview for review and approval before assembling the interview information for the final report. This further participation by each interviewee not only assures greater accuracy but also promotes each interviewee's acceptance of the interview/report/recommendation process, thus easing the eventual implementation of a sound RMIS.

Analyzing the Interview Findings. Analyzing the "small pictures" provided by each interviewee's perspective should yield an integrated "big picture" of the organization's RMIS needs, resources, and opportunities for improving information flows and risk management decisions. Knowledge of both present and future possible information flows, discussed subsequently, is essential to this analysis because an important aim of RMIS is to eliminate cumbersome manual data-gathering and management procedures, automating them to improve the accuracy and timeliness of managerial decisions. Achieving this goal requires detailed knowledge of current information flows and decision procedures.

Making a Report or Recommendations. This analysis, supported by interview results and other pertinent information, should be assembled into the completed requirements analysis or recommendations. With many possible adaptations for the particular customs or situations of any given organization, such a report or recommendations often addresses the topics shown in Exhibit 13-4. Because information flows—both current and proposed as well as computerized and manual flows—are so essential to the design of a proper RMIS, identifying these flows deserves recognition as a design step, which, while related inexplicably to the others, merits some separate discussion.

Identification of Information Flows

Given the ideal tasks for the RMIS to perform, an expert in management information systems from within or specifically hired by the organization can detail the flows of risk management information within the organization, into the organization from outside sources, and from the organization to outside entities. Exhibit 13-5 suggests one possible global perspective on these information flows through which the risk management department interacts with other departments within the organization and with several outside entities. Exhibit 13-6 focuses on one portion of this global information flow, dealing with how the information in the report of an accident covered by insurance reaches the claims administrator, insurer, and the risk management department. (Neither of these exhibits is designed to prescribe an ideal information flow, only to suggest some frequent patterns.)

Information flows, both current and recommended, should be indicated by flowcharts and supporting narrative. A flowchart can show simply the information flows from department to department or entity to entity. These charts and narratives frequently reveal how the underlying data is gathered and how it is processed to generate desired information.

Out of a great variety of detailed information flowcharts like Exhibit 13-6 emerge the detailed specifications for the RMIS—specifications re-

Exhibit 13-4
Sample Format for RMIS Report

I. Identification of Users
II. Description of Current System Information Flows
III. Requirements Definition
    A. Objectives
    B. Required Reports
    [Note: "Reports" should be defined broadly to mean
    "information needs," including day-to-day ad hoc
    queries as well as regularly scheduled reports.]
    C. Required System Functions and Operations
    D. Performance Requirements
    E. Data Requirements
    F. Constraints
    G. Expected Benefits
IV. Description of Proposed System Information Flows
V. Recommendations
    [Note: Recommendations can deal with manual procedural
    concerns as well as with computer-related matters]
VI. Appendices
    A. Interview Results
    B. Data Source Documents
        1. Manual Data Source Forms
        2. Automated Data Source Documentation (file layouts
            and coding schemes from existing computerized
            components)
        3. Data Sourcing Summary (summarizing sources and
            volumes of various categories of data over time)
    C. Required Report Samples

garding (1) the content of information flows, (2) the RMIS hardware and software needed at various locations to process this information, and (3) the skills of persons needed at various locations to operate the hardware and software. These specifications can be analyzed to project the resource requirements—technological, financial, and human—of the ideal RMIS.

Determination of Feasibility

The resources the ideal RMIS is likely to require can be detailed, probably by the risk management and information system professionals

Exhibit 13-5
Possible Global RMIS Information Flows

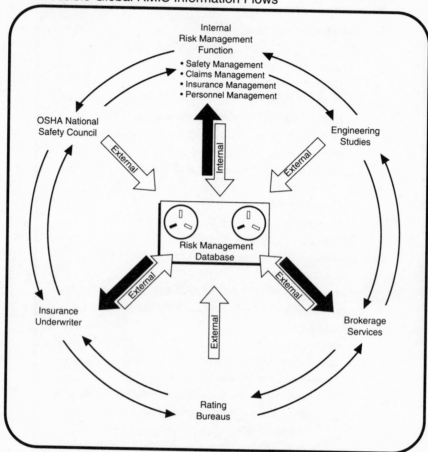

Reprinted with permission from Laurie Weiss, Kay Goodier, and Marvin Gwinn,
"Identification of Data Flow," in James D. Blinn and Mitchell J. Cole (eds.),
Pathways to RMIS (New York: Risk Management Society Publishing, Inc., 1985),
p. 37.

working together, into various cost components, such as those suggested in the upper portion of Exhibit 13-7. These costs should be projected for each of at least the first three years and totaled for the life of the system to recognize the importance of the time value of money to the organization.

Similarly, the benefits projected for this ideal RMIS can be estimated following the format suggested in the lower portion of Exhibit 13-7. While the cost information is likely to be more detailed and concrete than that for benefits, forecast costs and benefits of the RMIS presented

Exhibit 13-6

Possible Information Flow Regarding Accident to Claims
Administrator, Insurer, and Risk Management Department

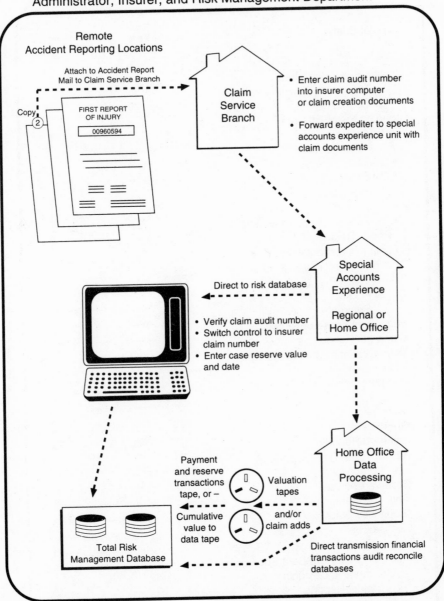

Adapted with permission from Laurie Weiss, Kay Goodier, and Marvin Gwinn,
"Identification of Data Flow," in James D. Blinn and Mitchell J. Cole (eds.),
Pathways to RMIS (New York: Risk Management Society Publishing, Inc., 1985), p. 41.

Exhibit 13-7
Cost/Benefit Analysis of an RMIS

	COSTS			
Type of Cost	Cost in Year			Total
	1	2	3	
Design/Feasibility Study	—	—	—	—
Data Conversion (Existing Insurers or Claim Administrators)	—	—	—	—
Loading Historical Data	—	—	—	—
Particular Data Entry	—	—	—	—
Specialized Reporting	—	—	—	—
• OSHA	—	—	—	—
• Safety Monitor	—	—	—	—
• Exposure Monitor	—	—	—	—
• Cost of Risk	—	—	—	—
• Property Valuation System	—	—	—	—
• Policy Tracking	—	—	—	—
Training/Documentation	—	—	—	—
Administration/Quality Assurance	—	—	—	—
Travel	—	—	—	—
Out of Pocket	—	—	—	—
Subtotal	—	—	—	—
Equipment Lease or Rental	—	—	—	—
Computer Resources	—	—	—	—
Comunications (Connected Time Changes)	—	—	—	—
Computer Storage	—	—	—	—
Printing	—	—	—	—
Microfiche	—	—	—	—
Graphics	—	—	—	—
Standard Reporting	—	—	—	—
Ad Hoc (One-Time Reporting)	—	—	—	—
Loss Forecasting	—	—	—	—
Reserve Analysis	—	—	—	—
Financial Planning	—	—	—	—
Graphic Displays	—	—	—	—
License Fee	—	—	—	—
People Resources	—	—	—	—
• Loading/Verifying Data Sources	—	—	—	—
• Assistance in Designing or Product Reports	—	—	—	—
• Maintenance of Software	—	—	—	—
Subtotal	—	—	—	—
TOTAL COSTS	—	—	—	—

BENEFITS

Type of Benefit	Savings in Year			Total
	1	2	3	
Tangible				
1. Staff Reduction	——	——	——	——
2. Claims Administration	——	——	——	——
3. Financial	——	——	——	——
Intangible				
1. Reduced staff time	——	——	——	——
2. Improved response to special requests	——	——	——	——
3. Better marketing by control of data	——	——	——	——
4. Improved morale in the risk management department	——	——	——	——
5. Opportunity to do some valuable "back-burner" projects	——	——	——	——
TOTAL BENEFITS	——	——	——	——

Reprinted with permission from Richard F. Denning, "Cost Benefit Analysis "" in James D. Binn and Mitchell J. Cole (eds.), *Pathways to RMIS* (New York: Risk Management Society Publishing, Inc., 1985), pp. 78 and 80.

in this way can give senior financial and other executives the soundest possible information on which to evaluate the financial desirability of any particular RMIS to the organization.

To this point, the design decisions and financial analyses have focused on an ideal RMIS—a system that senior management may find unacceptable because of a high cost/benefit ratio or low projected time-adjusted internal rate of return. Gaining senior management support may require that one or more system alternatives eliminate the need for some expensive hardware, software, or personnel. These alternatives may forgo some less essential tasks and may be designed and presented as "fallbacks." Rather than attempt to gain approval for an extensive, expensive system, the risk management professional could begin with a basic, economical system to be upgraded or expanded at a later date. Anticipating the possible need to present such "basic" alternatives, those conducting the initial RMIS requirements interviews may ask interviewees to categorize or rank the desirability of each of the tasks they would like the ideal system to perform.

Buy/Lease/Build Decisions

Once senior management has given its approval for a specific RMIS and its related software, hardware, and personnel, the next crucial design decisions are whether to buy existing software programs or to construct ("build") these programs and whether to buy or lease the RMIS hardware. These decisions lead, in turn, to a choice between developing RMIS capabilities within the organization's own personnel or, alternatively, relying on vendor support.

Software Decisions. In choosing the specific programs or capabilities for an organization's RMIS, there was an era when the arguably most important decision was between generic types of software—for example, whether to select a mainframe program that emphasized primarily numerical analysis or one that emphasized word processing and report writing, thereby requiring more words than numbers. Such a choice is no longer necessary because currently available multi-purpose programs generally provide a "package" of a diverse set of capabilities desired by large numbers of users in many organizations.

Instead, the most fundamental software decisions now typically involve a choice between buying some unified software "package" available from one vendor versus custom designing individual programs for specific tasks. If a unified standardized program is chosen, the next decision is to select a particular vendor. On the other hand, an organization that opts for a series of customized programs may be able to "target" software acquisitions for particular tasks, provided these various programs are compatible in allowing communication and a transfer of data from one program to another.

All these choices must be governed by the eventual ability of the system to meet the organization's requirements; beyond this fundamental concern, other decision criteria include (1) budgetary constraints (both one-time and ongoing); (2) the time required to make its software operational; and (3) the compatibility of the software with the organization's present, computerized MIS.

A variety of brokerage organizations, insurers, and independent software and hardware vendors stand willing to provide "prepackaged" RMIS software that will perform most of the tasks required of an RMIS for most small and medium-sized organizations. This software, already tested and usually backed by the provider's warranty or service agreements, is usually available for purchase for less money than an organization would need to develop a software program on its own.

Thus, the only organizations for which designing their own software is a cost-effective option tend to be these that already have (1) substantial MIS expertise on staff, (2) a substantial volume of risk management data in computerized form that is not compatible with the computer language or programs that the brokers, insurers, or other vendors have used to develop their software, or (3) some specialized RMIS needs that cannot be addressed by "prepackaged" software.

The risk management professional for an organization that meets the first of these three conditions should explore the costs and benefits of developing RMIS software internally to (1) utilize existing personnel, (2) assure the compatibility of the RMIS with the overall MIS, and (3) establish and maintain good working relationships with the in-house information system staff. An organization in the second category may wish to consider the relative merits of transforming its data to make it compatible with outside software, or ask the outside provider to transform its existing software, rather than develop new software within the organization. For an organization that falls within the third category, the cost-effective option may to be purchase the outside software for most of its RMIS needs and to develop its own software only for those special tasks the pre-packaged programs cannot easily perform.

When an organization chooses to rely on ready-made or customized, externally generated software, its choice of a supply source should concern price and more importantly, the following:

- The reliability of the software (based on the proven experience record of the particular programs or of the supplying firm)
- The adaptability of the software (both to potential new uses within the organization's RMIS and to technological advances through "upgrades" in the supplier's software)
- The supplier's ability to provide support, training, and service as new persons join the risk management staff, as the RMIS evolves, or as software problems may develop in the future

Although there are few definite rules for making software decisions, the experience of many organizations suggests the following:

- If facing both hardware and software decisions, make software choices first because hardware commitments often limit software choices
- Choose widely used software over relatively obscure software because of the greater availability of trained personnel and more frequent software upgrades
- Enlist the cooperation of the organization's own computer personnel to gain their expertise and their support before the choice is made
- Remember the option to not computerize—to continue manual operations—if software/hardware or other RMIS options do not promise greatly increased efficiency

Hardware Decisions. When computer hardware was much larger and more expensive than it has become recently, most organizations chose to lease rather than buy their computer equipment to avoid large cash outlays for its purchase, to leave the risk of loss (principally through technological obsolescence) with the owner/vendor, and to assure the vendor's continued servicing of the equipment. These considerations still apply to large mainframes, which frequently are leased rather than purchased. However, as stand-alone micro and minicomputers have dropped in price and size and have risen in popularity and reliability, an increasing number of organizations now purchase this equipment.

For an RMIS, the lease/purchase decision is typically made on a basis consistent with the organization's choice for its overall MIS. Using the same (or at least compatible) hardware and software for both the RMIS and the MIS facilitates integrating the two systems and promotes exchanges of information throughout the organization's computer network and among all its managers. Thus, while not feeling bound to the machinery of an existing MIS, a risk management professional contemplating a separate system for special risk management needs should be confident of, and be able to document fully, the advantages of the separate equipment for the RMIS.

In an organization without an existing MIS, the decision whether to lease or to purchase the hardware should be made like any other lease/purchase decision, giving due consideration to such factors as follow:

- The difference in the expected net present value of the cashflows over the projected life of the equipment
- The way the organization's various loss exposures—including both physical damage and technological obsolescence—are affected by the choice between buying and leasing
- The flexibility that both the buy and the lease options give the organization to update its RMIS (or MIS) in the foreseeable future as the organization or computer technology changes

Personnel Decisions. The three fundamental options any organization has for finding people to operate its RMIS are to rely on (1) the organization's own employees, (2) the personnel of an outside organization, such as an insurer, agency, brokerage, or consulting organization, or of a hardware/software vendor, or (3) some combination of the organization's own and other's personnel. Because the objective is to secure the expertise of specific individuals who can make the RMIS perform to meet risk management needs, no textbook—and no risk management professional—can generalize about the best sources from which to locate the needed person(s). Nonetheless, the following are the essential factors to consider in staffing the RMIS function:

- Management information expertise sufficient to operate the RMIS as desired
- Knowledge of the organization and of its RMIS needs
- Integrity and honesty in protecting any confidential aspects of

the information in the RMIS or the aspects of the organization's operations

- Ability to respond promptly to any unplanned immediate needs for risk management information or to work with risk management personnel in modifying the RMIS to meet other special needs
- Personnel costs, including direct compensation and employee benefits, in both the long- and short-run

How an organization staffs its RMIS activities may be influenced greatly by its choice of hardware and software vendors and its lease/purchase decisions. A supplier of particularly complex hardware or software, or one that only leases rather than sells its computers and related materials, may provide personnel to operate the system as part of its overall "package." Here, the choice of the system dictates the source of the RMIS personnel, but not necessarily the particular individuals who operate the system. Thus, the software, hardware, and personnel decisions often are not three independent choices but, instead, are closely linked.

IMPLEMENTING RMIS

Implementing or installing an RMIS is analogous to the step in the risk management process of implementing chosen technique(s) of risk control or risk financing. The precise moment of implementation is when the "old way" of doing things is discarded and replaced by a "new way."

In implementing either an RMIS or a new technique of risk management or risk financing, the successful risk manager will have to use proper management techniques of planning, organizing, motivating, monitoring, and communicating to achieve the following.

- To reduce initial resistance
- To effect a smooth transition
- To respond to the changes caused by implementation

In both kinds of implementation, the risk management professional will secure the necessary commitment from key management, colleagues, and staff by the time the decision is officially made and responsibilities and schedules are announced. Going from the "decision to implement" to "completed implementation" requires much work.

Although much of this actual work will be done by others, the risk management professional will be reviewing the progress and the results of that work, making sure that it meets the results standards and the activity standards that have been established. There will be much com-

Data Problems. Three potentially important problems in the data with which an organization's RMIS operates are data integrity, data ownership, and insufficient data.

Data Integrity. Perhaps the greatest data problem is assuring data integrity. Proper collection, verification, and entry of accurate information for the RMIS are essential, as are adequate built-in editing routines in the software (to prevent such errors as February 32) and security procedures to protect against sabotage.

To preserve this integrity, the procedures for entering data into the RMIS should include the following:

- Personal verification by the risk management professional of major changes in the parameters (such as for establishing reserves for open claims) that the system uses to project risk management budgets and to develop reports of risk management results
- Restrictions on the numbers of persons authorized to enter data into the RMIS, to manipulate the data, or to access the system for output
- Periodic auditing of the loss records and other information in the system, such as by asking individual departments or geographic locations to confirm the accuracy of the data applicable to them, so that any erroneous data can be corrected or eliminated promptly.

Data Ownership. When the underlying data in an RMIS is compiled from a number of sources—such as the organization, its insurer(s), and its agent/broker/consultant—questions may arise about who "owns" this data, that is, who may extract it from the system for any particular purpose and who is responsible for updating it or removing errors. The same questions may arise when an organization works with an outside software vendor whose personnel help operate the RMIS. Here, an important additional concern can be separating ownership of the programs from ownership of the information generated by applying these programs to raw data or losses and other measures of risk management performance. All these questions gain added complexity when an organization seeks to change insurers or vendors or when the organization itself becomes involved in a merger.

Insurers and software vendors generally take the position, in their sales and service agreements and in their day-to-day dealings with an organization's risk management department, that they own the data and the information that the RMIS produces from that data. (In return, these insurers and vendors agree to maintain and correct the basic data.) Therefore, the risk management professional for an organization that wishes to maintain control over its own data or to extract from the insurer's or the vendor's systems particular information reports should pay special attention to contract provisions on data ownership and control for two purposes: (1) to assert the organization's ownership and the insurer's/vendor's custodial responsibilities and (2) to establish procedures for removing the organization's data from the insurer's/vendor's systems, and appropriate fees the organization will pay under these situations when the organization wishes to terminate or continue (perhaps on some modified basis) its relationship with the insurer/vendor.

Insufficient Data. For the many sophisticated RMIS now on the market to meaningfully use their analytical modules capable of predicting expected losses or plotting trends, these systems must contain sufficient data to produce "statistically significant" results. The amount of data required for statistical significance depends on the probability of error that management is willing to tolerate. Producing results that have only a 5 percent probability of being wrong by a given margin— that is, are "statistically significant at the 5 percent level"—requires much more data than is needed for results that are significant at the 10 percent level. Since gathering data imposes costs and because some data simply may not be available at any cost, designing an RMIS requires the risk management professional to join with senior management in deciding what choices they wish to make among the tradeoffs between the costs of data and the costs of perhaps making a wrong decision because of insufficient data.

System Problems. Apart from data and hardware incompatibility problems, the hardware/software of an RMIS may fail to perform as expected because the system is not matched to the organization's needs, because the risk management professional or other managers overemphasize the system's "gadgetry," or because the system generates an overkill of data/information.

System/Organization Mismatch. The organization's risk management requirements may not correspond with the capabilities of its RMIS. If, for example, the risk management professional has underestimated these needs, a "prepackaged" RMIS may not have the analytical or database management capabilities to meet these needs and generate the detailed reports that senior and other managers expect.

Similar incompatibility results if an outside vendor hired to develop and operate an RMIS lacks the expertise or insight into the organization's philosophy or objectives needed to fulfill its expectations. Similar disappointment with an outside vendor may result if the vendor's contract has been so rigorously negotiated that the fee paid the vendor does not enable it to fulfill its contractual duties, especially when the contract covers a long term and makes no provision for inflation.

Finally, the RMIS may not be sufficiently expandable or adaptive to avoid technological obsolescence. It may not have the capacity to accept new modules, giving it additional analytical and reporting capabilities or enabling it to exchange data or programs with other computers either within the organization, by the organization's insurers, or by other vendors the organization wishes to employ. In such a situation, the risk management department may become dependent upon an antiquated inefficient system that may be more expensive to maintain than would be a newer, more expandable, and more comprehensive RMIS.

Overemphasis on Gadgetry. A computer hardware/software vendor understandably tries to emphasize the unique or unusual features of its products. This tendency may conflict with the responsibility of a risk management professional to select wisely in purchasing an RMIS, choosing only the features that the system needs and avoiding unnecessary gadgetry. Alternatively, an organization's risk management or other official may become so enthralled with a system's sophisticated capabilities that they fail to be sure that the benefits of these advanced capabilities are worth their costs. To avoid either of these difficulties and to assure that RMIS selection and operation remain cost-effective, the procedures for determining and fulfilling the RMIS needs must be carefully drafted and conscientiously followed.

Data/Information Overkill. The capability of an RMIS to generate forty or fifty pages of data, or even five or six pages of information, does not mean that all these pages will contribute to the effectiveness of a risk management program. A risk management or other executive seeking an answer to a particular question or wishing to know the status of some aspect of the risk management program often will not have time to read a lengthy report. An RMIS, or the persons who operate it, should be able to provide specific answers targeted to particular questions or to generate an "executive summary" presenting and interpreting the highlights of a more detailed report, to which the executive may refer if he or she wishes. This ability to summarize information, and often to supplement it with graphs, enables the risk management professional to communicate quickly and effectively with senior management and other managers.

Hardware Problems. Two potentially important problems with RMIS hardware are mechanical failure and technological obsolescence.

Mechanical Failure. The mechanical failure of hardware can best be prevented and minimized by ensuring that competent in-house staff or external technical support personnel are readily available for system maintenance, servicing, and repair. As a safeguard against unpreventable breakdown, sound risk management calls for contracting with appropriate vendors or other organizations with comparable equipment for the use of backup facilities during hardware downtime.

Obsolescence.   Even though computer manufacturers constantly introduce new models or entirely new lines of hardware, the resulting obsolescence does not always present immediate problems. As long as the organization's present hardware performs as needed and parts and service staff remain available, the age of the present equipment often does not matter. Obsolescence becomes a definite problem only when parts or services are difficult to obtain or when expansion or modification of an RMIS calls for additional hardware.

Hardware advances very quickly; much of what was state-of-the-art equipment five years ago has gone through several generations of improvement. Therefore, upward compatibility—the ability to transfer data and software from older hardware to newer hardware—is vital to the decision of whether or not to acquire new equipment. Such compatibility through progressive models receives more emphasis from some hardware manufactures than from others, which may be an important factor in initially choosing among hardware vendors.

Software Problems.   Software may fail or develop "bugs," become obsolete, or prove inappropriate for adapting to an organization's changing RMIS needs.

Failure and Obsolescence.   Problems of software failure can best be handled by providing reliable, competent support staff—either within the organization or on-call from an external vendor—to advise the organization's personnel in overcoming "bugs" or, if necessary, to re-program the software to eliminate any defects in it.

Software obsolescence, like hardware obsolescence, need not become a problem until technical support for the "old" software is unavailable or the organization loses cost-effective access to hardware that would run the software. Lack of upward compatibility in hardware also can render dependent software obsolete. Choosing software that is widely used tends to reduce these problems of obsolescence.

Lack of Adaptability.   Because an organization's risk control and risk financing requirements and products change, as does the general technological and economic environment in which many organizations operate, an organization's RMIS needs may also change, rendering its software less than ideal for meeting new challenges. Because some change is inevitable, and because change usually marks progress, an RMIS that is never adjusted for change is probably a less than optimal RMIS.

An organization's risk management professional should therefore periodically update the software that supports the RMIS. He or she should regard these required changes as opportunities to upgrade the entire system and to correct any RMIS weakness that experience with the system has revealed. The best way to meet these challenges and to seize these opportunities is often to repeat the phases of the RMIS design process described previously in this chapter.

Personnel Problems. Employee turnover can create personnel problems for an RMIS because new employees must be trained before they can use the system. In addition, new or infrequently used software may require employee retraining. Carefully and clearly written operating manuals and software documentation provide consistency and efficient training. Another sound risk control measure is to cross-train several persons in the use of the same software, especially for infrequently performed tasks such as annual risk management cost allocations.

Frequent Applications of an RMIS

To suggest the uses an organization may make of an RMIS throughout the entire risk management decision process, the following discussion focuses on the uses of an RMIS in (1) identifying and analyzing exposures, (2) examining and selecting risk management techniques, (3) implementing the chosen techniques, and (4) monitoring the results of these choices.[6]

Identifying and Analyzing Loss Exposures. For this part of the risk management process, many organizations rely on an RMIS for accident/claim/incident reports, for property valuation, and for loss forecasting.

Accident/Claim/Incident Reports. In the gathering of risk management data, accidents, claims, and incidents are usually differentiated. In this context, an accident may be defined as an event that causes substantial loss to the organization; a claim is a legal demand against the organization growing out of some loss, usually accidental, suffered by another; and an incident is an event that, while it results in no substantial loss, could result in an accident or claim against the organization. Accidents and claims are losses to the organization; incidents, under somewhat varied circumstances or with less "good luck," could become losses. Incidents should be considered warnings of potential future accidents and claims.

Thorough, detailed data on accidents, claims, and incidents are at the heart of an RMIS because so many of the software programs rely on this fundamental data. At the least, the system will report on all past accidents and claims and will show the current status of unresolved (open) claims against the organization. Historical data and audit trails for past accidents and closed claims are also included in many systems.

Rather than simply generate a chronological "loss run," which is very difficult for its readers to analyze and, hence, often goes unread, an RMIS usually structures loss and claims data into more organized reports, such as a "large loss" listing. Such a report displays every loss or claim whose total exceeds some threshold value—for example, $5,000—and sorts them in descending dollar value so that the biggest accidents and claims (those that can be said to deserve the most attention because they cost the most) appear first.

These large accidents and claims may also point to the need for risk control action in certain locations or for certain activities. Similarly, reports bringing together data on certain types of losses or claims— those that, while initially apparently minor, may become much more severe, such as loss of hearing cases and back injuries—can alert the risk management professional to prime targets for loss prevention or loss reduction.

In addition to focusing on severe losses, an RMIS can be a valuable tool in identifying highly frequent types of losses that often go unnoticed because they tend to be individually small, or "routine,"—inventory shortages, employee back strains, and minor vehicle collisions, for example. These accumulations of losses often deserve as much attention as do single, dramatic large accidents. Because the aggregate dollar cost of the many small losses can total more than one large loss, risk control attention can be profitably focused on them. A well designed RMIS highlighting frequent losses can bring about this focus and can target cost-effective risk controls.

Incident reports can also flash an "alert" sign to the risk management department. While not actually causing a loss, an incident clearly suggests how a substantial loss might happen. Traditionally, hospitals have given the most emphasis to incident reports, such as of a patient receiving the wrong medication but, by good luck, suffering no adverse effects. Other organizations are beginning to give equal attention to incident reports because, according to Heinrich's "domino theory," there are about 300 "near misses" for each reported industrial accident. If one of these 300 were recognized as clearly signaling the need for improved safety, the one real accident or claim might be avoided. Thus, an organization of any size that is deeply committed to risk control should consider implementing a thorough, responsive incident reporting system grounded in its RMIS.

Property Valuation. Because most risk management decisions involving real or personal property should be based on the replacement, functional replacement, or reproduction value of that property, the historical cost of properties, usually shown in accounting records that adhere to generally accepted accounting principles, often have little risk management use. Therefore, to recognize and treat property exposures properly, an RMIS can be used to gather and update data on the replacement or reproduction values of property. Having a thorough inventory of property and the appropriate valuation standards for each item greatly facilitates the revision of this record—adding or deleting property, or bringing values up to date. For example, a computerized record of property purchases and sales is helpful in adding or deleting properties from the organization's records. Through an RMIS, property values can be regularly changed through either individual consideration of the value of each item or class of property or through a variety of formula techniques that recognize the combined effects on property values of both price level changes and depreciation.

Loss Forecasting. An RMIS can be used to forecast the frequency and severity of losses using probability analysis or regression analysis but with much greater speed and ability to consider several probability distributions or regression relationships simultaneously. For example, it is quite beneficial for a loss-forecasting program in an RMIS to perform the following sequence of projections:

1. Establish a statistical (regression) relationship between an organization's past levels of activity and its past frequencies of loss (such as workers compensation back claims).
2. Project the organization's level of activity for each of the next three to five years (using statistical techniques or management estimates) and apply that regression equation to these projected activity levels to forecast the frequency of employee back injury claims for these three to five years.
3. Project the total cost of these losses (aggregate back injury loss severity) by first projecting the cost of the average claim (based on historical costs adjusted for price level changes, technology, or other factors) and then multiplying this per-claim value by the projected number of employee back injuries or other losses.
4. Project the organization's aggregate annual cash outflow for these claims, taking account of the fact that each claim may take several years to settle, with only a portion of the total cost of each claim being paid in any one year. (The present value of these annual outlays for such claims or other accidents represents their true cost to the organization.)

These computations will generate *expected* future costs of accidents or claims; *actual* cash outlays could be significantly higher or lower. The RMIS can be programmed to take account of past differences between projected and actual losses so that future projections can be refined and, thus, improve the accuracy of subsequent forecasts.

Examining and Selecting Risk Management Techniques. The next two steps in the risk management decision process entail (1) projecting the likely operational and financial consequences of various risk control or risk financing alternatives for dealing with a particular loss exposure and (2) formulating net present value cash flow or other decision criteria for selecting among these alternatives or choosing combinations of them. At this point in the risk management decision process, a computerized RMIS can be particularly useful in financial modeling, analysis of alternative retention levels, and safety analysis.

Financial Modeling. Computerized financial modeling involves developing a set of relationships among the assets, liabilities, equities, expenses, and revenues within an organization's financial structure and then tracing, on a yearly or other periodic basis, the effects that given events would have—according to the assumptions underlying the model—on the organization's balance sheet, statement of profit and loss, and statement of sources and uses of funds.

Such models can forecast the organization's overall financial condition under various risk management "scenarios": the impacts that particular property, liability, personnel, or net income losses could be expected to have on the organization's financial strength, and how its viability might be improved by the use of various risk management techniques. Such modeling, really period-by-period simulation of the organization's financial health under given sets of assumptions, can be most helpful in drawing senior management attention to critical risk management decisions and in selecting risk management techniques that are particularly likely to generate desired results.

Analysis of Retention Levels. A frequent special case of financial modeling focuses on deciding what dollar amount or portion of particular kinds of losses the organization should retain (that is, pay with internally generated funds). This decision involves selecting retention levels for various kinds of losses so that the organization controls its overall loss costs without subjecting itself to excessively high levels of uncertainty about what these costs will be.

For this purpose, the RMIS can be programmed to assume various levels of retention and limits of insurance, simulate various loss frequency and severity patterns, and then compute the total costs of retained losses and of insurance premiums. The computer can then generate both the expected total risk financing costs (retention plus insurance expenses) for a given period and a range of possible outcomes around this total. Each outcome within this range also can be assigned its own probability so that senior management can appreciate the varying degrees of uncertainty for the various possible outcomes that may flow from the choice of a given retention level. Here, the RMIS can alert for injuries to persons who may or may not recover their health, the total amounts of payments for medical care and loss of income may be very difficult to predict or to reduce to a present value of an appropriate loss reserve.

Any organization having at least ten or twenty such significant claims a year can improve the speed and efficiency—as well as lower the ultimate cost—of paying these claims by relying on an appropriate claims administration package to assemble basic data on each claim; to track payments to date and current reserve values of the claim; to assemble the records pertinent to that claim; to generate routine documents and correspondence; and to compile statistics on the cause, duration, and costs of each claim for summary reports to senior management and other interested parties. For claims that reach litigation, computerized data will also include information on the legal representatives of all parties involved, the jurisdiction, and the ultimate legal and financial consequences of any suits.

While an RMIS will certainly distinguish among claims that are retained, those paid by insurers, and those paid by other parties, the system is likely to gather and process the same types of information for all types of claims regardless of the payor. In contrast to the claims-reporting function through which many RMIS assist in the exposure-recognition phase of risk management, the claims administration capabilities of many RMIS focus on forecasting, making, and monitoring actual claim payments by an organization or payments it receives for losses it has suffered.

Preparation of Routine Documents. Properly administering either the risk control or risk financing activities of a well-managed risk management program requires preparing many routine documents: incident reports; safety inspection forms; insurance certificates; and reports required by national, state, or local workplace safety or environmental protection regulations; among many others. Each of these documents typically has its own format that calls for inserting particular names, places, dollar or other quantitative measures, and perhaps brief, often standardized, explanations of events. Such reports lend themselves to ready computerization for easy preparation and quick and reliable dissemination. Before the RMIS, many of these documents and standardized reports were generated by hand or typewriter using preprinted forms. With computerization, the ability to program the production of both the form and of the information it requires has greatly increased the efficiency of these otherwise burdensome routine documents.

Monitoring Results. In tracing the success and identifying the shortcomings of a risk management program, an RMIS has many uses. Two of them are the production of reports for management and the allocation of risk management costs among an organization's departments or activities.

Production of Management Reports. Assessing the extent to which a risk management program is meeting its objectives requires comparing actual performance to activity or results standards. A computerized RMIS database is an excellent tool for gathering data on actual performance, compiling standards for desired performance, and performing the many calculations needed to properly compare actual with desired results. The computer also offers opportunities for consciously or automatically adjusting standards for changes in operating or economic conditions and for tracing performance over time. The resulting information must be reported to management for its evaluation and response. Being able to gather and analyze this managerial information significantly facilitates generating, and greatly improves the accuracy of, risk management reports.

Cost Allocation. A system for allocating costs of risk (retained losses + insurance costs + risk control costs + risk management administrative expenses) among the various departments of an organization can be a most powerful tool for motivating personnel within those departments to practice risk control. The underlying rationale for such a system is that, to the extent that a department's specific costs of risk can be identified, charging those costs against the budget of that department makes risk management a more meaningful responsibility of the manager of that department.

An RMIS can be an indispensible aid in designing and implementing a cost allocation system in three ways.

1. Programming the RMIS to allocate costs among departments provides an ideal opportunity for examining the assumptions underlying such allocation and gaining managers' understanding and support of the allocation system.
2. The RMIS acts impartially—indeed, mechanically—in allocating particular costs to particular departments according to the fixed rules in the computer program.
3. The RMIS can compute and allocate costs rapidly, thus making the system particularly responsive to individual managers' risk control efforts.

The allocation of risk management costs is a complex subject, involving numerous decisions and tradeoffs about the kinds and amounts of costs to be allocated and the formulas for their allocation. The essential point is that an RMIS makes feasible many cost allocation options.

MANAGING RMIS LOSS EXPOSURES

An organization's risk management professional and program can easily become dependent on a computerized RMIS for accomplishing necessary tasks that were once performed manually. This dependency creates its own loss exposures if access to the RMIS and its output is partially or fully interrupted. For example, an otherwise sound risk management program built on a computerized RMIS could be devastated by the disappearance of a major hardware or software vendor, the organization's intentional change of such a vendor, unauthorized access to RMIS data, computer viruses, other damage to computerized data, or physical damage to the software or hardware the RMIS uses. The material under this heading concludes this chapter by examining these loss exposure and how they may be managed, particularly through effective risk control measures.

Vendor Disappearance

Any RMIS vendor may cease doing business or may discontinue an RMIS product or service upon which an organization's risk management program depends.[7] Pre-loss prevention and reduction measures to cope with this exposure, particularly when selecting vendors or renegotiating contracts with them, include the following:

- Consideration of the vendor's financial stability
- Consideration of the present and probable future breadth of use (popularity) of the vendor's hardware, software, or other goods and services
- Service contract revisions that provide appropriate guarantees or procedural safeguards

Although the first two measures are prudent practice of good business judgment, they do not provide absolute protection against loss of RMIS capabilities. Like any company, an RMIS vendor can lose market share, be acquired by another firm under adverse conditions, or suffer other financial reversals that drive it out of business. Again, like any other organization, an RMIS vendor also can choose to discontinue a product or service, often primarily to improve its own overall financial position.

To safeguard against vendor disappearance, every RMIS should be structured according to the following recommendations:

- The original computer programming (the "source code") for the RMIS is available to the organization, held either by the organization or by an independent custodian.

- The software is written in a popular computer language.
- The RMIS operates on widely used hardware.
- There is daily cooperation between the organization and the vendor.

These common-sense recommendations are aimed at maintaining good relations with vendors, through procedures vendors are increasingly willing to accept. These recommendations protect the client organization if the vendor fails or makes a business judgment contrary to the client organization's best interest. These measures also serve the vendor's best interest because, if a vendor discontinues the product or service but remains in business, the favorable publicity resulting from a well-managed transition of the client's RMIS vendor/hardware/software can be a valuable business asset to the former vendor.

Intentional Change of Vendors

An organization may choose to change RMIS vendors for any number of financial, managerial, or technical reasons. However, when an organization's RMIS facilities are provided by insurers, brokers, or third-party administrators, an RMIS change is often inextricably linked with a change in an insurer, broker, or administrator: a decision to change one often forces a decision to change the other. Therefore, an important concern when changing insurers, brokers, or administrators is how best to maintain access to either one's present RMIS, or a suitable substitute.

To ensure such access and control of the confidentiality of the sensitive information that may be stored on an RMIS, it is wise to do the following:

- Be certain from the outset that any vendor-provided RMIS is offered on an "unbundled" basis, available independently of any other insurance coverages, brokerage services, or other commitments.
- Explain that the RMIS data—distinct from the vendor-provided RMIS software that typically remains the vendor's property—is owned by the client organization and that it will be supplied to the organization on request at a reasonable cost within a reasonable time on an industry-standard, computer-readable medium in a suitable format.
- Confirm that any new RMIS can accept data and software programs from the old system without significant manual re-entry of any input.
- Ensure continuation of the previous RMIS technical support ser-

Although computer viruses typically "live" in software, all elements of an RMIS or other computerized operation are vulnerable to virus infection; there is as yet no foolproof set of safeguards against them. Every organization should therefore have a "computer disaster recovery plan," including procedures for restoring pre-infection versions of files and backup copies of data files and software programs from original system disks and other documentation.

Other Computer Related Exposures

Data stored on computers is vulnerable to destruction, theft, or scrambling from most of the hazards already described in this section. Beyond these general hazards, data is particularly subject to loss because of failure of personal computer hard drives and user error.

PC Hard Drive Failure.[9]   Many personal computers come with hard drives—physically inflexible storage media for data and programs that reside within the computer (in contrast to floppy discs for data and program storage that are easily removed from or inserted into the personal computer through the disk drive.)

For both "floppies" and "hard drives," many experienced computer operators believe that the significant risk management questions are not about *if* the drive will fail but, instead, *when* it will fail. The principle precaution against such failure is to back up the work of a personal computer—that is, to faithfully make copies of the software a personal computer is using and its most recent output for storage on a "backup disk" outside the personal computer. Then, when the personal computer fails, the resulting loss is limited to work done since the last backup was performed.

The backup schedule need not be daily, but it should be frequent and, more importantly, faithfully followed. Not every RMIS (or other computer operations) requires a daily backup, but every operation does have an appropriate backup interval. The more intensely an RMIS or other computer program is used, the more valuable and difficult it becomes to reproduce its output, and the more frequently should its product be separately stored.

When a hard disk, floppy disk, personal computer, or other component of a computerized system fails, the failed component should not be used again until the defective element has been restored and the cause of the failure has been determined and eliminated. Any data, but particularly RMIS data, is likely to be so valuable that it should not be entrusted to a disk or other equipment that has once failed. Another reason for not using a failed storage disk is that, even though the disk is faulty, experts may be able to recover much data and software from it, thus reducing the severity of the failure. However, once the failed disk has been overwritten through reuse, any information it once contained is lost forever.

User Error. A mistake by a system user—often colloquially but quite accurately called the "Oops Syndrome"—is perhaps the most frequent cause of loss of data, occurring whenever a user deletes a record, file, or program that should have been retained or mistakenly reformats a personal computer's hard drive instead of a floppy diskette (thereby erasing perhaps a month's work, which should be backed up in some other storage medium).

The keys to preventing data loss through user error include the following:

- Training all users
- Each user's frequent "backing up" of his or her work
- Ready access to a "help desk," "hotline," or other source of human "hand-holding" help in case of any real emergency
- Software features to prevent or cancel errors, such as computerized requests for user confirmation prior to deleting material; on-line, context-responsive, computerized "help"; well-chosen defaults, such as saving information unless otherwise instructed instead of only saving information when instructed; and a "cancel-preceding action" or "undelete" option.

Damage to Software. Software, which instructs a computer how to organize and manage data, is stored in files within a computer's memory or on removable floppy disks. Like data files, software files are vulnerable to loss or corruption and need to be backed up. Software can fail in two ways: (1) bugs can be discovered and (2) new errors may be introduced through modifications, enhancements, or attempts to fix existing bugs.

Many bugs can be prevented by thorough initial testing, but some will only be discovered through actual use. Any bug found must be reported and corrected. Many suppliers of standard software routinely send out upgraded versions of their software, which correct bugs discovered and reported by their entire client base.

When programs are modified or enhanced—either to meet changed or expanded needs or to fix a bug—new errors can be introduced: software that once worked well—and that has no apparent connection to the enhancement—no longer functions properly.

It is therefore good practice *always* to back up software before replacing it with a new version (so that the old version can be restored just in case the new one is seriously defective). Similarly, *always* thoroughly test new software before putting it into the production mode.

Damage to Hardware. Hardware can fail through age. It can also be stolen or damaged by accident or vandalism. Pre-loss treatment methods include the following:

- For vandalism, using security measures (including locked doors, security guards, cardkeys or other devices that screen unauthorized entry, and locking devices on PCs) to prevent unauthorized access to hardware.
- For accident prevention, instituting proper location controls (locating hardware on a high floor to safeguard against floods or in an interior room to safeguard against wind damage) and proper environmental controls (sufficient air-conditioning as required for larger machines to prevent damage from overheating and halogen systems to control damage from fire and natural perils).
- For system damage due to age or malfunction, employing a computer repair service for regularly scheduled preventive maintenance and repair visits. If the "downtime" caused by regular preventive maintenance presents a problem, the risk manager may want to arrange for the use of backup computer facilities.

SUMMARY

An organization's risk management information system (RMIS) consists of data (usually computerized) and the procedures for manipulating and interpreting that data. The particular functions for which an organization relies on a computerized or manual RMIS may vary: some systems only perform repetitive tasks in processing transactions with insurers and claimants; other systems generate standard reports that the risk management department issues periodically to insurers, senior executives, and other managers throughout the organization; still more advanced systems give the risk management professional or other managers the ability to make "random access" inquiries to the RMIS database to answer particular questions or to generate reports on a virtually instantaneous (on-line) basis. Finally, the most advanced type of RMIS currently available contains in its software programs many of the decision criteria on which a particular organization's risk management choices are based.

Possessing both the appropriate data in suitable form and the relevant decision rules, these RMIS can make, or recommend, suitable choices on such matters as selecting retention levels or directing risk control efforts to the most significant hazards. Not all RMIS perform all these functions—based on the organization's risk management needs and the costs and values of gathering and computerizing particular kinds of risk management information, an organization may wisely choose a less expensive and more basic system without incurring the expense of a more sophisticated one.

Regardless of their costs or their capabilities, all RMIS possess four common components: (1) the database (usually divided into loss, exposure, legal, financial, administrative, and risk control data), (2) software elements for organizing and manipulating this data, (3) hardware elements (computers, printers, and the like), and (4) personnel who operate the RMIS. An organization has a number of specific choices with respect to each of these components. Its selection from among these choices should enhance its ability to achieve the benefits that an RMIS can provide (increased efficiency, reduced costs, and improved communications throughout the organization) while minimizing the potential disadvantages of an RMIS (excessive cost, system inadequacy, incompatibility with an MIS, and adverse personnel effects).

Designing an RMIS for any particular organization involves a variety of considerations, including detailed analysis of its specific RMIS requirements, identification of the information flows required to fulfill those requirements, analysis of the costs and benefits of the feasible hardware/software alternatives that reliably can generate those information flows, and decisions on the most cost-effective sources of the software, hardware, and personnel to operate the RMIS.

Once the RMIS has been designed and is in place, managing the system entails securing the greatest potential benefits from the system while controlling the system's potential limitations throughout each of the steps in the risk management decision process. The benefits of an RMIS include increased efficiency, reduced costs, strengthened communication throughout the organization on risk management matters, improved credibility for risk management activities, and higher quality information on which to base better risk management decisions. The limitations of an RMIS frequently stem from human failures in not recognizing that a computer can only perform analysis; it cannot make decisions and cannot necessarily reduce the organization's actual losses or cost of risk. Successful reliance on an RMIS requires diligence in overcoming various problems that may arise from the underlying data of the hardware or software, personnel operating the system, or the entire system. Because an RMIS is exposed to the same potential accidental losses as any other computer facility, managing an RMIS requires appropriate risk management of the loss exposures that the RMIS creates or intensifies.

Tweedy, David A. "Do Homework Before Choosing RMIS; Overlook Bells and Whistles, Focus on System Needs." *Business Insurance*, 19 March 1990, p. 24.

_____. "Planning Eases RMIS Vendor's Exit." *Business Insurance*, 27 February 1989, p. 21.

"26 Killed in Flash Fire in Westchester Hotel, Majority of Dead Were Corporate Executives Trapped in Meetings." *New York Times*, 5 December 1980, pp. 1+.

Waddell, Jim. "It Went Data Way." *Insurance Review*, February 1990, pp. 45-46.

Williams, C. Arthur, Jr.; Head, George L.; Horn, Ronald C.; and Glendenning, G. William. *Principles of Risk Management and Insurance*. 2nd ed. Malvern, PA: American Institute for Property and Liability Underwriters, 1981.

Williams, C. Arthur, Jr. and Heins, Richard M. *Risk Management and Insurance*. 5th ed. New York, NY: McGraw-Hill Book Company, 1985.

Index